Thomas Purnell

Literature and its Professors

Thomas Purnell

Literature and its Professors

ISBN/EAN: 9783337205195

Printed in Europe, USA, Canada, Australia, Japan

Cover: Foto ©Thomas Meinert / pixelio.de

More available books at **www.hansebooks.com**

LITERATURE AND ITS PROFESSORS.

BY

THOMAS PURNELL.

LONDON:
BELL & DALDY, YORK STREET, COVENT GARDEN,
AND 186, FLEET STREET.
1867.

NOTE.

THE Author avails himself of this opportunity to express his obligation to Mr. C. R. Newman, for many literary and intellectual benefits received from him during several years.

It is right to add that a portion of what is here presented to the reader has already appeared in print.

CONTENTS.

VIII. - MONTAIGNE.

IX. THE MAN OF LETTERS AS A STATESMAN.

ROGER WILLIAMS.

LITERATURE AND ITS PROFESSORS.

I.

MEN OF LETTERS.

ITERATURE is a term which has, like many others, been wrested from its original meaning. At one time it was supposed to have something to do with learning; but step by step it has been degraded, till at length it has become synonymous with writing; and now every person, who describes current events or reports another's speech, or gives us his opinion about a book or a picture or a poem, claims to be a man of letters. Just as the taking a shilling from a person in a red coat makes a soldier of Hodge, so, it seems, does the printing of his opinions make a man free of the republic of letters. From the moment when his production appears in a book or periodical publica-

tion he occupies a new position—he has attained to
the dignity of an author. He allows his hair to grow
long, and thenceforth becomes a man of genius by
profession.   As a consequence, the area of literature
has been so extended, and books have become so
numerous, that the most resolute reader finds himself
unable to make himself acquainted with a tithe of
what issues from the printing-press; works are
publicly advertised as guides and pioneers through
the chaos which has resulted from the overabun-
dance of the literary faculty; and plans have at
various times been suggested by distracted students
for lessening the pernicious effects upon our literature of the shoals of books that are weekly added to
our stock.   Amongst other proposals, I have seen
without surprise that, for the benefit of our per-
plexed descendants, there should be an annual as-
sessment, and that every copy of all worthless works
should be ruthlessly burnt. Some such scheme seems
warrantable ; is, at all events, worthy of consideration, notwithstanding the obvious difficulties that
would be encountered were it seriously proposed.

Literary men notoriously entertain a very exalted
opinion of their calling.   They profess to consider it
so important in its nature and results, as to entitle it
to a rank far in front of most others; and they would
even lead us to infer from their writings, that a

sort of sacredness attaches to the very humblest of its professors. Some of them, indeed, boldly maintain that the man of letters is, now-a-days, " your true king of men ;" whilst there is none but imagines himself to be a component part of that band of illuminati which is said to form, by some unexplained and inexplicable arrangement, a fourth estate within the realm, superior to, and regulating the rest. They all seem to be persuaded, that by printing his notions a man acquires a degree of importance to which he would not be entitled had he abstained from sending them to the press.

Ostensibly the man of letters does not, it is true, demand so much consideration as the professor of theology, who prefixes to his name a notice calling upon us to do him reverence; but he is sufficiently forward in magnifying his office and functions. His pretensions will be found to permeate our literature, sometimes openly avowed, sometimes by sublime innuendo. They were openly and with much indignation expressed by more than one critic of a recent volume of poems, wherein the editor had mentioned that the poet had renounced letters for more important matters. The critics did not, of course, question the accuracy of the statement made by the editor, but their censures were directed against his implied assertion, that any pursuit is to be considered of

more importance than that in which they are themselves engaged. On the other hand, in their treatment of Mr. Disraeli, to whom they bear the same
relation as the young divines of the time of Charles
the Second bore to Hobbes of Malmesbury, writers
exemplify these pretentions by innuendo. Ambition
to become a statesman is surely not reprehensible,
nor, as Mr. Disraeli's novels professedly deal with
political matters, is it strange to find in them a hero
whose aim is the acquirement of senatorial distinction. The author of " Coningsby" may think that
delivering a speech or performing an action is as
dignified a proceeding as criticising it ; but it is well
known, even to those who are only moderately familiar
with modern literature, that his critics are of contrary opinion. They characterize the aim he imputes
to his heroes as of a gross nature, and the reward he
makes them covet as far beneath the dignity of right-
thinking men.

This undue assumption of superiority and exaltation of their own calling may constantly be detected
in numerous other forms throughout our literature.
A large proportion of our public writers assume a
boldness that is sometimes more than amusing. No
sense of decency restrains the arrogance of their
pretensions. With pen in hand, they seem to be
different men from what they are in ordinary times.

There is then nothing too great for their attempt. With politics they are more conversant than professed politicians ; if they write on morals, they pronounce judgment as if they had been favoured with a special revelation from heaven for the occasion ; on social manners, *les petites morales*, they dogmatise with a confidence they would not venture to exhibit in the presence of their friends; and, even in novels, they irrelevantly discuss legislation, law, divinity, military and naval matters, and every other subject under the sun, with the airs of a referee, and in a manner which plainly indicates their conviction that the faculty they possess of being able to put their observations into print is identical with that of being able to form correct judgment on men and things.

Whilst, however, literary men thus magnify their office, they lament that, even from those who acknowledge the high rank claimed for the printing of opinions, they, the individual representatives of the practice, fail to receive the personal consideration to which they believe themselves entitled. Their complaint is, doubtless, in some degree true ; but the reason, I venture to remark, is not that usually given and generally accepted.

Thackeray was fond of attributing the personal disesteem, in which men of letters are sometimes held, to a tradition that dates from the time of Swift

and Pope. "It was Pope, I fear," he says, " who
contributed more than any man who ever lived to
depreciate the literary calling. It was not an un-
prosperous one before that time, as we have seen; at
least there were great prizes in the profession which
had made Addison a minister, and Prior an ambassador, and Steele a commissioner, and Swift all but a
bishop. The profession of letters was ruined by that
libel of the Dunciad. The condition of authorship
began to fall from the days of the Dunciad; and I
believe in my heart that much of that obloquy which
has since pursued our calling was occasioned by
Pope's libels and wicked wit." In the interval that
divided Pope from Johnson men of letters undoubtedly laboured under a cloud, and found it impossible to
emerge into that pleasant official sunshine which had
warmed the hearts of their immediate predecessors;
but even then the supply equalled the demand, and
if nothing we are proud of, except what came from
the men who owed their culture to the era of Queen
Anne, can be referred to this gloomy period in our
literary annals, we must attribute the result to other
causes than the publication of a clever satire. Men
hitherto had relied on patrons for the countenance
which led to ultimate reward. But already in France,
as well as in England, private encouragement had
become only occasional; a new system was about to

arise; and patrons that paid for dedications, either in money or places had become scarce. "Men of "quality have mended that fault," says Asmodeus, "and thereby done acceptable service to the pub-"lic, which before was continually pestered with "wretched performances; the greatest part of the "books being formerly written for the lucre of their "dedications." In England, moreover, there was special cause for the departure at this juncture from the established usage of long generations. Neither George the First nor George the Second could speak English, and as few Englishmen spoke German, the language of the court became, of necessity, a kind of bastard Latin. The sovereign despised the literature of which he was himself ignorant, and the court was too polite not to follow the example of the sovereign. If, then, literary men had not learned to wean themselves from the system that had prevailed, with good results, from the time of Aristotle to their own day—and there was then little hope of successful endeavour by other means—how could it be expected that literature could thrive?

The presumption that the great prizes are no longer within the reach of the class amidst which they fell in the days of Anne, is as groundless as the notion that the profession of letters was ruined by Pope and his Dunciad. A literary man's chance

of success is as great now as it ever was. It is true
he does not, nor should he, obtain political and ecclesiastical preferment solely by virtue of the literary
ability he may have evinced ; but if he possesses the
qualifications which in this country are expected of
aspirants to posts of dignity and high emolument,
his literary merit will undoubtedly aid him in the
accomplishment of his desires. The truth is, literary
men have lost no opportunity they ever possessed of
advancing themselves; but, on the contrary, have
attained to positions they had not hitherto occupied.
Against Addison, who became Secretary of State, may
be placed Mr. Disraeli, who has become leader of the
House of Commons; and if Swift became " all but
a bishop," by reason of his literary abilities, we have,
at the present moment, two archbishops who would,
I think, have had less chance of the great preferment they enjoy had they not displayed eminent
literary ability. From an organized literary guild
or the establishment of an academy, were the idea
practicable, I can anticipate little benefit either for
literature or its professors. Its decrees would be
inoperative, however unanimously concocted. What
would be the effect, then, of the legislative measures
of a board, composed of literary homœopaths, allo-
paths, apprentices, vendors of patent medicines, one
is quite unable to predict. Every man's literary

power is proportioned to his desert, and so is his personal weight. If he is endowed with those personal qualities which fit for social intercourse, what is to prevent him exercising them and gaining the influence he covets? But, from a delusion, incomprehensible by others, that something is owing from society to their vocation as a vocation, the most meagrely equipped professors are disappointed at not receiving the consideration that is due only to those of their brethren, who, to the highest literary culture, have united successful literary performance. They consequently blame the public for their own nonsuccess, or sit down to revile Mr. Tupper, partly because they have never read his productions, but chiefly because his books have gone through a provokingly large number of editions.

There is, however, a specific reason, not usually considered, for the continually decreasing importance of literary men. Those who write books are so numerous that they are no longer prodigies in the eyes of their neighbours. What all can do none reverences. Even the poet is fast losing the prestige that once attached to his office; and there are signs that the time is not far distant when he will be regarded in a light not different from that in which any other of the world's workers are regarded. The aim and object of art being to give pleasure, the artist, whether he expresses himself in words, or on canvas, or in marble, must learn to renounce the high pretensions he successfully advanced when he really discharged the functions of a teacher. The sooner he sees the necessity for this, the better will it be for us and for him. If a man has anything to say, let him say it in the clearest and most direct way he is able. The manner is unimportant. A well-dressed man must not be confounded with a good man. What is said will more and more become of greater importance than how it is said; and the advance made in civilization by our generation will hereafter be judged by the value we attach to the form of a speaker and writer. Metrical composition is no longer required to enable us to preserve what is worthy of preservation, any more than plays are necessary to teach us history, or pictures to give us a narrative of the chief events in the Scriptures. People have already ceased to consider a writer synonymous with a wise man; and although they still express surprise that Sir Thomas Browne or Sir Matthew Hale, and other of our elder writers, were unable to see impropriety in customs common to their day, and thus implicitly avow their disappointment that those worthies were not better than the time in which they lived, similar illogicality is seldom exhibited with respect to men of our own era. Nobody now expects Mr.

Dickens to be in advance of his age because he is the most popular author of the time. But numerous writers still delude themselves with the belief that they are intellectually superior to those who abstain from writing, and demand recognition accordingly. Men who write elaborate essays "concerning" nothing, or, in tortuous phraseology meant for style, spin out nothing "concerning" everything, cannot reasonably, however, expect the reward due only to great achievements in literature, simply because they belong to the same profession as those who have accomplished them,—any more than a small retail tobacconist in Whitechapel can expect the social importance of a wholesale dealer in the city. And yet they do.

When the elder Dumas, appearing as a witness before a court of justice, was asked his profession, he is reported to have said, in a tone of modesty that did not conceal his magnificent self-conceit, " Monsieur, je dirais auteur dramatique, si je n'étais dans la patrie de Corneille." Whereupon the President, with true French irony, replied, " Mais, Monsieur, il y a des degrés,"—a reply that is, unfortunately, as applicable to not a few English men of letters as to the gorgeous Frenchman.

I never heard of a poor money-lender flattering himself he was a millionaire because he was of

the same profession as the Rothschilds; and yet the
humblest private in the ranks of literature believes
that, by a kind of reflected greatness, he participates
in the glory that has been achieved by his illustrious
predecessors and contemporaries. He insists upon
claiming flattering recognition for merits not his own,
and expects applause solely because he belongs to the
army in which others have victoriously fought—just
as I have seen in the streets the master of an im-
mense mastiff taking to himself the attention and
admiration meant by passengers for the powerful
brute he was leading by a string.

The pretence that the literary calling is more
sacred than others, or should be regulated by different maxims from those by which men of any other
profession are guided, is a tradition derived from
past ages, and, as might be supposed, originated with
literary men themselves. At one time, however, it
had foundation on fact. The priesthood were the
sole literary men. Its members united in their persons the writing and the sacred functions. They
alone were clerks. It was not, therefore, unreasonable they should require and receive the respect due
from ignorance to obvious and transcendent superiority. But nobody will seriously maintain that a
similar reason exists in our time for its continuance,
since, to speak with designed discretion, the clergy

are certainly not more intelligent than the laity, nor are those who print their opinions better informed than those who do not. It would be for the interests of literature and of literary men themselves that the pretence should now be abandoned.

II.

CRITICISM.

THE number of literary men having increased to such a degree as to include almost everybody with literary tastes, it is manifest that all who are addicted to being clever could not advantageously employ themselves in original composition; their genius, therefore, with convenience to themselves, and it is thought with advantage to the public, has taken a critical direction. Their activity chiefly displays itself in criticism; the age, in literature, as in other matters, is nothing if not critical. Seeing the competition that within these circumstances must necessarily exist, it is not unreasonable to expect the art to have reached the degree of perfection of which it is susceptible. But it is notorious that it has made only a slight advance in that desirable direction. Although more than two hundred years have now elapsed since what may be called the invention of periodical criticism by Denis de Salo and his foot-man, little progress seems to have been effected in it, as far as England is concerned. In Germany—and, only in a less degree, in France—it has under-gone great improvements; but, as all who pay atten-tion to its development among ourselves cannot fail to notice, its condition in this country is most de-plorable. This misfortune is, no doubt, partly owing to the exigencies of daily or weekly publication. The press, like time and tide, waits for no man; and it will not be denied that the views of a man who writes with the printer at his door must neces-sarily be hastily and prematurely expressed. But it is chiefly due to the false notion entertained by critics of the aim and objects of the art they profess, and to the fact that they form their judgments from a local and temporal point of view instead of from a universal and permanent. Criticism, regulated by fashion, must be inoperative, just as the creative lite-rature of every age, disfigured by such a blemish, has become inoperative.

Practising critics, when they do not philosophise from their own idiosyncracies, become advocates of a cause. They found their opinions on what is inci-dent, and not permanent. They are without an intelligible and trustworthy standard whereby to test the merit of works that come before them; but

grope their way to the misbegotten verdicts with which
we are undeservedly distracted. And so it happens
that the history of our literature abounds in well-
remembered examples of their ridiculous blunders.
So near-sighted, indeed, have been the majority of
them, that one age has seldom ratified the verdicts
delivered by its predecessor; and, in innumerable
instances, reversals of judgment have taken place
during the lifetime of the critics by whom they
were pronounced. It is well known that—according
to the Scottish reviewers and their friends, who, at
the beginning of our century, stormed the strong-
holds of literary criticism, and infused into the profession an amount of confident assertion that has
since appeared astounding—Wordsworth was a dolt,
Southey a common-place rhymester, Coleridge a
madman, and Byron a writer whose productions were
unhealthy rubbish or worse. Opposed to these not
over-cautious arbiters of literature were other arbiters equally certain on the other side. Such sorry
discordance is, unfortunately, still occurring, and
will continue to occur so long as criticism is founded
on principles dependent on fashion.

Of the flourishing condition of musical, dramatic,
and fine arts' criticism I shall not now venture to
pronounce. From presumably competent persons I
hear, on all hands, loud and deep complaints of its

shortcomings and overgoings. What most concerns us at present, however, is this—that, here in England, there is—I may venture to say so without claiming for myself exclusive information—little real literary criticism. We get opinions instead; and week by week there is opportunity of being amused at the wide diversity between them. Except in rare instances, when an author appears of such transcendent merit that not the worst critic in England can gainsay his genius, two verdicts on a book are seldom alike. One writer informs his reader that the work under his review is the most powerful he has ever read; another, that he has examined it with great care, and cannot find a line he could conscientiously praise.

It is very commonly, and, to judge from these discrepancies, not unreasonably believed that friendly bias or personal malice influences the tone of the critic, and prompts him to praise or disparage the work he is reviewing. When party feeling rose high, this probably was the case; but I conclude, from accurate attention to facts, that the belief is now rarely well grounded. Critics do not at the present day, as they did at the commencement of the century, attack a writer they have never seen simply because he belongs to a coterie with which they are at enmity, or from which they have themselves been excluded. Personality has fortunately ceased to be an observable feature in our literature. The time when the personal peculiarities, or moral qualities, or obscure birth of an author influenced the judgment formed of his works has happily gone by—never, let it be hoped, to re-appear. One may still detect occasional revival of the custom; but the improved taste of the public mind preserves us from the risk of being subjected to that truculent, openly-avowed sort of disdainful personality which in the last generation characterized the writings of our predecessors. It now displays itself only at long intervals, and in a very modified form; it is latent; keen; usually directed against a rival and friend; and is meant less for readers than for the edification of him at whom it is aimed. With the prevailing belief that criticism owes its present deplorable state to the frequency with which critics suffer their judgment to be swayed by personal feeling I am not inclined to agree. Prudential reasons, if nothing higher, act as a too influential check upon the display of jealousy or favouritism. In rare instances, bias with regard to the writer reviewed undoubtedly regulates the proportion of praise and blame awarded to his book— the editor or critic being content to sacrifice the legitimate influence of his paper for the sake of gratifying his predilections, just as there are theatrical managers who are ready to withdraw a successful piece from the bills **because**, being **actors as well as** managers, their *rôle* **is not** sufficiently prominent **to** gratify their inordinate self-love. A journal regulated by feeling would not, however, exist **for six** months; and this is so well known to press **managers** that such literary wrong-headedness as would make the attempt is daily becoming less frequently exhibited. Indeed, were I to judge solely from my own literary experience, I should say it has entirely ceased. I have more than once reviewed books by men whom I have known to be in feud with the editor of the journal in which my criticism would appear; but no hint has, even implicitly, ever been given me as to the treatment it was **desired the** works should receive. **On** the contrary, I am happy, for the honour of English critics, in being **able to** recal numerous instances of a quite **contrary tendency**. Authors not unnaturally are apt to suppose every notice of their works that is not laudatory is designedly disparaging, and the public side with them in abusing the **two** or three journals which persistently and consistently refuse to be of so angelic a nature as to be able to detect merit in the books that week after week are offered for their imprimatur; but in the **present** state of literature amongst us there is unfortunately little opportunity for the manifestation of undue severity. Excessive leniency, rather, is the vice with which periodical criticism can with more justice be charged. In addition to the tendency inhering in some minds, to deal tenderly with one who, in demanding their judgment upon himself makes them his patrons and benefactors, there is the incidental probability that the critic of a work is personally known to the author, or that he has succumbed to the importunities he was subjected to by the author's friends. The experienced eye at once detects the criticism that results—as, indeed, it was meant to be detected. The praise is abundant, but provokingly vague; the censure is deferentially advanced; the whole criticism is so indeterminate that it might be applied to almost any book in the language. Potentialities and not performance is the theme. We read of the author having evinced "decided indications of possessing marvellous power;" of much to be found in the work that cannot fail to exert "direct influence on the age;" of the critic not being surprised to hear "great things of Mr. Author hereafter;" and of the great delight he has for the present in "cordially recommending the work to his readers;" how it is "the book of the season." Even here, however, in his dishonesty, the critic is too honest to point out defects as beauties, or indicate specific but imaginary merits. He contents himself with overlooking shortcomings and expressing a hope that the author's future works will be better than that he is reviewing, and will not disappoint the expectations he has formed from this.

If, then, we may in great measure credit critics with the first requisite of criticism, the avoidance of partialities, and acquit them of the discredit of exhibiting malice and undue commendation in their judgments—how are we to account for the low condition of their art in England? How is it that the weight exercised by critical opinion is so slight that it is unappreciable? Readers, finding it impossible to consult every book, in order to ascertain the commodity they want, are obliged to resort to the critical reviews for assistance, and the assistance is in such matter equivalent to directions. What we call criticism has, I am aware, enormous power. It can sell off an edition of a book; by reiterating praise (or blame) it can send a book through several editions; it can spoil the sale of a book it ignores. Critics, however, confound the power they possess of selling a book with the ability to determine its merits. They deceive themselves but not their readers; each of whom, while conscious that the opinion of his guide does not influence himself in forming his verdict, still believes that it influences others, and thus favours the delusion that power is weight. Authors, smarting under the effects of a severe or inadequate review, accuse their critics with being self-appointed instructors. For the reproach that underlies the accusation there is not the least ground. By purchasing his journal the public, or that section of it which forms his constituency, sanctions, as far as it can sanction, the reviewer's assumption of judicial functions; and the author, by personally sending his work, or by directing his accredited agent, the publisher, to act for him, implicitly enters into an agreement that an opinion should be pronounced; tacit and implied only—but still morally as binding as would be a more formal agreement to submit it to arbitration. When the decision of the referee is adverse, there is, within these circumstances, no valid cause for complaint. On the other hand, by abstaining from sending a copy of his work the author makes indirect declaration that he declines to submit to the customary ordeal. In this case I do not see that the critic has the right of interference. Duty to his customers, if he has only that plea, will not excuse the obtrusion of his opinion where it is not asked. The question is, however, of little moment. The number of deserving books that appear—and of these almost all of late years have been by non-professional authors, who have made special study of certain branches and confined their attention thereto—

is so few that there is seldom need to look beyond the
works themselves in order to discover a motive for
the unfavourable verdicts complained of. Let a reviewer be severe, and the chances that he is right
will be in proportion to the severity of his criticism.
Journalism that resolutely confined itself to the consideration of deserving productions would flourish—
not like a tree planted by the rivers of waters.

The deplorable diversity of opinion of which I
have complained is, I think, less the result of wilful
perversity than of misconception on the part of critics
as to their true function, and of ignorance as to
their true method. They regard criticism as only an
art, and refuse to recognize it as a science. It nevertheless has its methods and its laws; and all judgments founded on true principles—principles which
have been successfully enunciated by more than one
German writer—would necessarily be symphonious.
English writers, however, will not see this. They think
criticism to be a matter of taste, and not a matter of
knowledge; and, if they conceive themselves to be
men of taste, give their opinions fearlessly, having
no misgivings that they are right. If a book is bad,
they feel it is bad; but are utterly unable to tell us
wherein it is defective. Their procedure is as varied
as are their verdicts. Some deal out half praise and
half blame, and think they deserve commendation for

their judicial **fairness.** Others, of whom Lord Macaulay **was a** conspicuous example, are little more than elegant **précis-writers.** They give themselves **the airs** of men who can say on a dozen pages what the poor author could not say **on a** hundred, and do **not review** the **book before them** at all, but re-describe the subject-matter. The majority, however, are **not so** magnanimous. They regard themselves as the police **of** the republic **of** letters, and, like the police, **seem to feel personal** interest in a conviction. They accordingly devote themselves to **the** detection of blemishes; **employ** their ingenuity on the rectification **of a** date, **or the** orthography of a name, or the **discovery of plagiarism; or** proceed to elucidate some **minor detail** with which they happen to be acquainted, but of which they imagine their author to **be** ignorant, because **he** has not said all that could be said on the **point.**

From what has been advanced no one will fail to see **that English criticism** reposes **on** a false estimate **of its office and** scope, and that its professors evade their legitimate functions. We **do** not require **from them more than is necessary.** With the current notion, **which demands from the** reviewer of a **book a** knowledge **co-extensive with the author, I do not agree.** It **would be** equally unreasonable **to require** a judge at **Nisi Prius to** be acquainted with the innumerable subjects upon which he adjudicates. It is, of course, well for him to have a decent acquaintance with the subject-matter, and what had previously been written thereon; but the essential characteristic of his profession is judicial, and it is no part of his duty to give the subject-matter from his own point of view. This would be dissertation, and not criticism.

It is obviously impossible, in most instances, for the reviewer to be as well acquainted with the subject-matter of the book as the author who has made it a special study, and devoted years, perhaps, to its production; but the complete knowledge possessed by the original writer is not required to enable him to ascertain whether what was undertaken by the author has been satisfactorily accomplished, any more than it is necessary for me to serve apprenticeship to a cabinet-maker, in order to discover whether the chair I occupy answers the end designed in being a comfortable seat. What we need in a critic, in addition to the power of writing intelligibly, is a judicial mind trained for the particular purpose of his profession. It would, in my opinion, be disastrous to the best interests of literature to insist, as is frequently done, upon the reviewer having a more complete acquaintance with the subject than the writer he is reviewing. Even the belief that the critic is

expected to **possess this** extraordinary knowledge is
injurious, inasmuch **as it** tempts him to assume a
virtue if he has it not.   Artists are even more peremptory than authors in their demands for " experts"
as critics, and are loud in their denunciations of what
they indignantly term " presumptuous patrons" and
" **committees of taste."** Men who have themselves
failed as practical **artists they** disparage, without considering that, **as** in Goethe's case, some acquaintance
with the technicalities of art-practice does not weaken
a man's insight, **or** impair his critical faculty.   If
Phidias had been under the necessity of propitiating
a jury of expert Phidiases, and Michael Angelo of
submitting his designs to Raphael, or his other competitors and rivals, instead of to their several unpro-
fessional patrons and critics, **the** result would probably **be** less satisfactory to artists **and** ourselves
than it is. Dramatic criticism, seldom performed by
ignorant patrons, is, we know, almost entirely confined
to the experts; and instances have occurred when men,
by the necessity of the system, have been obliged to
criticise their o**wn** plays.   I see no valid reason why
the plan should be adopted in literature.   Reviews of
works of fiction, of poems, of **the various** branches of
science, performed by men specially interested in the
several departments, **have usually been** failures ; the
writers having either treated the subject anew from

their own point of **view**; **or** praised and condemned on ground utterly unintelligible by the reader, **in** whose service and for whose benefit they professed to work. If we could combine the expert with **the** critic—if, **that is,** we could unite special faculties with perfect knowledge—it would be a desirable consummation. Until that is attainable, we must either abolish criticism, or cease to blame the reviewer because his knowledge is inferior to the man on whom he is in judgment. Literary questions are not the only questions that must be relegated to the laity for final decision.

Criticism, as I conceive it, has to do solely with the disposal of the materials, and but incidentally with the quality of the materials themselves. **In** fine, it should concern itself with the method of **an** author, and not with the elucidation of the subject.

The critic should be guided in his decision by **certain** fixed and intelligible principles. Above all, he should know no more of the author than is revealed to him by the work under his review. Women who write are so well aware of the disadvantage to which a revelation of their sex would expose them, that they not unnaturally resort to innumerable **expedients** for the purpose of keeping themselves **unknown**. Most readers will remember **with** pain the earnest entreaty made **to a famous critic by** poor

Charlotte Brontë, that he would discuss her book without reference to her sex, and the indignation she exhibited upon finding that her entreaty had been disregarded. A critic, who has unofficially become acquainted with the personality of an anonymous author, has several temptations to use his knowledge. In the first place, he is enabled to make discoveries which exhibit his penetration, and thus secure journalistic as well as personal advantage. He is enabled to show such skill in the selection of illustrative passages to support his views as to the sex or condition of the author, that he imposes upon the reader, and appears " to possess very unusual insight." His unofficial knowledge will almost invariably be found to colour his verdict. He becomes what may be called a shirt-collar critic ; deducing his conclusions, not from the evidence before him, but from his personal knowledge of the author. If the latter moves in a humble sphere, some passage will be discovered that proves his ignorance of the usages of society ; if he belongs to the upper classes, something will be found to indicate that he is unacquainted with the habits and feelings of some of the characters he has endeavoured to represent. The discussion of anything further than what is derivable from the book is, I humbly submit,—for here I know I have against me general opinion—a gross transgression of the ethics of criticism. Such discussion may interest the reader; it may gratify the author himself that his progress should be traced from the first public exhibition of his genius to his triumphant conquest of all difficulties, and his assumption of general approbation; but this, like many other interesting experiments, is not within the limits of criticism, and should be eschewed by the reviewer—whose duty lies in scrupulously confining himself to a consideration of the particular work he is reviewing. I do not think it will be denied in theory that every book should be judged absolutely and not relatively—either with respect to the author's position at some former period, or to the circumstances of its production. By dramatic critics the opposite practice is pursued. One of the most eminent of them has avowed to me (and his statement is confirmed by the practice of the whole body) that he always regards a performance from " the point of view of the House " where the actor appears. If, for instance, Cholmondeley Lascelles, (*né* Smith), who is a very mediocre actor, played with applause at a small uncritical east-end theatre, where even he is a " star," the critic would pronounce favourably on the successful performance. If, on the other hand, Cholmondeley performed the same character at Drury Lane, he would esteem it his duty to denounce the attempt as an impertinence.

The pursuance of this "point of view" sadly affects the importance and power of dramatic criticism; and is equivalent to a reviewer criticising a book, not on its absolute merits, but from "a publishing-firm point of view." ᐳA work of trifling merit, published by an unknown tradesman—were the same principles applied to literary as to theatrical criticism—would be tenderly treated, whilst the same, issued from one of our great publishing houses, would be abused as unworthy of the literary fame of the establishment. Such a practice does, however, prevail; not alone with respect to the selection of books for review, but in some degree with respect to the mode of their treatment. But it takes a different direction. A work coming from an eminent firm is sure to receive greater consideration than if it had been the venture of an ignoble bibliopolist. By such practice the very first principle of criticism is completely violated. Everything foreign and irrelevant should be kept external. There must be no extenuation of shortcomings. Let it not be urged, in favour of a work and in mitigation of its faults, that the writer was environed with disheartening difficulties during its composition, or that, being a peasant, his meagre and defective education precluded him from participating in the advantages usually possessed by authors. The self-taught man, debarred

in his youth from the attendant privileges of a royal
road to learning, is notoriously disposed to over-value
his hard-earned acquirements, and to disparage the
easily-won achievements of those for whom a clearer
path had been made. But **the** judicious critic **is**
wholly free from such bias. Were he called **on to**
judge a man's enterprise, and estimate the extent
and power of his resolution, it would be fit for him
to take into consideration extenuating circumstances;
but his office being to judge of results *per se*, **it**
would be unfair to those who have not had disadvantages to surmount, **if** he were to judge a production
by the difficulties **of the** producer. The productions
of a man must **not be** over-rated because he is a
prodigy. Literature has no concern with prodigies.
We do not think the Iliad the first of epics because
we say Homer was blind, or the Divine Comedy
great because its author was **an unfortunate exile.**
Posterity has short recollection, and declines load-
ing its memory with the names **of** horses that would
have won the race had they not been over-weighted.
It can remember only winners. **If the work** of **A,**
the prodigy, is not intrinsically of superior excellence
to that of B, who has had no difficulty to contend
against, in any estimate we are called on **to form of**
him, he should not be credited with the result **he has**
accomplished, *plus* the difficulty he has triumphantly

encountered. So prevalent is this method, especially in the treatment of poetry, that temporary success has been secured for works that deserved utter and instantaneous oblivion, solely because their authors were considered prodigies. Armless street artists procure halfpence for chalk drawings executed with their feet on the pavement. It is the devious skill of the draughtsman, however, and not the beauty of his production that attracts patrons.

But to leave general for specific sins of current criticism, I notice as a cardinal defect the tendency habitually manifested by reviewers to consider the minute details of a work to the exclusion of its general whole. I do not decry the obvious advantages to be derived from able detection and representation of latent beauties, and from the discovery and due appreciation of new gifts of expression in an author; or of a faculty showing itself in an unusual and unexpected form. But I beg to insist that a part is not the whole. The detection of the beauties and defects of passages is not a review of a work. Upon the critic is imposed a higher duty. Gross errors in detail notoriously heighten the effect of some of the most famous sculptures that remain to us; and so in literature, the impression intended to be produced by the author is frequently and designedly intensified by similar means.

The best books in every language abound in the gravest faults. Were a critic, then, to fasten on transparent defects, and conclude that the book is poor, or to deduce, from beauties he has discovered, that it is deserving of praise, he has his business yet to learn. It is true there may be defects of detail which, by destroying congruity, ruin art. Had the Venus de Medici the lips of a negress, it would cease to give pleasure; and the substitution in some of Shakespeare's plays of blemishes less glaring than those by which they are distinguished, would have the effect of destroying the efficaciousness of what is now congruous. In criticism regard must be had to the combination attempted by the author, and his success or failure must be explained. Beauties and blemishes should be massed, for it is the sum of the impression produced by a writer that is the criterion of his powers. I do not say the general effect should blind the critic to the existence of partial defects and beauties; I merely remind him that he should consider them partial defects and beauties, and nothing more. He must not judge of a work as a cheese-man tests his cheese—by tasting it.

III.

THE PROVINCE OF THE ANONYMOUS.

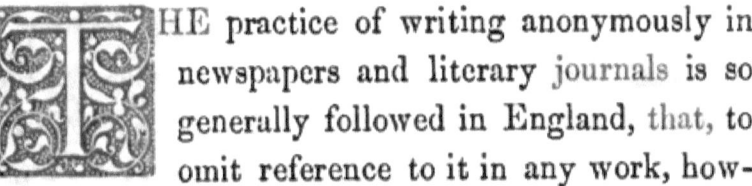HE practice of writing anonymously in newspapers and literary journals is so generally followed in England, that, to omit reference to it in any work, however humble, that has literature for its subject-matter, would be inexcusable. There is little need, however, to say much, since the scope and limits of anonymous writing have often been discussed, and more than once, I believe, been accurately defined. They may be briefly stated thus. In matters of fact the name of the writer is essential; in matters of opinion—in questions, that is, that are to be decided by argument—the writer may give his name or withhold it, as seems fit to himself. For instance, if the Teheran correspondent of the *Illuminator* tells us that the King of Persia has been intriguing with

Russia, or has killed his favourite wife, or has set fire to his palace, or charges him with any other scandalous proceeding, we have right to demand the name of the writer. We have right to say to him, " Off " with your mask, Mr. Correspondent, let us see " who you are; let us know what are your means " of information; give us the opportunity to ascer- " tain if you are trustworthy, and have no sinister " motive for your communication. It is not suffi- " cient for the conductor of the *Illuminator* to know " this. Everybody to whom you address yourself— " that is to say, all your readers—have right to be " equally well informed." The publication of the name would bring us double advantage. It would tend to repress the exuberant egotism of the correspondent, and have the effect of curtailing the redundancies of his communications. Were we, literally, to believe him, the foreign correspondent of a newspaper should be at once the happiest and most miserable man in existence. He is intimately acquainted with the secrets of foreign governments; nothing of importance " transpires" without his cognizance; indeed, the representative of majesty itself has fewer opportunities of learning the origination and progress of events, and not half the ability to use the information when it is acquired. In the social life of the capital to which he is accredited, he is *facile princeps.* He is killed with incessant kindnesses and attentions of the fashionable world; he has to ruin his health by agreeable excesses in which he is encouraged by the most agreeable companions; and, to crown all, he is enabled to enjoy the supreme felicity of giving himself the airs of martyrdom in the columns of the newspaper he represents. What state can be more enviable than his? A king retired from business excites our pity,—how much deeper, then, should be our commiseration with the newspaper correspondent who has relapsed into common life? Why he obtrudes upon us a narrative of his personal confidences, furnishes us with a catalogue of his whims, tells us how he relaxes himself, and what he eats, drinks, and avoids, is a question not easily answered. Even the word "gossip" is degraded when applied to his daily sermon; for it is not idle talk but offensive pretension that is generally placed before us. The legitimate and only cure for this state of things is a disclosure of the writer's name, so that those to whom he addresses himself may have the means of ascertaining whether the chronicler is to be implicitly trusted, or whether his confidences and revelations are to be taken with many grains of salt.

Even at home, where greater facilities for verification exist, the same information as to authorship is desirable. If a writer in the *Illuminator* charges himself with the responsibility of giving a daily or weekly report of what is being done at the principal Clubs, or of gossiping about literary and political notabilities; if he reveals the secrets of studios, publishing houses, and cabinet councils, we ought to have his name. We ought to know who he is that frequents the Clubs, and carries off what he hears therein. We should like to ascertain whether the unpublished book which he announces as about to create a great sensation is by himself or a member of his family; whether the information he has given touching the dissolution of Parliament has been derived from a member of the Cabinet, or from the less trustworthy medium of the porter's hall. Here, his credibility is at stake—he is dealing with facts— his name is essential. But, on the other hand, when the same gentleman in a leading article discusses politics—tells us that he considers Mr. Disraeli an adventurer in politics, and Lord Russell a great statesman—it is his own affair, and he has right to shield himself under the anonymous; he is dealing with arguments, and not with facts; the force of his reasoning can be neither strengthened nor weakened by the revelation of his identity. To the reader it is a matter of perfect indifference whether he gives or withholds his name.

Clearly just, however, as this limitation must

appear to all who consider the matter dispassion-
ately, the question is constantly re-opened by public
speakers and by writers in the press. Among
those who favoured signed articles was the late
Lord Herbert, who believed that for the mission
of public instruction anonymous writing in the
newspapers is a great disadvantage. " It puts on
" a par," he argued, "in point of weight and
" authority, the most scrupulous and the most un-
" scrupulous writer, the most exact and the most
" inexact. . . . . If we knew who the writers
" were, we should know, in the case of a man whose
" character is established, that everything he says
" might be taken for gospel, while we should also
" know in another case that the writer was neither
" so accurate in his statements nor so careful in
" sifting his facts. I think we should derive great
" advantage from such a state of things. . . . .
" Then, again, there is something in the English
" character that dislikes secrecy. Men are ashamed
" to a certain extent of writing anonymously, and if
" they do so, they conceal it. I have known many
" gentlemen take a leading part in public writing ;
" but I have always found them unwilling to admit
" or to be known as writers of such and such ar-
" ticles. They don't like the impression which would
" be produced if they were known as anonymous

" writers. In the House of Commons an impression
" prevails that a man who can speak in his own
" name upon any question takes an unfair advantage
" if he says something under cover of an anonymous
" article."

Something very similar to this has been urged by
Mr. Thomas Hughes, M. P. "Our readers," says
that gentleman,* "would derive the greatest benefit
" [from the abolition of the anonymous system], for
" they would pretty soon take our measure, and
" would read the lucubrations of some of us, and
" skip those of others: just as they treat the
" speeches of our brethren of the third estate of the
" realm already. (By the way what right have we
" of the fourth estate to such an advantage over
" them? The greatest bore in the House is not
" allowed to shout in a feigned voice from behind a
" door.)"

One can scarcely imagine objections of so little force
as these could have possibly been advanced in seri-
ousness against the anonymous system. A writer is, I
presume, to be tested by the quality of his arguments,
and not by our opinion of his character. If Lord
Herbert correctly represented the prevailing impression of the House of Commons, his announcement

---

* *Macmillan's Magazine*, December, 1861.

gives us a sad opinion of the liberality of members of Parliament. When a man becomes the representative of an English borough he surely is not to be debarred from advancing, by the most powerful means within his reach, principles which, from the few opportunities he can have of being " on his legs " in the House, he could only feebly advance by speech. Mr. Hughes's notion implies that his readers are unable to take his measure till they become acquainted with his name. I hope, for the sake of his admirers, that the estimate he has formed of their capacity is false. The parenthetical assertion that anonymous writing is equivalent to a shout in a feigned voice behind a door is more curious than true, and does not demand serious comment. The author of an unsigned article in a newspaper speaks in his natural voice as truly as he who prints in name in flaming capital letters. It is his personality and not his opinion, or unfeigned voice, that is concealed.

The subject has engaged the pen of Mr. Anthony Trollope, too, who appears, however, to be only a semi-believer in the benefits that are promised from the total abolition of anonymous writing. He thinks " any one can understand that a leading article in " the *Times* must be written as a part of a combined " whole. It must support certain views to which " the *Times* is committed. It must be subject to,

" and compatible with, the prevailing spirit of the
" *Times.* That is the valid reason for anonymous
" writing in political journalism ; but no such reason
" operates in regard to magazine articles." In periodical literature he believes the public should have
the means afforded them of knowing " what they
get " for their sixpence, shilling, two shillings, or
five, and thinks " it is absurd to argue that readers
" should judge by the matter and not by the name
" of the writer." People differ as to what it is
absurd to argue, and I have the misfortune to be one
of those who think it right that readers should judge
of the matter by the matter. What does it signify
to us who it is that occupies a dozen pages of
our magazine with fiction? or pens the critique or
the stanza? or gives us his opinion about politics,
or religion, or art? Not the most powerful name
on earth can make twaddle anything but twaddle ;
nor can the absence of a man's name lessen the
weight of his sentence. It is singular that the very
number of the magazine* in which Mr. Trollope
discusses the subject contains convincing evidence of
the wholesomeness of the limits I would assign to
anonymous writing. " In this Review of ours,"
says Mr. Trollope in the concluding sentence of his

---

* *Fortnightly Review,* July, 1865.

article, " we intend to try what signatures will do " for us. Our editor will, at any rate, not be " ashamed of putting forward the names of his con- " tributors; and we, on our part, will not be " ashamed to put forward our names under his " authority." After this frank avowal of a frank intention we know what to expect. On the page facing Mr. Trollope's name is an article on " Public Affairs." Now, if it is desirable that any communi- cation should be signed by the writer it is that in which public men and public events are freely criti- cised. One of our statesmen is accused of attempt- ing to lead his party to commit political suicide; another is said to have resigned his seat in a " fit of petulance," and his objection to being a Treasury dependant is sneered at. Members of Parliament are spoken of as " a" Mr. Blank, and the " notorious " Mr. Blank; and an unfortunate Cabinet minister is described as " born in narrow-mindedness, he has " grown mature in it, and he will never change." The whole is characterized by the same taste. Every other article has the writer's name scrupu- lously appended to his communication. But here, when we anxiously turn over the pages to see who is the author, no name appears; when we are desirous of learning whether we are listening to Snug the joiner or to the Royal beast, to the Bishop of Oxford or to Mr. Pifken the curate, our curiosity is piqued and not satisfied.

Fortunately, in this country, no decision on this point at which disputants may arrive is binding upon others. As a result, the greater portion of current literature is anonymous; and the obvious and legitimate advantages of the practice are so great that men of letters will, doubtless, continue to oppose any modification that may be proposed to them, either by following the example of French writers, and signing every article that contains an expression of opinion, or of American journalists who print on the face of their newspapers the names of proprietors and editors. The opponents of the anonymous system necessarily agree with me in requiring the names of a writer in matters of fact; but they decline to agree with my limitation. They insist also upon the critic and the writer on public affairs affixing their names to their productions, complaining that, under the present system, an article is influential in proportion to the reputation of the paper in which it appears, and not, as they would have it, in proportion to the status of the writer. In some measure I agree with the validity of their complaint, but I must altogether dissent from the remedy proposed of substituting the authority of a name for the authority of a paper. In both cases the influence would be de-

rived from an illegitimate source, as the consideration
should be, not " Who says it?" but " What is said?"
If the arguments adduced by a writer are judicious,
it is a matter of complete indifference by whom they
are advanced, and I therefore think it an impertinence in any writer to suppose his name can give
additional weight to a sound conclusion. If the public persist in attaching fictitious importance to anonymous writing, and give to opinion the weight of fact;
if they take Jones's unsigned crudities to be more
valuable than they would, had that gentleman's
name appeared as the author; if they like illu-
sion,—the fault is clearly with them. It can hardly
be supposed that, within these circumstances, Jones
would voluntarily relinquish the advantage to be
derived from writing anonymously. If, on the other
hand, Jones thinks his opinion would derive additional weight from declaring his name, or is fearful
of receiving more influence than he deserves if he
abstains from avowing it, we have no fault to find
with him. He is free to choose. There is a class
of writers, however, who would not permit him the
choice. They themselves—" the champions of a free
press"—affix their names to what they write and
call upon others to do the same. Their pretence is
that the proceeding gives a guarantee of good faith,
and prevents a man from saying anonymously what

he feels indisposed to say openly. In reality, however, their practice arises from an undue estimate of
their own importance, and springs from the same
source as that which induces vulgar persons to cut
their initials on seats and to deface with their names
monuments and places of public resort; it is usually
called personal vanity. For my part, I believe it to
be no disadvantage to literature that a writer—within
the province that has been already indicated—should
have the opportunity of saying anonymously what he
would be indisposed to say openly. If A, who is a
critic, knows B, the author of a volume of very
indifferent poems, he would not like to sit down and
say the truth of poor B's book, were he obliged to
affix his name. But he could do this anonymously
without, I think, being justly liable to the charge of
cowardice or want of friendship. It is allowable for
him to maintain his social relations with B, and yet be
honest in his calling in not thinking B's poetry good.
If, however, he had to affix his name and expressed
his disapprobation of the work, the poet would forthwith tax his memory to ascertain what he could have
done to offend the critic, never supposing a writer to
whom he is personally known could speak except in
laudatory terms of his work.

To resume. Questions of policy or principle, of
art and science, of literature, of morals—questions

which have to do with argument—are within the province of the anonymous. Questions of fact, dependent upon evidence and the credibility of witnesses, are without the province.

IV.

LITERARY MEN IN PARLIAMENT.

NGLISHMEN are reputed to be a practical people. No revolution in their history has been the result of a desire on their part to effect constitutional changes in order to obtain some contingent theoretical advantage. They are said to pride themselves on their inability to be influenced by an idea. Indifferent to abstractions, they are moved solely by practical, which mostly mean physical, reasons. Sometimes, indeed, out of a confused sense of duty, they attempt to act from other considerations, as on the occasion of the tercentenary of Shakespeare's birth. But it is in vain. The living Garibaldi will ever be more influential than the dead Shakespeare. Whatever they may profess to the contrary, however, they feel half ashamed of their stolidity. When rallied by their more enlightened friends on account of their inacces-

sibility **to advanced** ideas in politics, they excuse themselves with **the plea** that **the** ideas have reference to what they do not understand, and decline to become converts till they are in a position to test **the** validity **of the** ideas in their own practical way.

At this moment **they have the** unusual good-fortune **to be presented with a** cardinal opportunity of applying **their** favourite **test.** An eminent literary man, **and one of the** most prominent of **the** advanced philosophers, **is a** candidate **for a seat in** Parliament, and, having expressed **his views** on practical politics, he **has furnished them with** the means of examining his ideas when applied **to a** subject with which they conceive themselves **to be** familiar.

I have no **desire to** undervalue the high functions of **the** philosopher. **In any** estimate of the practical man, as compared **with the man** of thought, **I agree** with Mr. Emerson, **that** the ordering of **a bale of** goods from **Smyrna to** New York, or the **running up and down to** procure a company of subscribers to set going **ten** thousand spindles, or any other practical action, is not to be preferred to a life of contemplation. **But I** hold that the life of contemplation **is an** altogether different thing from the ordering of goods; that **it** requires **in** those by whom **it is** undertaken a different set of **faculties**; bespeaks **a different** training **and a** different experience; that success in one department depends upon the exercise of qualities of mind different from those which presumably and really make a man successful in the other ; that, in a word, the theoretical is wholly distinct from the practical. The philosopher has to do with the discovery and elucidation of right principles of conduct. His function is to reason out what he conceives to be the best course for mankind. His attempts are directed to the discovery of a fixed standard of morals. He has in his calculations no respect for idiosyncrasies. To him the agriculturist of Suffolk is as the iron worker of Wales; the Catholic of Munster as the Protestant of Kent. He propounds theories. But theories, even should they be correct, are not the most essential requisites in a legislator. No government that could be devised can be universally applied. So few are the general principles that have been ascertained, that regard must be had in legislation to the circumstances of the particular government. The condition of affairs must be thoroughly mastered ; the aspect of the times and the temporary disposition of the nation must be considered. The mood of a people is evanescent, and, therefore, what is expedient to-day may be pernicious to-morrow. These popular barometrical changes the generator of correct principles is incapacitated from dealing with. He deals with

men as if they were counters of fixed value, whilst
in practical legislation such a course would produce
dangerous consequences. Here principles must vary,
to be in harmony with the governed. It would obviously be injudicious, for instance, to apply the same
laws to ourselves as to our Indian fellow-subjects, or
to ourselves at one time as at another. At the present
moment every Londoner is, politically speaking, in
the possession of complete personal liberty; circumstances, however, may at any time arise when it will
be found necessary to suspend the *habeas corpus*.
Now the philosopher would, to judge from his ante-
cedents, be an unfit person to determine the moment
when the changed relations between the governors
and the governed have reached the point to make
the suspension necessary and salutary. For this
duty another class of man intervenes. This is the
statesman. He does not profess to be guided by
absolute right and wrong—is doubtful, indeed, if
there is an absolute right and wrong—but his conduct is regulated by what is called Expediency. He
makes a choice, that is, of what he judges to be the
least of several evils. The philosopher, on the other
hand, whose profession is to discover what is right,
persists in advocating what is right, and disdains to
concern himself with what is expedient. By *à priori*
reasoning he has gone and discovered, for example,

that every man and woman who can read and write should have a voice in governing the country. The practical man tells us such a notion, if carried into effect, would be dangerous to the State. Which of them is right?

Of the philosophers, the candidate for Westminster, Mr. John Stuart Mill, has for a long time been considered one of the most eminent. He is what, in the slang of his admirers, is termed " the greatest thinker" of the age. In strict accuracy he can only be credited with being the most eminent of the performing thinkers, of those, namely, that print their thoughts on philosophical questions; just as poor Tom Sayers—who, by the exaggeration of friends, was said to be the best man at fisticuffs in England —was only the best of the ten or twelve that battered each other for the delectation of the public. But, admitting Mr. Mill's eminence in the direction and to the extent claimed, is it expedient for him or for us that he should hold a seat in Parliament?

All who appreciate the fact that the destiny of organized nature is amelioration, will agree that it is highly advantageous for the public that men are found to devote themselves to abstruse speculations, for the purpose of discovering the form and processes of this amelioration; and that it is well for the public to acknowledge their obligation. I must, however, in the interests of literature, dissent from the form in which that acknowledgment is, in Mr. Mill's case, attempted to be made. Those of this gentleman's admirers who are connected with Westminster have invited him to come forward as a candidate for their city. They evidently belong to that class of minds which considers a man eminent in one department to be equally well fitted for any other, and they esteem a seat in Parliament to be the most appropriate reward for transcendent merit of all kinds. Hence the increasing number of successful lawyers, soldiers, gold-diggers, and tradesmen, that are returned to the House of Commons. In Mr. Mill's favour, however, they urge that he is not only a theorist, but has written very successfully on practical subjects; that, in short, he has, in numerous instances, looked at things from the same point of view as ordinary men. I reply—So have all newspaper editors; but neither they nor the public would benefit by their translation from their editorial chairs to the benches of the House of Commons. Mr. Mill, however, I venture, with much diffidence, to think is more than most eminent men unfitted for those benches. Fortunately, it is within our power to test his validity to the claim of being a statesman. He takes the opportunity, in reply to some questions put to him by his supporters, of expressing his earnest hope that they

intend " to include in their adhesion the principle of
" an individual appeal by circular to every elector,
" laying other names before him as well as mine,
" and requesting him to select from among them, or
" from any others, the person or persons whom he
" would wish to be brought forward as candidates."
Could any request be more illogical and trifling? If
Mr. Mill were an autocrat, to whom lists of candidates
had to be submitted for approval, he would deserve
high respect for the generosity by which his conduct
was dictated; but as it happens that the electors are
competent to elect almost any able-bodied Englishman, I fail to see his object in recommending the
proceeding. For his supporters to issue, under their
sanction, and explicitly with their recommendation,
the names of other candidates, would, if it meant
nothing, be a silly farce; if it meant anything, it
would militate against their own interest, inasmuch
as they would be setting up rivals to their own candidate. They have already decided, by their selection, that Mr. Mill, in their opinion, is the fittest
man to be their representative; and now they are
naïvely requested by that gentleman to announce to
the constituency that there are others they consider
equally eligible. The document to which this recommendation forms the preamble is all that was
wanted by the stolid Englishman to enable him to

see the deep gulf that separates the " great thinker"
from the statesman.   It is divided into ten heads.
With some of them all men will agree; but the
most important of them are characterized by a strange
boldness that is astonishing, even coming from a philosopher.   I can only indicate their tendency.

With respect to Reform, Mr. Mill would confer
the suffrage upon every man and woman who can
read and write and do Rule of Three.   This plan is
very simple and intelligible.   It would almost give
equal power to everybody in the State—noses would
count.   But not so.   It is evident that, by counting
of noses, the lower orders, who in every country
have the most, would inevitably outnumber the other
orders; so he would impose restraints by allowing
minorities to be represented—that is, he would, by
skilfully devised checks, in effect bring the representation to where it is. Noses would be neutralised.

He prefers a mixed system of direct and indirect
taxation.   So do we—so does the Chancellor of the
Exchequer; but practical men are needed to determine how far each mode can safely be pursued.   His
views with respect to intervention in the internal
affairs of another country are unique—he will not
interfere *unless others had interfered.* He is of opinion
that on account of religion there ought to be no disabilities.   This I believe to be unwise.   If the

principles of the religionists are noxious, disabilities should certainly be imposed; if they are dangerous to the State, or are immoral, they ought to be repressed. His most important paragraph, however, relates to the ballot, which he opposes, on the ground that the elector is a trustee of the non-elector. The *onus probandi* clearly lies with him; but, although he is emphatic in his assertion, he gives no reason for his belief. Is it possible he thinks it a first principle? The aim and object of the franchise he appears altogether to misapprehend. I have to offer him two reasons for differing from him. If the voter were a trustee of the non-voter, the latter—*cestui que trust* —could exercise legal supervision over him, and would have the power of calling him to account for his actions; secondly, by conferring on a man the privilege of voting, the object of the Constitution is simply to get from him *his opinion of the merits of the candidates*, and, therefore, he is a representative of himself alone.*

---

* Let us suppose there are three brothers with votes. A, who is a retired tradesman, and independent of the commercial influences of the town in which he resides, wishes to record his vote openly, believing his example will be followed by many who have good opinion of his judgment; he is, of course, enabled to do so. B, however, who is a small shopkeeper with trade relations, does not wish to give his vote in public. Some of his cus-

I do not believe Mr. Mill to be a man of aspiring vein. His intellectual underlings, by persuading him that he will best serve his country by entering Parliament, have, I am confident, done him injury. There is no occasion for him now, any more than heretofore, to impound his wisdom. He can still enunciate his views through the press more appropriately and with an effect more commensurate with their value than he is likely to do by his voice in the House of Commons. As far as the merits of the opposing candidates have been disclosed, he may make as good

---

tomers imagine that, by purchasing his tea and coffee, they make it necessary for him to think as they do in politics, and will cease to deal with him if he practically differ from them. Others who buy of him their eggs and bacon, think that therefore his views should coincide with theirs. Were they, then, to discover, at election-time, that his principles were opposed to what they profess, they would assuredly discontinue their custom. It happens that the tea-and-coffee customers favour one candidate, and the eggs-and-bacon customers his rival. What is poor B to do? He is anxious to vote; but he knows that he will lose half his profits were he to exercise his privilege. Not being fully assured, however, that there is intimate connection between politics and eggs-and-bacon, he wishes to retain his customers, and to give his vote. He demands permission to vote by ballot. C, the third brother, is at a distance of two hundred miles from his home on the day of election—ill at the seaside. Although he is desirous of voting, it would be greatly inconvenient, and perhaps dangerous, for him to undergo the fatigue

a legislator as any of them; but I am unable to see
in what respect he is their superior. When what is
best in theory becomes coincident with what is practicable in legislation, salutary consequences may
result from the election of such a man as **Mr. Mill.**
It will then be time to invite " the greatest thinkers
of the age" to the direction of affairs. **Mr. Mill has,**
doubtless, rendered great services to the science of
politics, and Mr. F. W. Newman and others are willing, on this account, to accept " his large mind,"
notwithstanding its aberrations. But this condonation

---

of a long journey. Why should not he register his vote with
the returning officer of the town in which he temporarily resides, and thus declare his choice of candidates? I know no
valid reason why each of the brothers should not vote in the
manner most convenient to himself. If, as I assert, the right
to vote has been conferred on him in order to obtain his views
on public affairs, it is of little importance *how* he delivers his
opinion—whether openly, as is the present custom ; or by ballot, as is practised in clubs and other private societies; or by
certified papers sent through the post, the plan adopted in the
election of members for the universities. It surely is unnecessary for him to appear in person and at a certain place.

To compel a man to vote by ballot in the election of a member of Parliament, as is proposed by the Ballot Society, is so
manifestly unjust and tyrannical, that there is little fear of the
bill, annually introduced into Parliament, being carried. Why
should A be deprived of the legitimate influence exercised by
his example, because B requires the protection of secrecy?

appears to me unreasonable—as unreasonable as it would be to appoint a man teacher of arithmetic who deliberately propounds the notion that two and two make five.   The admirers of Mr. Mill should find another way of rewarding him than by sending him to the House of Commons.

Since the foregoing was written, Mr. Mill has served for one session in Parliament—has been for that period the six-hundred-and-fifty-eighth part of a king; with what result to the high reputation he had deservedly earned as a philosopher all of us have cause to lament.   I could never bring myself to believe it would be well for us if philosophers were kings, and kings philosophers.   Much better will it be, I presume, for each class to remain in its own sphere, mindful of the maxim, " Ne sutor ultra crepidam."   As was predicted, he has been less successful as a politician than was anticipated by his too sanguine friends.   Liberal organs of public opinion, which at the time of the contest were over-hard upon those who opposed his candidature, and urged upon the constituency the duty of rejecting any man possessing only the ordinary qualifications, for one of Mr. Mill's conspicuous and exceptional merits, have latterly confessed their disappointment.   I am not sure whether the two I quote were among the number of Mr. Mill's more enthusiastic backers, but I

subjoin their remarks, as they furnish us with the
opinions of very influential and presumably educated
writers as to the degree of success achieved by one
of our wisest men of letters who has deserted his
study for the senate.

" The old saying, that no man can safely be called
" fortunate until death has placed him beyond mis-
" fortune's reach," says the *Saturday Review*, " seems
" in some danger of receiving a painful illustration
" in the career of Mr. Mill. The contrast between
" Mr. Mill the philosopher and Mr. Mill the politician
" is deplorable, but it is really a question whether it
" is not even more ludicrous. It is so absurdly sug-
" gestive of Molière's inimitable scene in which the
" innocent M. Jourdain calls in his ' Maître de
" ' Philosophie' to calm the dispute raging between
" his other masters as to the merits of their respective
" arts. The philosopher begins by referring the
" disputants to Seneca's masterly treatise on ' Anger,'
" and assuring them that in this world there is no-
" thing worth striving for but ' *la sagesse et la vertu ;*'
" but in less than five minutes, to M. Jourdain's
" horror and amazement, he is furiously pommelling
" and being pommelled all round. The British nation,
" struck by Mr. Mill's writings, summons him, amid
" loud acclamations, into its Parliament as the great
" philosopher of the age, and innocently congratulates

" itself on having among its advisers at least one man
" who understands the virtues of moderation and self-
" control; and, on the first grave crisis which calls
" for both, is amazed to find him the blindest and
" most furious of partisans.   Molière deliberately
" intended to make philosophers ridiculous, but this
" can scarcely be the intention of Mr. Mill.   And
" yet his appearance at the Agricultural Hall the
" other night might almost furnish grounds for
" even this supposition.   We admit that this asso-
" ciation between Mr. Mill's philosophy and his
" speeches is not strictly logical.   The ' Represen-
" ' tative Government' and the ' Essay on Liberty'
" would remain exactly what they now are if their
" author were in open Parliament to pull Mr. Dis-
" raeli's nose, or offer to ' take off coats' with Mr.
" Walpole.   But, logical or illogical, it is the way of
" the world to measure the value of what a man says
" or writes by its practical estimate of his character."

" We are half inclined to regret," says the *Pall
Mall Gazette,* " that philosophers are not, like cler-
" gymen, excluded from the House of Commons.
" Philosophers are beyond price, but philosophy is
" frail, and party-politics are seductive. And as ' good
" ' things corrupted are the worst,' so philosophers,
" when they are once off the poise, are apt to rush
" into intolerance with the fury of renegades. Mr.

" Mill's late exhibitions illustrate this very pro-
" vokingly. As Liberals, we regret this, because
" whereas formerly in Mr. Mill's alliance we had the
" sentence of a judge in our favour, we feel that we
" have now, so to say, only the protestations of an
" advocate. But we are deeply sorry for the trans-
" formation on other grounds too. Henceforth,
" when Mr. Mill writes of social or political mat-
" ters, even his old admirers will read him with mis-
" giving. What he would write would be in too
" flagrant contradiction to his present practice. But,
" indeed, just now the philosophical faculty has
" departed. He is a lost philosopher. . . . . .

  " No doubt Mr. Mill receives large compensation
" of a kind in his political importance. But what a
" falling off there must be in philosophical temper if
" such compensation can ever be sufficient! He has
" given up to party, and party in its pettiest sense,
" what was meant for mankind. All that abstraction
" and disinterestedness which gave him authority has
" vanished. He is no longer umpire, but a party to
" the squabble. Instead of hardly condescending
" *laudari laudatis*—instead of the cold proud atti-
" tude which seemed to show he thought it almost
" too mercenary even to accept the esteem of the
" estimable—we see Mr. Mill now readily ' helping
" ' to make a mob,' and apparently rewarded quite to

" his taste by a popularity which would have once
" seemed to him misconception, if not an insult. Of
" course Mr. Mill has not suddenly ceased to be a
" clever man ; but his words now have no more than
" their own weight, and that weight is not always
" great. The false oracle is detected by the false
" prosody. It is not only the philosophical temper
" which is impaired in Mr. Mill, but the logical
" cogency. The fallacies he has been all his life
" exposing he now finds very handy weapons."

The writers I have quoted so well express what
all feel who are interested in the well-being of the
literary class, that I need not add one word to their
testimony. Mr. Mill's political career will not have
been fruitless if it has had the effect of convincing
his admirers that the literary character and the politician are not necessarily identical, and of dissipating
the injurious notion that philosophers should be kings
and kings philosophers.

V.

LITERARY HERO-WORSHIP.

THE present age, often accused of scepticism, shows itself to be, in some respects, fully as credulous as any of its predecessors. Without stopping here to multiply examples in support of this assertion, it will be sufficient to instance the firm belief it displays in the doctrine of hero-worship. Nor is this belief professed merely by the vulgar and illiterate. It is extensively current even among the intellectual and the refined; it has found its way into books; it forms the text of some of the most popular works in our language; it is echoed in every direction; and, in fine, has become so prevalent, that if one should venture to doubt the existence of " great " men, one would be regarded much in the same light as if one were to question the reality of one's own existence, or deny that all men are mortal. " It is natural to

" believe in great men," writes Mr. Emerson. "No
" sadder proof can be given by a man of his own
" littleness," says Mr. Carlyle, " than disbelief in
" great men—it is the last consummation of un-
" belief." There can be no doubt, then, of the
existence of this belief. It is notorious that public
opinion selects certain personages to occupy the
highest place in its regard, and upon them confers
the title of " great men." And in making out the
list of what are termed great men, public opinion
appears to be actuated by a spirit of the utmost im-
partiality. It liberally selects names from almost
every country under the sun, esteeming none too
remote or too insignificant to furnish a representative. Even China has Confucius; and Switzerland,
small as she is, is credited with Tell, notwithstanding
that hero labours under the somewhat serious dis-
qualification of never having existed in the flesh.
The praise of liberality does not, however, exclusively belong to the nineteenth century. It must be
shared with the eighteenth, which was even more
lavish in the bestowal of this title. It was with it
Voltaire paid his physician, Tronchin; and upon
losing Madame Chatelet, as he could not in good
French call her *grande femme*, it is still *grand
homme* (great man) that we find him styling her,
when, in writing to the King of Prussia, he says,

" I have lost a friend of five-and-twenty years'
" standing, a great man who had but one fault—
" that of being a woman."*

We have now established with certainty the existence of a belief in "great" men; let us next ascertain, if we be able, what is a great man? Let us see what constitutes a great man, and discover wherein he is like ordinary men, and wherein he differs from them.

But it is here, at the very point where the inquiry becomes of some value, that we are fated to meet with disappointment. In former ages no doubt existed as to the meaning of the term. It was conferred only upon a man of exalted social or official rank—the Xerxes, the Alexander, the Cæsar. In ancient Rome, no one could have thought of calling Virgil and Horace great men, because they were poets, even though he entertained a higher opinion than we of their literary merits. The term was confined in its application solely to those who were powerful by reason of their influential relations to the State, or of their social rank. And down so far as to the time of our own Elizabeth it had, I believe, the same confined signification. Thus limited, the term had a just, precise, and well-

---

* Bungener—" *Voltaire and his Times.*"

F

known meaning. **But** now that the traditional and ordinary idea **of a great man** has been abandoned, and the title indiscriminately and capriciously conferred upon other grounds, it has lost its significance and **become utterly** unintelligible. Almost everybody **professes to believe** in great men as decidedly as he believes, say, in sky-rockets. But the basis of **his belief in the one case** must be essentially different **from what it is in the other; for** almost everybody **knows what a** sky-rocket **is,** can describe one, and **is able** to recognize **one when he** sees it; whilst, as to what constitutes **a** great man, there are irreconcileable **varieties of** opinion. **No two** persons will be found **to give** the same definition of a great man, or (what is the **same thing** in amount) agree upon those to whom **the** title **shall be** applied. Many, affecting catholicity **in their views, make out a** long list; others, more **particular in their choice,** select only a few for the honour; **while some are** so fastidious as **to exclude all names but** those of two or three of the most famous personages **that** have ever lived. **Nor is this the sole** difficulty that **besets our inquiry.** There is another and **a more** formidable **one. Not** only **are we** presented with **a variety of** lists, but each list in itself varies **in accordance with** the different stages of its owner's mental culture. No man pretends to be in possession of a list that is permanently fixed. Now, a name is added thereto; now, it is displaced or degraded; and now, again, it is struck out altogether, to make room for another which is thought to be more worthy of honour. The heroes of a man's youth are no longer heroes in his manhood, and the names he most esteemed in the prime of life come to be regarded with indifference in his declining years.

It plainly rests with those who have an idea of a "great" man and call upon us for our belief, to prove the existence of such a thing, or at least to enlighten us as to the meaning of the term. They do neither, however. The widest possible diversity of opinion exists amongst them, and every attempt on our part to arrive at a satisfactory conclusion must therefore, of necessity, be fruitless. Mr. Carlyle —who appears to be regarded, and to regard himself, as the high-priest of hero-worship—contends that earnestness and sincerity constitute a hero; and, accordingly, his "great" men, let them differ ever so widely in other points, are yet all sincere and earnest men. One may be a despot, another a staunch opponent of absolutism; this may be an apologist of Catholicism, that other its deadliest enemy—but in one respect they are all alike: they are eminently distinguished for earnestness and sincerity. If we turn from Mr. Carlyle's idea of a great man to that

of his American admirer, Mr. Emerson, we shall
have another, and a widely different definition. Mr.
Emerson supposes a great man to be "one who has
" a large stomach,"—" one of great affinities, who
" takes up into himself all arts, sciences—all know-
" ables—as his food; who can spare nothing; who
" can dispose of everything." Such a man we confess never yet to have known—for the assertion that
" Plato, like every great man, consumed his own
" times," is manifestly incorrect—and such a man is
an impossibility. Mr. Ruskin also believes in great
men, and is of opinion that the " first test of a great
" man is humility." Not that he therefore supposes
a great man to be ignorant of his greatness: " For,"
says he, " all great men not only know their busi-
" ness, but know, usually, that they know it; only
" they don't think much of themselves on that ac-
" count." Professor Ranke, again, the historian of
the Popes, contributes a fresh notion. In speaking
of Alfred he indignantly asks, " What right has he
" to be styled ' the Great?' That title belongs only
" to those who have fought, not merely for private,
" but, at the same time, for great general interests."

Such are some of the various opinions entertained
in reference to the subject of our inquiry. I have
quoted these authors only because they are those
whose works happen to be by me whilst I am writ-

ing. Were I to quote as many more, they would be found to differ amongst themselves quite as much as these. They might all agree that there is such a thing as a "great man:" but here their agreement will end; they will be at issue on the meaning of the term; they will all use the word in widely different senses.

The progress of our inquiry has, thus far, been but slow; or, rather, it has been in a backward direction. We are, in fact, at the very point from which we started. Can it be, then, that this term—spoken so trippingly on the tongue, and falling so easily from the pen—has, after all, no idea to correspond with it in the mind? Are we to conclude that it has no meaning, and that it is constantly used without being understood? We shall see.

Speaking broadly, there appear to be two classes of men to which general opinion is willing to assign the highest and most honourable title in its power to bestow. First, there are those in whom certain active, masculine qualities are developed in a very high degree, and successfully made patent to the world. In this class (to take notable examples) are Dante and Napoleon. These men are "great" in the worldly sense of the term. Next, there are those who are esteemed great in proportion to their goodness, and the beneficial effect they have exercised on human virtue and **human** happiness. In this latter, which is the theological sense, Washington **is a** greater man than Napoleon, and John Howard, or the inventor of lucifer-matches greater than either.

Now, whilst admitting that Dante was a great poet, **and** Napoleon a great warrior, one must, at the **risk of being characterized as** "**a critic** of small " vision," and " **a promoter of** spiritual paralysis," confess one's inability **to perceive how** any greatness, except of this partial kind, can justly be claimed for either of them. And that no man is "great," other than in this partial sense, may be deduced from the simple consideration that *no man can be an exemplar of all greatness.* An instance will make the meaning clearer. **Let us take, as our** example, the first Napoleon. **Here** is one whom **all classes** of hero-worshippers **will most** readily **agree** to admit into their several lists of heroes ; **he was** as great a man, they **say, as** any that ever lived. Without derogating in **the** least degree from the just fame of this celebrated character, and crediting him with the possession of **all** his rare and brilliant qualities, we cannot concede **to him** the title of " great man." **He was** no poet, no artist, no orator, no philosopher, no handicrafts-man; **or,** if he was, **and more, he was much ex-**celled **as** such by many of his contemporaries for **whom the title** is not claimed. He was a military man, had pre-eminently the genius of a soldier, and possessed all the various qualifications requisite for the successful carrying on of war. But this does not constitute a great Man; it makes only a great Soldier. There may be some, too indolent to perceive any difference between these expressions, who will object that I am playing upon words—that it is a mere verbal dispute—and that to call a man a great warrior is substantially the same as to call him a great man. But the dispute is something more than a dispute about words; it is essentially a dispute about things. If it be admitted that the qualities that appeared in Napoleon are the identical qualities that constitute a great man, it must follow that warriors only are to be called great men; and it must follow that Dante, and such as he, who were in possession of none of these qualities, have no right to the title. If, instead of Napoleon, we make Dante our example, we shall of course arrive at a similar conclusion. Grant that Dante's qualities are those that give a man a claim to be called great, and you exclude Napoleon, and all who have not been poets. Both these men we have mentioned are pre-eminent in their several departments, and it has been suggested to me that, after all, this only is meant by the term—one, namely, who has been successful in arriving at the first place in his particular walk. The

great man "must be good of his kind," says Mr.
Emerson; "able men do not care in what kind a
"man is able, so only that he is able." This test is
intelligible—it would admit Mr. Thomas Sayers and
M. Blondin, and would not exclude even Mr. Bar-
num. But few hero-worshippers will consent to adopt
it. Lord Macaulay, one of the most eminent of them,
repudiates it. In one of his essays, he says: "Homer
"is not more decidedly the first of heroic poets,
"Shakespeare is not more decidedly the first of
"dramatists, Demosthenes is not more decidedly
"the first of orators, than Boswell is the first of
"biographers. Many of the greatest men that
"ever lived have written biography. Boswell was
"one of the smallest men that ever lived, and he
"has beaten them all." This dictum is elegantly
and plainly expressed; the meaning cannot be missed
—but, is it just? If Homer is a great man, because
decidedly the first of epic poets, why, it might be
asked, should Boswell be precluded from occupying
a similarly elevated position, seeing that, notwithstanding he has for competitors many of the greatest
men that ever lived, he is the first of biographers,
and has in his calling immeasurably surpassed them
all? The essayist, however, did not see the difficulty,
or, seeing it, he evaded it; he was too brilliant to be
expected to be accurate.

Not only, however, are we called on to believe in
great men, but, it seems, we must esteem them, or we
shall suffer penalties. " Our religion is the love and
" cherishing of these patrons," say all true worship-
pers; " woe be to him who believes not!" But just
as we have seen these professors to be guilty of
a provoking ambiguity and want of accuracy in
the definition they give of their patrons, so now, in
demanding our esteem for them, we shall find they
are equally unreasonable. We are ordered to esteem
" great " men for the qualities they possess; but if
we require a reason for doing so, we get no reply.
And can we hope for any that is satisfactory? The
qualities that go to make up a man's greatness,
whatever they be, are gifts, are accidents—just as
health, wealth, or strength are gifts. " He is great,"
Mr. Emerson confesses, " who is what he is from
" Nature;" and again, in speaking of Shakespeare, he
says, " His principal merit may be conveyed in
" saying, that he of all men best understands the
" English language, and can say what he will. Yet
" these unchoked channels and floodgates of expres-
" sion are only health, or fortunate constitution."
Qualities of the intellect are as much gifts as personal comeliness is a gift, or as a healthy constitution
is a gift. They are external to the man, and esteem
is no more due to him for the possession of the one

than it is for the other. Why, then, should we esteem
him? Riches are admirable; but are we to give our
esteem to the man who is rich? Health and beauty
are admirable; but are we to tender our respect to
the healthy and beautiful? Mr. Carlyle's synonyme
for greatness has even fewer claims on our esteem than
these have. Heroism, he tells us, is sincerity; we
must reverence the sincere. Before, however, ten-
dering to any man our reverence, we should first
ascertain what his principles are; we should know
whether they are good or bad—whether conducive
to the happiness or misery of mankind. Sincerity,
in itself, is a quality neither to be commended nor
blamed. It matters not how sincere or conscientious
a man may be in his opinions; it matters not how
earnest he may be in his conduct: if the opinions
are erroneous, and the conduct noxious, on what
ground can esteem or respect with any justice be
claimed for the possessor? Yet it constantly happens that men treat with consideration the advocates
of a principle they believe to be false and wicked,
solely on the ground of their presumed conscien-
tiousness. Mr. Bright, for instance, is admitted to
be a sincere and earnest man. Competent authorities, however—competent by reason of education,
long acquaintance with affairs of State, personal experience, and intimate knowledge of our history—

deny his right to be considered a statesman, and look upon his principles as dangerous. What course, then, should they naturally pursue in reference to Mr. Bright? Not, surely, any course that would tend to elevate him in public opinion. Yet this is the very course they follow. On their last accession to office, Mr. Bright's chief opponents, the Conservatives, retaining as firmly as ever their decided objections to the honourable member's policy, thought fit, in more ways and on more occasions than one, to express their high esteem for the honourable member himself. And why? Why, because Mr. Bright is distinguished for earnestness in advocating the very doctrines they most condemn. The measure of esteem is, I presume, proportioned to the earnestness of the advocacy; if, then, the advocacy should turn out to be successful—if, that is to say, the party should be overtaken by political death, the esteem should rightly be doubled. Again, there is no doubt that Mary Tudor was eminently sincere in her religious professions—there can be no doubt that she was equally earnest in their propagation; but how can we esteem her personally, whilst we are forced to disavow her tenets and reprobate her conduct? To do so would plainly be irrational. Now this is what Mr. Carlyle in numerous instances does. Such a course, as might be supposed, leads him into incon-

sistencies and **contradictions. It** leads him also **to**
commit positive acts of injustice; it leads him,
amongst other things, **to** speak of the poet Byron
with contempt, **and to** celebrate the ploughman
Burns as a king of men.

It **must now be clear that the** popular notion of a
"great" man is **liable** to many **and** serious objections;
that, in fact, if we consider rightly, **it has no** more real
existence **than** those famous " general terms " which
formed so prominent a feature **in the** philosophy of
Plato, but in which there have long since ceased to be
a believer. It must be equally clear that the only
sense in which **a** man can justly be called great is **in**
the sense suggested above—that, namely, which cre-
dits him with being supreme in his particular depart-
ment or departments. This **view of the** question has
much **to** recommend **it.** Whilst leaving room for
asserting that Dante was **an** eminent poet, and Bacon
an eminent philosopher, **it would** confine the meaning of the term to its proper limits, and would preven**t**
the senseless comparisons instituted between " great "
men who have often nothing in common except their
humanity. And it is productive, indirectly and incidentally, of other benefits. It would **put** an end to
the presumption that success in one line or pursuit
indicates **power** for success **in** all lines or pursuits,
and render impossible the **absurd** and unjust **cen-**

sures people are in the habit of passing upon a man
eminent in one department for disappointing their
expectations in not being eminent in another department. What complaint is more frequently heard
than that of some hero-worshipper who expresses his
surprise at the " great " Napoleon's many littlenesses
of character under captivity; or at the cowardice of
Cicero when pursued by the emissaries of Antony?
A juster estimate of the pretensions of either of these
celebrated men would have dissipated all surprise.
It would have made it clear that the former, who
was a soldier and man of action, never advanced
any claim to be considered a moral philosopher; and
that the latter, who was a philosopher, is not to be
blamed for not having the qualities of a soldier. But
this distinction it is impossible for the hero-worshipper to make. He looks for a " whole man " whose
faculties are co-ordinate, whose *function* it is to be
great—a man who is excellent in every circumstance and in all respects—a Brahmin of the race.

Nothing less than this in a man will, it seems,
satisfy the strong popular appetite for hero-worship.
Ignorant people, in all ages, require some tangible,
some personal, representative of the qualities they
admire. They cannot see a principle until it is
personified—they cannot discriminate between the
qualities and their possessor; and as, of old, Deme-

trius the silversmith made gods **for** the people **of** Ephesus, so to-day Mr. Carlyle, or somebody else, supplies the public exigency with respect to heroes. People cry for gods, and there is never wanting an Aaron to gratify their wishes.   They add the cubits **to a** man's stature, and then pay their money to see a giant they have themselves created. Nor does it much matter **to** hero-worshippers what **the** claimants for their regard **may be**— " Scourges of God," or, " Dar- " **lings** of the human race,"—only they must make **a** great noise, or have a great noise made for them ; let them **be but** " sufficient " men, whether of sword, **or** of tongue, **or** of pen, and they cannot fail to be apotheosised.

A " great " **man**, indeed, **is nothing** more than one who has achieved **a great reputation ;** his " greatness " being **in** the **ratio of his fame.**   So **we** find Swift making **the avowal to Bolingbroke** that all his en- deavours **to distinguish** himself arose from want of a **great** title **and** fortune, **that** he may be used like **a** lord by those who had an opinion of his parts ; for, he **adds, " the** reputation of wit **or** great learning " does **the** office **of** a blue riband, **or of a** coach and " six horses,"—that **is**, it carries **power.** The favour- ite design **of** Napoleon also was **to** make a great noise.   " A great reputation," **he says, "is** a great " noise ; **the more there is made, the** farther off **it is**

" heard. Laws, institutions, monuments, nations —
" all fall; but the noise continues and resounds in
" after ages." He was right, and he made a great
noise accordingly; he is the best-heard man of all
times.

Much and very general abuse has been showered
upon the celebrated valet who was not able, like the
rest of the world, to see in his master a great man.
I have often tried to be very indignant with him,
but whenever I made the attempt, it must be confessed that my rage refused to rise. It always
struck me there was too much to be said in the
fellow's favour. Clearly the valet did not regard his
master as a hero; but how can he be blamed? His
master had never come before him in the character.
In breaking the shell of an egg, or in buttoning his
braces, there is little room for the display of the
heroic side of a man's character. This the poor valet
had never witnessed. Must we abuse him, then, for
not regarding as a hero a man who to *him* has never
exhibited himself as a hero? Shall we not rather
praise him for being wise enough not to see a hero
before he appears?

This exaltation of heroes—this sycophantic homage
to great names repeated from generation to generation till they are depressing—has become detrimental
to the best interests of humanity. It breeds habitual

contempt in one class of people for the pursuits and actions of another; it tends to encourage the absurd popular notion of some "coming man," who, in any emergency, is expected to set things right; it tends to discourage the recognition and ready acceptance of the fact that association, organization, and division of labour, are the truest means that can be adopted for the material and moral progress of mankind; it praises the past at the expense of the present; in a word, it is an incubus upon civilization itself.

VI.

ON TAKING A MAN'S MEASURE.

THE attainment of correct judgment on men and things is proverbially a difficult task. The readiest disposition to arrive at a true issue concerning the simplest event in every-day life is very frequently altogether ineffectual. Some mental bias, unrecognized, perhaps, by the sufferer himself, will have the effect of shunting a man off the right track, and diverting his mind from the solution which afterwards he will clearly perceive was the true one. So common, indeed, are errors in judgment, that most men admit their liability to them, and many even pride themselves upon the readiness with which they avow their mistake when it has been discovered. There are directions, however, in which this admirable temper is no longer manifested. A man, however deferential he may be in other respects, is prone

to esteem, as of highest trustworthiness, the opinion
he forms of the moral and intellectual qualities of
another. The conclusion at which he arrives—
notoriously liable from its difficulties to be un-
founded—is, however, precisely that on the correct-
ness of which he is most disposed to place reliance.
In whatever else he may be defective, he has a
knowledge of character. A knowledge of character,
just as a knowledge of politics and religion, comes,
he thinks, by nature; and he who runs may read.
In this respect he believes himself to be infallible.
He will take your measure whilst you stand.

There is some truth in this conceit. A man could
not, it is clear, get on without the occasional exercise
of discrimination, and some sort of reliance upon his
own capacity in judging. Without being an official at
the Mint, he knows he can tell a good shilling from
a counterfeit. He is, of course, sometimes right; but
he is inclined to believe himself never wrong. In
other matters he does not display this excessive self-
confidence. Unless specially trained, he would not
pretend, for instance, to discuss the merits of a race-
horse; or to decide upon the authenticity of a doubtful picture; or to treat one of his friends afflicted
with some dangerous malady. Herein he would confess his inability. But the slightest acquaintance with
his neighbour is sufficient for him to make himself

familiar with the quality of his neighbour's intellect. His penetration in this direction is as boundless as that of the Duchess de la Ferté, who once confessed to Madame de Staël, " It is strange, but I find nobody " except myself always in the right."

What country linen-draper, or pot-house politician, when the merits of a statesman are discussed, but will undertake to estimate his ability to a T ? What young templar, as yet inexperienced in the sensation derived from the touch of a confiding client's handsel-guinea, but will exactly tell you the capabilities and deficiencies of the several judges, assign to each of them his relative merits at law and equity, and supplement his information, if you will, by cataloguing every silk gown according to its worth? We might find examples of this arrogance in every profession. In literature it is offensively prominent; but, whether he confesses it or not, almost every human being fancies himself able to measure, if only by rule of thumb, those with whom he is brought in contact, or to whom he thinks it worth while to apply his attention. Every one may be candid enough to own his practical inferiority to him whom he thus unhesitatingly criticises. He is free to confess he cannot write poems like A, or novels like B, or paint like C, or lead the House of Commons like D ; yet, by some peculiar process, inexplicable, I believe, even to him-

self, he is firmly convinced that whatever judgment
he has formed of the intellectual rank of these persons, and consequently of their performances, is invariably and unassailably correct.   Indeed, the very
readiness with which he recognizes his own inferiority is an incentive to self-esteem, and tends to
make him set a higher value on the discrimination
he has exhibited in thus discovering their superiority
to himself.   Strange as it may appear, he possesses a
sort of inner judgment which applauds the insight he
has displayed in the decision.   His favourite axiom is
slightly varied from that of the elder Shandy's—" An
" ounce of one man's judgment is worth a ton of other
" people's."

Notwithstanding this reliance commonly placed by
a man on his own judgment, innumerable instances
of false verdicts are well known.   Some of these have
been pronounced by men from whom better things
were to be expected.   We all remember Coleridge
meeting at table one of noble brow and sober demeanour, and immediately concluding that his *vis-à-vis* was
a man of parts.   Afterwards, when the gravely-com-
ported diner expressed his delight at the appearance
on the table of apple dumplings, he forfeited the good
opinion of the illustrious opium-eater, who thereupon
pronounced the man to be a fool.   Can anything be
imagined more unjust?   Coleridge in both instances

judged on insufficient evidence; and in both instances he was undoubtedly wrong. In the first
place for judging a man to be wise from his outward
behaviour and personal appearance, and next for suddenly abandoning his first impression and considering
him a fool because he exhibited a liking for apple dumplings. In reality nothing had occurred by which the
man's intellect could be measured. From what had
happened only his taste could fairly be ascertained.

Such verdicts, however, founded, as this by Coleridge was, on insufficient evidence, are the rule and
not the exception. Men are prone to form their judgments of each other by the cut of their coat or the
fold of their shirt collar, and to gauge one's capacity
by the manner in which one enters a drawing-room
or carries one's head in the street. But such a test
is almost invariably found to be defective. The
mental and moral character of a man seldom exhibits
itself in such form. The external signs from which
the inference is drawn frequently depend in no degree upon natural disposition, but upon habit—i. e.
the external force to which a man has been subjected
—or upon the position, perhaps accidental and only
temporary, he happened to occupy at the time when
the judgment was formed. I need not waste the page
by enumerating examples. You may to-morrow see
half a dozen guardsmen, all unhesitatingly bold

fellows, **all** self-contained, all equally steady; **yet** had you seen any **one** of them twelve months ago, you would, probably, have seen a waddling, loutish ploughboy, as indecisive in his movements as the most timid country maiden when walking along the streets on her first visit to London.   Nor is this unsatisfactory way of judging, followed only by ordinary men and confined in its application to the concerns of every-day life.   It pervades **our** literature; and the recorded instances of men who have suffered from its effects, are too numerous to be mentioned.   *Ex ungue leonem* appears to be the favourite maxim of an Englishman's criticism.

As we have seen, there is a general tendency to make a man a hero for the successful exhibition of some one desirable quality.   If he has acquired celebrity as a poet, his opinion of a great-coat is likely to be taken in preference to that of an unknown writer; or, if he is renowned as a general, his testimony concerning a piano-forte is more highly prized than that of an obscure subaltern, although the latter may be a connoisseur in musical instruments, **and the** general be ignorant of the difference between a bassoon and a cornet-à-pistons.   So, for the possession of some undesirable quality, or the absence of what is conceived to be an element of greatness, there is a disposition to credit him with being a fool.   Such inferences are usually erroneous. On the other hand, there are occasions when the process—this drawing a general conclusion from a partial examination—may, to some extent, be legitimately employed. If, for instance, a friend assured us of his belief that twice seven makes fifteen, we want no further proof of his ignorance of figures, but are justified in saying he is no arithmetician. It would, however, be very unfair were we to infer anything more. If, again, our friend confessed he derived pleasure from the discourses of Boanerges, all we could legitimately conclude would be that he was deficient in good taste ; or, if he thought his tailor an authority in political economy, that his political education had been neglected. A man may like Boanerges, and be a first-rate cook, and he may admire his tailor, and yet be an excellent market-gardener. A certain portion of the public, however, and their representatives in the press, do not acknowledge this limitation.

I recollect, some years ago, a member of Parliament for one of the metropolitan boroughs made a sad slip in his history. Honourable gentlemen smiled at the error, as was natural. But outside of the House the blunder became a matter of serious importance to the unfortunate member. Mr. Punch, especially, was very severe upon him. That gentleman (who himself, probably, would have failed to

answer five out of every nine historical questions
that one might easily put to him) reminded us week
after week of the gravity of the offence. From this
lapsus linguae he deduced that the unlucky culprit
was—I won't say a pickpocket—but almost anything
as bad; and whenever, under emergencies, fun was
wanted, he took down his telescope, peered into it the
wrong way, and then proceeded to give us his representation of the member for Finsbury with his queer
notions of English history.

We must look to the same source for this undue
appreciation as for the undue exaltation mentioned in
the last chapter. Men instinctively like the exercise
of power, especially in intellectual subjects ; and,
having in their nature a fixed amount of praise and
blame, they must expend it with risk of consequences.
Most frequently they do this capriciously, or are
guided in making their decision by some accidental
fact; but they must expend it, and it is fortunate for
him who wishes to earn their applause if some lucky
accident should occur to dispose them in his favour.
It is proverbial that human nature, after too highly
praising a man, revolts against its own verdict, ignores
its favourite, and in time comes to depreciate him in
the proportion it previously exalted him. Examples
in our literary history will occur to everybody. The
popular treatment of Byron is a case in point.   In-

stead, however, of depreciating the idol they have set up, it occasionally happens that men console themselves with vilifying some would-be idol that comes before them. But whether exercised upon one person or upon two, this duality of passion—co-existing simultaneously at all times—must inevitably be expended. It happens, however, that, instead of applying the wrong end of the telescope at one time to one man and the right end at another, they content themselves with directing the right end towards the one man and the wrong to another. In the latter case their feelings of praise and blame are excited and exhibited contemporaneously.

One might fancy there is no room in literary matters for the display of these feelings; but literature here, as in most other respects, is a faithful reflex of the society in which it is produced and to which it is addressed: and the way in which literary verdicts are returned is notoriously and disgracefully wrong. The cardinal fault seems to be that of estimating a writer and ranking him according to the idea formed of him as a man; or, if he is dead, from what his contemporaries said of him personally whilst he was alive. This judging an author from the man, or, what is as unjust, the judging the man from the supposed revelations of himself in his works, is obviously a defective way of judging. Few men are the same in books

as they are in conversation. A friend of the late John
Stirling tells me that promising author's works are
infinitely inferior to his conversation, and we, therefore, who are acquainted with him only through his
published writings, are surprised to find so much
said of him, and so high a rank assigned to him by
those to whom he was intimately known. His
physical debility and want of robust temperament
stood in the way of his performance. The younger
Hallam will readily occur to the reader as another,
who, like Sterling, was greater in capacity than in
energy. The clear insight of these men, known to
friends, was conspicuously absent in their books. On
the other hand, excellent literary performance does
not insure adequate recognition of merit when personal greatness is absent. If, for example, one man's
writings were ever superior to another's in wisdom
and in form, in intellect and in art, they are those of
Goldsmith to what were produced by Johnson. And
yet what is the result? We know the one was
through life—and the echo of that eighteenth-cen-
tury applause still lingers in our ears—universally
regarded as Dr. Minor, whilst the other, seen through
the right end of the telescope, was everywhere hailed
as Dr. Major. The idea men formed of Goldsmith's
work was perhaps insensibly influenced by what they
had heard or knew of Goldsmith's life. Volatility

or stupidity being considered to be the mark of a
fool, it is thought the volatile man, or the stupid man,
must manifest himself in all he undertakes, and that
his peculiar failings and virtues will unconsciously
betray themselves in his writings.   The public look
for homogeneity in a man, and consistency between
his character and opinions.   They conceive it possible, not only to determine a man's mental ability
from his deportment, but to infer his moral character
from his literary productions.   They will not see
that the literary character and the personal character
may be antipodal, and should be judged apart.   A
man must practise what he preaches, or his gospel
will be disbelieved and his sincerity questioned as
well by the upper vulgar as by the lower.   This
was so well known to Steele, that, upon relinquish-
ing the publication of the *Tatler*, he gave as the
true cause for the discontinuance of its publication,
the discovery by the public of its author.   " I considered," said he, on taking leave of his readers,
" that severity of manners is absolutely necessary
" to him who would censure others; and for that
" reason, and that only, chose to talk in a mask."
Steele might have discontinued his publication from
prudential motives; but in recognizing the illogical
disposition of his readers, he appears to have himself
acted illogically.   The public he addressed resemble

those ladies who fear to be introduced to their favourite
author, lest a personal knowledge of the man may
spoil the high opinion they have formed of his works.
They would probably consider a man insincere who
argued against drunkenness, whilst he himself was
a confirmed drunkard, and fancy what he said to be
less true than if uttered by a teetotaller.

A man's nature is composed of so many various
and often conflicting elements, that it is impossible
to deduce his true character from the revelation of a
single phase.   We shall be puzzled to discover
which is the predominant that colours and modifies
the rest.   The popular mind, shared in to a great
degree by men of letters, is disposed to infer a
man's character, not from his ordinary action and
every-day conduct, but from some unusual and extraordinary exhibition, altogether at variance with
his usual behaviour.   If he exhibits himself in some
exceptional way, it is supposed that thereby he has
shown his true nature.   Should he once in a lifetime act in a manner contrary to his usual custom—
treat his neighbour ungenerously, or behave meanly—
his friends at once, and with no further evidence in
support of their view, conclude that they obtain
a glimpse of his true character, when in reality he
was only acting under altered circumstances.   The
discordancy which results from his nature meeting

the unfamiliar conditions, and unsuccessfully attempting to adjust itself, is only temporary ; but it is taken to be indicative of the whole man—a particular circumstance is thus regarded as the index of a complete nature.

Books are even a less safe criterion than exceptional variation in conduct. In works produced by the exercise of the art-faculty, the author displays only his intellectual power, and sometimes merely the æsthetic side of it. In proportion as he progresses as an artist will he be enabled skilfully to conceal even this from his reader. If his sympathy is wide and deep, and easily aroused, he can portray what is foreign to him with as much accuracy as if he were describing his individual nature. His greatness and his success will, indeed, be in the ratio of the ability he possesses to make his representations strictly objective. Accurate resemblance, then, between the man and his book is missing. Intellectual sincerity is exhibited ; but we search in vain for that conformity between practice and precept which we have been usually taught to expect. In forming our estimate of a man's character, were we strictly to confine ourselves to a consideration of his literary productions, we should be under the necessity of re-writing the lives of most of our great authors. Luckily, external materials exist which enable us to gain a much more trustworthy portraiture of them, than it is possible to obtain from their **works**. Horace wrote verses we esteem licentious; and the author of " The " Christian Hero" produced a work in which the virtues are admirably set before us in their true light. Did we know no more of these worthies than is to be derived from their several productions, our opinion of the two men would, I presume, be different from what it is now. We find that the little Roman satirist, although he had a big paunch, and his hair was grey before its time, was no *roué*, and was the last man to go out at midnight and whistle at the door of a deceitful mistress. Nor, unhappily, was the author of " The Christian Hero" a perfect model of the virtues he sets up in that work for our imitation. We cannot take the measure of either by what he himself has furnished. In the case of Horace, all that we can safely infer is, that he writes as if he were what he pretends to be; and, in the case of Steele, that he aspired to what he was unable to be.

I conclude, then, that a clear and broad distinction should be made in any estimate we have to form of a man, between his life and his opinions. If I have to criticise a book, it does not concern me what its author was. I have to do with his precepts, and not with his practice. If he has aided my culture,

and given me advanced views of life which he himself was unhappily unable to exemplify in his own
person, my thanks are equally due to him for the
benefit and the discovery; and I credit him with
being a wise man.   If, on the other hand, I concern
myself about his life, my estimate should not be
modified by the value of what he has produced.   If
he was a bad man, I must not ignore or extenuate
his faults because his works are of highest excellence.
The Ayrshire ploughman was a very great poet, but
a very unwise man.   Goethe was a very wise man,
but a very mean artist.

VII.

THE MEDIÆVAL MAN OF LETTERS, GIRALDUS CAMBRENSIS.

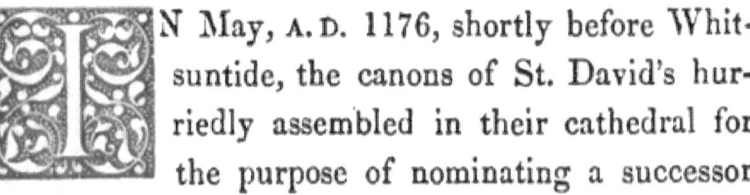

IN May, A. D. 1176, shortly before Whitsuntide, the canons of St. David's hurriedly assembled in their cathedral for the purpose of nominating a successor to their diocesan, David Fitz-Gerald, who had just died. Entering the Chapter-house, they proceeded to their deliberations with bolted doors; and, after long and anxious debate, unanimously fixed on Gerald de Barri, nephew to the late bishop, a young man who had not yet completed his twenty-ninth year, as their nominee to the vacant see. Thereupon the conference came to an end; the doors of the Chapter-house were flung open; and the *Te Deum*, that had been raised, was greedily caught up by the impatient crowd without.

The reason for this secresy, and for this selection, may be stated in a few words. From the days of its

patron Saint to the time when, by the settlement of
Normans in South Wales, the way was prepared for
the introduction of foreigners into Welsh sees, St.
David's had been in possession of archiepiscopal privileges. It was the Holy Sepulchre of Wales. Two
visits to its shrine were esteemed as efficacious as
one to Rome itself:—

> " Roma semel quantum,
>   Bis dat Menevia tantum."

Its privileges had now been lost; the see was
included in the province of Canterbury, and every
attempt made by the Welsh to regain ecclesiastical
independence had signally failed. The clergy at the
commencement of the turbulent reign of Henry II.
had conceived hope of freeing themselves from cano-
nical subjection to England. But Henry was too
politic to be a voluntary party to their design. Nor
was he to be moved to their purpose by persuasion,
or by entreaty, or by money: " As long as I live,"
said he, " I will never furnish a head for rebellion in
Wales by giving the Welsh a metropolitan." He
well knew that the first Norman kings in subjugat-
ing Wales had failed to subdue it; that its people
threw off the yoke and carried devastation into the
English borders; that the severest measures of re-
pression devised had been ineffectual against them;
and that every effort made to check rebellion by

opposing chieftain to chieftain had been utterly unsuccessful.   He decided, therefore, upon adopting
measures of a different nature from what had hitherto
been pursued.   He resolved to rule Wales not by
its chieftains, but by its clergy; not Welshmen, but
Normans, should be appointed to the various sees;
not patriots, but courtiers, should be the means of
all promotion.   In pursuance of this design he was
inexorable; to the highest ecclesiastical posts he
advanced men whose interests were widely or altogether distinct from those of the people, and who
were totally unfitted by birth, education, and inclination for the duties that belonged to their high
office.   From Henry, then, it was hopeless to expect
a concession of metropolitan privilege to St. David's.
But the clergy did not therefore despair.   Disappointed in their hope of obtaining a metropolitan in
name, what was to prevent their having for a bishop
one who would be a metropolitan in effect—one who,
by reason of his princely lineage, extensive and profound learning, undoubted talents, and tried courage,
should be able successfully to cope with the Archbishop of Canterbury ?   Their scheme seemed not
impracticable; the man who, above every other, was
thought to possess the requisite qualifications, was at
hand; all they waited for was fit occasion to put into
execution their well-pondered project.   At length

the much-coveted opportunity came. Bishop Fitz-
Gerald died; and the Chapter at once, and unhesitatingly, and without even apprising the king, or his
justiciary, of the vacancy that had occurred, unanimously elected Gerald de Barri to fill the see of St.
David's.

The bishop-elect — sometimes termed Giraldus
Sylvester, but best known to us by his literary
title, GIRALDUS CAMBRENSIS—was undoubtedly
one of the foremost men of the twelfth century.
Thierry ranks him with Thomas Becket; and to no
one who has made himself acquainted with the particulars of his strange career will that position seem
too elevated. His undaunted self-assertion and
determined perseverance; his unwearied industry,
activity, and energy of character; his many romantic
adventures; his numerous and varied literary productions; and, above all, the disappointments he
experienced during a long and eventful life, made
him a remarkable man in the eyes of his contemporaries; and the interest with which his life and career
were regarded by them has not ceased even now, but
increases year by year as his motives become more
apparent, and a more thorough acquaintance is formed
with his works. He is the best representative of a
mediæval man of letters.

Giraldus was a native of Pembrokeshire, where he

first saw the light in the year 1147. But it happens
that although he was born in Wales, and styled himself " Cambrensis," he cannot with rigorous accuracy
be considered a Welshman. The stranger, who, to-
day, traverses the principality, and finds with surprise at its furthest extremity a district inhabited by
a people whose vernacular is English, would have
found there much the same phenomenon in the
middle of the 12th century; he would have found, as
he will still find, that if—speaking generally—a line
were drawn from east to west through the centre of
Pembrokeshire, it would divide that county into
two totally distinct regions; he would have found on
the north of this line a people speaking the Welsh
language, and having the well-defined characteristics
of the Welsh race, whereas on the south the inhabitants would be unable to speak a word of that
language, and would possess a physiognomy that
proclaimed them to be of a different race from that
of their neighbours in the hill-country; he would
have found, in fine, on the one side, sons of the soil,
and, on the other, a mixed population of foreigners.
These latter, again, he would have discovered were
composed partly of Anglo-Normans, who, soon after
the Conquest, had subjugated that portion of the
country, and partly of colonists from Flanders, who
had been planted among them " to be a barrier and

"an assistance" against their restless and watchful foes—the Welsh.

It was on the south of this line, then, in the district spoken of, even in his time, as Anglia Transwallia, that Giraldus was born—the exact place being the Castle of Manorbeer, at that time, as at the present day, one of the most picturesque spots in Britain. By birth he was fortunate. His family were people of exalted rank, and exercised considerable influence, as well at the remote English court as over the affairs of the district in which they resided. His father, William de Barri, was a Norman Baron, and enjoyed the favour of the English monarch; by his mother, who was the descendant, through the famous Lady Nesta, of Rhys-ap-Tewdwr, he was closely allied to the Welsh princes; the see of St. David's was held by his uncle; the line of the De Barri, with their direct and indirect kindred, were the chief instruments in the conquest of Ireland under Strongbow. Favoured by such circumstances, it will create no surprise to find that he aspired to play a conspicuous part of the transactions of his time. But the direction towards which his aspirations tended was not perhaps what will be very generally anticipated; for he resolved, at an early age, upon entering the Church. Even as a child he showed a decided predilection for the ecclesiastical profession. The castle

of Manorbeer is on the coast; within a stone's throw
is the Irish Sea, and on its shore the young De
Barri, whenever they could escape from the monotony that reigned within the castle walls, were in the
habit of amusing themselves. Here each of the
boys manifested his peculiar bent. The two elder,
we are told, were accustomed to construct mimic
forts and castles in the sand, but Giraldus, it was
observed, invariably amused himself with the erection of churches and monasteries. His father, who
appears to have been a man of judicious and good
understanding, perceiving, by this and other indications, the inclination manifested by his youngest son,
was delighted at the boy's disposition, and—partly
in joke, partly no doubt with a belief the prediction
was not unlikely to be fulfilled—used to style him
" The little bishop." To regard ecclesiastical benefices as hereditary property had become fashionable
in Wales; why then should the great preferment
held by the family pass away into the hands of stran-
gers? Why should it not be retained by a De
Barri? His three other sons would embrace the
profession of arms — Giraldus should be spared to
the Church. The desire was not beyond the possi-
bility of accomplishment. The boy was accordingly
removed from the wild rocks, and hazel groves, and
fishponds, and dovecots, of his childhood, and trans-

ferred to the care of his uncle, the prelate, who readily undertook the superintendence of his education. At first the young noble was slow at learning; and, subsequently, more than once, according to his own confession, he exhibited decided inclination wholly to abandon the pursuit upon which he had entered, and to follow that which the heat of the Crusades, and the restless spirit of the times, pointed out as more suitable for a youth of his high degree. But these indecisive fits were only temporary. Encouraged by the bishop (just as we might suppose an uncle in our own day, who has rich livings in his gift, would be likely to encourage his nephew) and reprimanded for his idleness by the episcopal chaplains, he afterwards applied himself with so much diligence, that, when he left his uncle's roof, he had mastered all his instructors could teach him, and had surpassed most of his contemporaries in the learning of his time.

Paris was then emphatically " the city of letters." It was the first and greatest of universities. Students flocked thither from all parts of Christendom; its schools furnished opportunities of forming friendships that could not have been formed elsewhere; and if any of its students became famous in after life, they were almost sure of being known personally to the rest of their famous contemporaries. Its professors

were of European reputation, and often excited enthusiasm in their hearers equal to what we ourselves
have seen excited by Cousin or Villemain. What was
published from the chairs, moreover, had a circulation
more immediate and quite as extensive as that which
the printing press is able to afford—for it included the
whole of the learned world.   It was to Paris, therefore, that Giraldus repaired, after leaving his uncle,
to pursue those higher branches of study for which
it seems his own country afforded no facilities.   He
tells us that he placed himself under the most effi-
cient teachers, and he appears to have been a very
assiduous student, and to have made rapid progress
in theology, philosophy, and the canon law—for he
obtained great reputation as a lecturer.   Of his three
years' residence in Paris we know little.   When,
about A.D. 1172, he returned to this country, he was
a young man of twenty-five years.   With a hand-
some person, a tall and commanding presence, of
high rank, and possessed of all the learning and
accomplishments of his time, he could well hope, had
he chosen, to make no mean figure in the profession
of arms, and to achieve conquests in a field generally
far more agreeable to one of his age than any in the
domain of theology.   But he had now fully and
definitely determined upon the profession he would
follow.   He would be a soldier, it is true, but it

should be a soldier in the army of the Church Militant; he would make conquests, too, but they should be in and for the Church alone. To an ambitious man with less resolution—or to a resolute man with less ambition—than he possessed, the Church would, at that moment, have offered little inducement. It was passing through a great crisis. It was engaged in a struggle, wherein, in the person of its chief champion, it had received a deep wound.

The blood of Thomas Becket had just been shed on the altar at Canterbury, and the foul act was regarded by all friends of the Church as one of a series of measures that were designed to be enforced for the reduction of the power and pretensions of the clergy. The astonishment of all Europe at the audacity of the crime which had been perpetrated by barbarous nobles, at the suggestion of a barbarous king, had not yet subsided; and upon the mind of a young man just about to be ordained the fatal incident must have made deep impression, and suggested the expediency of reconsidering his determination. Giraldus, however, did not pause. Besides, even had he been inclined to sacrifice his own hope, was he prepared to disappoint the expectations of relatives and friends, who, from his childhood, had been accustomed to look upon him as their future bishop? No; it could not be thought of; it was plainly incumbent upon him to endeavour to fulfil at once their hope and his own desire. He took orders, therefore; and, as might be expected, at once obtained considerable preferment. But he was not content with a fixed locality. His active mind could not rest within the narrow limits of a parish or monastery. In anticipation he already regarded St. David's as his, and, like a man who is heir presumptive to some rich inheritance which through long neglect had fallen into disorder, he was anxious to redress the abuses of the diocese against the time when he himself should succeed to its control. And these abuses were then many and great. The clergy, he observed, amongst other irregularities of which they were guilty, for the most part married; sons, on the death of their fathers, succeeded to livings not by election, but by inheritance; and "if a bishop " attempted to institute a stranger, the whole family " were up in arms against institutor and instituted." The laity, too, were troublesome. The people of Pembroke and Cardigan refused tithe of wool and cheese, and the Flemings had even been able to procure from the king exemption from archiepiscopal jurisdiction. Giraldus, resolved to repress such enormities, with much indignation betook himself to the Archbishop of Canterbury, at that time Legate of the Holy See, and directed his attention to the scandalous proceedings. The archbishop, delighted, it appears, with the zeal of the young churchman, sends him back into Wales armed with the legatine authority—*ad hos excessus et alios quos ibi invenerit emendandos.*

The new legate was not long idle. He first applied himself to the refractory tithe-payers, whom he soon succeeded in bringing to submission. No man, however, is a prophet in his own country; and Pembrokeshire was not, and is not, in this respect much in advance of the rest of the world. Whilst Giraldus was discharging the duties of his office in the Priory at Pembroke, the high sheriff—to show contempt for him and his authority—insolently carried off eight yoke of oxen belonging to the monastery, and, on being required to restore them, added insult to injury by threatening repetition of such ungracious conduct. Giraldus, of all men the least likely to submit to this unbecoming and outrageous behaviour, menaced the offender with instant excommunication; but the sheriff laughed at the idea of the king's officer being excommunicated in his own castle by a young ecclesiastic, and showed no sign of repentance.

The legate, however, like his compatriot, Picton, in after years, was one of those who, whenever they threaten, mean to perform to the full, even if the performance involve more serious consequences than were likely to follow from the act meditated by Giraldus. Having thrice summoned the sheriff to restore his plunder—and thrice without effect—he thereupon convened the monks and clergy, and forthwith solemnly executed sentence of excommunication against William Karquit, high sheriff of Pembroke. His bravery, on this occasion, was rewarded as it deserved to be. On the day following, conscious of his success, he left Pembroke, and took himself off across country to Llawaden Castle, one of the seats of his uncle the prelate, overhanging the Eastern Cleddy. Hither he was followed by the crestfallen and repentant culprit, who, now making humble submission to Giraldus and restoring the plunder, was birched; and then—and not till then—received the absolution for which he had come. Next came the turn of the clergy. As he had selected one in high authority to be an example for the obstinate laity, so now the young commissioner resolved to choose an equally suitable victim to be a warning for contumacious churchmen. There happened at the time to be at Brecknock an aged archdeacon, who lived in open concubinage; that is to say, he had a wife whom he refused to put away at the bidding of Giraldus. Upon this the latter, finding that not only were his advice and remonstrances vain, but that the clerical old sinner ventured to defend the propriety of his course of life, and presumed even to abuse his adviser, resorted to means similar to what had been found so effectual with the king's sheriff. He unhesitatingly suspended the archdeacon, and afterwards deprived him of his benefices.

When Giraldus, in A. D. 1175, resigned his extraordinary powers into the hands of the archbishop, the primate, in order to show approbation of the manner in which the commission had been executed, presented him with the preferment of the deposed archdeacon. The new office afforded a wide field for energetic exertion, and his activity knew no bounds. He traversed the country in all directions to make himself acquainted with existing abuses, and then set himself to reform them. At one time the Flemings troubled him, at another disputes among the clergy engaged his attention; but he was equal to every emergency. This period of his life is an example that may be followed with advantage. Disregarding all personal discomforts, he spared himself no inconveniences, but, on the contrary, frequently incurred considerable risk from bad roads, robbers, storms, swollen floods, and personal foes, in the performance of the duties to which he had been called. His zeal knew no bounds. The Church never had a more vigorous champion to enforce her rights. He was unwearied in rectifying abuses. In carrying out

reforms he could not help making many enemies;
but he always displayed a desire to conciliate when
conciliation appeared to be for the interest of justice.
His promotion to the archdeaconry entailed on him
many difficulties. One of the most formidable was
an attempt made by the Bishop of St. Asaph to
invade the rights of St. David's. A new church
erected on the borders of the diocese of St. Asaph
became the subject of dispute between the bishop of
that see and the chapter of St. David's. The prelate had determined on the following Sunday to
dedicate the church, and thus substantiate his claim.
But the archdeacon was not the man to be vanquished.
He goes to the church, orders the bells to be rung in
token of investiture, celebrates mass, and then, having
left his retinue in the church to keep it and bolt
the doors, he sallies forth and meets the bishop, who
has just arrived—to find himself out-manœuvred.
Then there was an ecclesiastical battle, as acrimonious almost as any that have been fought in our
own day. The bishop threatened to excommunicate
the archdeacon; but Giraldus, having commanded
the priests and the clergy, whom beforehand he had
attired in their stoles and surplices, to come forth from
the church with cross and lighted candles, suddenly
faced the bishop, and solemnly excommunicated all the
enemies of St. Asaph. The bishop and his attendants

thereupon mounted their horses and fled, pursued and pelted by the rustics, who had mustered in crowds to witness the strange ecclesiastical encounter.

It was in the midst of such conspicuous and successful services to St. David's as these that his uncle Fitz-Gerald died, and the choice of the canons called him, as we have seen, to fill the vacant see.

This event was the crisis in his life—the grand object of his existence. To this his whole previous efforts had been directed, and from this his whole future exertions were to take their colouring. Giraldus, as I have said, was unanimously elected. Here, then, and at an age when he was yet capable of enjoying the realization of his ambition, he was so fortunate as to complete it. The predictions of his family and the high hopes of friends were fulfilled, and fulfilled so soon, so easily, and so much as a matter of course, as scarcely to be even credited. The expeditiousness of the transformation, and the very simplicity of the process that converted him from an archdeacon to a bishop, seemed to one of his temperament to be cause for alarm. At the time of the election he was at St. David's, and that same night he began to survey his position. To his calmer judgment the act of the chapter appeared to be too precipitate; the royal assent to the nomination had not been obtained; the whole proceeding would be

regarded as an insult to the royal dignity. Influenced
by this consideration, he resolved on the following
morning to renounce the election.   But he was too
late, for the king had heard from another source of
what had happened.   Henry, as we know, was not a
man of amiable disposition, and any attempt to out-
wit him he was not inclined to tolerate. He dreaded
in Giraldus another Thomas Becket.   He was very
wroth (*multum excanduit,* says the bishop elect), and
vowed vengeance against all concerned.   As for the
nomination he could not think of accepting it.   Giraldus, it is true, was well fitted by learning, zeal, and
irreproachably good character for the episcopal chair.
He fulfilled the principal requirement exacted by the
early Norman kings, who, in the distribution of ecclesiastical preferment, were well aware of the strength
to be derived from a clergy attached to them by a
community of interests—he was Norman. But, alas!
he was also Welsh; connected by marriage with the
Welsh princes; by birth a De Barri; of an ambitious stock altogether. Henry asks advice of the
bishops; they unanimously urge the nomination of
Giraldus: but the king, who secretly betrayed his
fear, is of a different opinion.   After silently and
patiently listening to all that was said, he rejects their
counsel, and swears he would banish every one who
had taken part in the matter. " As they have allowed

" me no share in the election, I will take care they
" shall have no part in the promotion." No sooner
had the chapter of St. David's learnt the result of
their unlucky act than they repented ; and, to save
their livings and avert the king's anger, professed
profound sorrow for their presumption, promising
meekly to accept whomsoever the king liked. Giraldus held his peace, and—only that he secretly urged,
first the papal legate, and then the archbishop, to use
his influence that the appointment should be conferred
on a man of good character, and acquainted with the
language and habits of the people over whom he was
called to preside—took no part in what was being
done. At length Peter de Leia, **" a certain** black
" monk of the Cluniac order," and Prior of Wenlock,
whom the canons had never seen, and whose name
only they knew, was elected in the presence of the
king at Winchester; and Giraldus, finding by experience that his exhortations to support the independence of St. David's and evade the oath of subjection to the archbishop, were altogether lost upon
the new bishop, collected his books, and set out in
disgust for Paris, to devote himself assiduously to the
study of the Imperial Constitutions and the Decretal.
We know little of him at this period of his career. It
appears that, like Thomas Becket, he intended to have
completed his studies at Bologna ; but the design

was unromantically frustrated: for finding his remittances irregular, and pressed by numerous creditors, he abandoned his intention, and, regardless of the danger he incurred, after an absence of several years returned to England. This was about A. D. 1180. He at once hastened into Wales, where he found things in a worse condition even than he had expected. Peter de Leia, fallen out with his clergy, had deserted his post, leaving his diocese to take care of itself. By the advice of the archbishop, prompted probably by Giraldus, Peter was induced to nominate the latter administrator during his absence of the affairs of the see. But this friendly arrangement was not of long continuance. The bishop, without previous warning, having suspended certain of the canons and archdeacons of St. David's, and refused to revoke his sentence, Giraldus sided with the chapter, and representing to the archbishop the illegality of the proceeding, procured a reversal of the sentence. He did more. Rejecting all attempts at reconciliation, he convened at St. David's a synod, and by his influence was able to enforce restitution of all the lands that had been alienated by the bishop, and to annul the illegal interchanges that had been made between the canons. He appears not to have lost his influence with the king, for in the year 1184 he was nominated king's chaplain, and invited to court;

and when the expedition to Ireland was planned, he was selected as the companion and counsellor of Prince John. Afterwards, in 1188, when Henry assumed the cross at Gisors, he accompanied Baldwin and Ranulph de Glanville, the justiciary, into Wales —his presence being thought a guarantee of the good faith of England. His services, successfully exerted in these offices, should undoubtedly have procured for him the object of his desire; the death of the king in the next year, however, dissipated hope of such reward. When the event occurred Giraldus was in France, whence he was sent into Wales, to prevent, by his personal influence, any disturbance that might arise from the change. But the reward for which he thirsted, and which would not have been too great for the eminent services he had rendered the English crown, did not come. He had, it is true, been offered an archbishopric in Ireland, and through the interest of his former pupil, Prince John, Bangor and Llandaff were afterwards proposed for his acceptance. All these, however, he refused, there being no station or office he coveted save one. In July, 1198, Peter de Leia died, and there seemed another chance of his obtaining this. The chapter of St. David's, thinking perhaps that Richard would be more tractable than his father, had the courage once more to nominate the great champion of their see. Giraldus expressed

no desire for the honour, and disregarded for a
long time the solicitations and importunities of his
friends. At length he consented, the chapter having
previously dispatched to Hubert, Archbishop of Canterbury and justiciary, their letters, in which Giraldus
was nominated. Hubert, however, who had designed the see for one of his friends, refused to accept
the nomination. Then commenced a long and acrimonious struggle which lasted for years. Giraldus,
now that he had again embarked in the cause, was a
stubborn antagonist, and the canons held out manfully. Two of them hastened to Normandy to present themselves to King Richard. That restless
sovereign was not to be found ; and when, after many
journeyings, they discovered his whereabouts, they
received at the same time intelligence of his death.
The new king, John, whom they met on their return,
heartily acknowledged the services of his former tutor
the archdeacon, and promised to ratify his appointment, and give them letters to the justiciary not to
molest the canons in their election. Giraldus, about,
at last, to gain his end, now transferred himself from
Lincoln, whither he had retired in ill humour, to St.
David's, and there, on the 29th of June, he was again
elected with great solemnity.

The new prelate was urged to ignore the pretensions of Canterbury, and to proceed to Rome to be

consecrated by the sovereign pontiff himself. Meanwhile, however, the canons received a command to elect as their bishop the prior of Lanthony, who would, otherwise, be sent down to them already consecrated. This was enough. John's meanness was apparent. Giraldus, who before was lukewarm, now roused himself for the contest that was inevitable; and, taking hearty leave of his brother Philip, whom he loved much, and to whom he constantly refers in terms of endearment, resolved to go to Rome. Six days before the expiration of the time allowed the canons for making choice he set out on his journey, and, skirting Flanders and Hainhault through Ardennes, thence into Champagne and Burgundy, he crossed the Alps, and, after many vicissitudinous adventures, arrived in Rome at the latter end of November. Alexander III, then pope, who received him with much graciousness, gave him many friendly interviews, and Giraldus was beginning to anticipate successful issue from his mission, when a hitch occurred. In the middle of December, a courier from Canterbury brought letters containing the archbishop's version of the dispute. Then commenced an acrimonious contest. It was apparent that the suit would be tedious. Giraldus seemed to make ground; but then, so did the agents of Canterbury. In the person of Alexander the Church was complaisant to excess. She had received her eminent son and champion with distinction. But pontifical mediation resulted, as usual, in her own triumph; she frequently sided with the weak, but never until she had ascertained that the weak was about to become strong; she invariably awaited the crisis, being ever ready to issue formal commissions on any disputed point, but always delaying her decision till the question had decided itself; she never refused to afford accommodation, but only when accommodation was not disadvantageous to her own pretensions. What could the supreme pontiff do in this dispute? To oblige both parties he at length offered to refer the election to a commission of the judges in England, entrusting to Giraldus in the interim the administration of the temporalities and spiritualities of the see. The suit was wearisome and heartrending. Giraldus incurred many dangers and made several unsuccessful journeys to Rome. At last the dispute, when it had reached almost the dimensions of rebellion in Wales, was terminated by the pope quashing the nomination of St. David's and of Canterbury, leaving to either party to recommence it *de novo.* I need not say that Giraldus was disinclined to renew the contest. His struggle for the independence of the see had failed, but not before all the powers of Church and State had been brought to bear against him. He seems finally to have become reconciled to the king and the archbishop, and is said to have ended his days in peace. The date of his death is unknown. He himself tells us that in his seventieth year he was engaged upon his treatise, " De " Principis Instructione." He probably died soon after.

Such is a brief outline of the career of Giraldus I have abridged from the admirable Introduction to the works of this extraordinary man, now being edited by Professor Brewer for the series of Chronicles and Memorials published under the direction of the Master of the Rolls.

The rewards of literature were as precarious, and the fate of a man of letters often as lamentable in the twelfth century as they are in the nineteenth. Then, as now, effort frequently failed to secure for an author the applause to which he believed himself justly entitled; and then, as now, the disappointed aspirant was forced to console himself with visions of posthumous fame to compensate contemporaneous neglect. Of this, Giraldus Cambrensis is a conspicuous example. He was a voluminous writer; his works—consisting of history, biography, topography, poems, letters to eminent men, prefaces, dedications, charges to his clergy, and works on divinity—are of cardinal importance to the student of our history; he confines his attention to what, from his position and opportunities, he, of all men, was most competent to undertake. **The** best picture of the state of society in England during the latter half of the twelfth century is to be found in his pages. **Yet his** literary labours, although **properly** estimated by the learned of his **time, were never crowned** with adequate reward. To his earliest production, the well-known " Topographia " Hiberniæ," **a result of his tour with** Prince John, we **are indebted for all** that is known of Ireland during the whole of the middle ages. "It is," says **Mr. Brewer, " the solitary text** book from which all " **writers in succession** to the present day have " **derived their accounts** of that country previous to " its final **conquest by** England. **It** may be con- " sidered as **the prototype of those** numerous pro- " **ductions which,** under the different **names** of foreign " scenes and incidents, personal recollections, sketches " of different lands, have **occupied** so large and im- " portant **a space in the literature** of Europe since " **the reformation."** This famous work is divided by **the author into three** books. In the first he gives **an account of the physical** features of the island and **the history of its remarkable productions ;*** the second

---

* As a specimen of the author's credulity, and of the state of ornithological knowledge in his time, I give an extract :—

" There are," he says, " in this country, a great number of

he devotes to the marvels of the land; and in the third he narrates the first peopling of Ireland, and describes the manners, dress, and condition of the inhabitants. " The History of the Conquest of " Ireland," that followed the " Topographia," and

---

" birds called barnacles, and which nature produces in a manner " that is contrary to the laws of nature. These birds are not " unlike ducks, but are somewhat smaller in size. They make " their first appearance as drops of gum upon the branches of " firs that are immersed in running waters ; and then they are " next seen hanging like sea-weed from the wood, becoming " encased in shells, which at last assume in their growth the " outward form of birds, and so hang on by their beaks until " completely covered with feathers within their shells, and when " they arrive at maturity, they either drop into the waters or take " their flight at once into the air. Thus, from the juice of this " tree, combined with the water, are they generated, and receive " their nutriment until they are formed and fledged. I have many " times with my own eyes seen several thousand of minute little " bodies of these birds attached to pieces of wood immersed in " the sea, encased in their shells, and already formed. These, " then, are birds that never lay eggs, and are never hatched from " eggs ; and the consequence is, that in some parts of Ireland, " and at those seasons of fasting when meat is forbidden, bishops " and other religious persons feed on these birds, because they " are not fish, nor to be regarded as flesh. And who can marvel " that this should be so ? When our first parent was made of " mud, can we be surprised that a bird should be born of a tree?" —*Historical Works of Giraldus Cambrensis.*—Bohn's Antiquarian Library.

generally considered the most valuable of the author's
works, is a masterly production in every respect.
Judged even by the most advanced canons of criticism, it is surpassed by no work of its kind in existence.   Giraldus, closely allied to that heroic little
band by whom the eventful conquest had been
effected, and consequently impressed with a high
sense of the importance of his undertaking, had
opportunities of obtaining information at first hand,
which, with his acute habits of observation and his
clear judgment, he was so well able to turn to the
best account.   The "Itinerarium Cambriæ," in which
he recorded his progress through Wales to preach
the third Crusade, and the " Descriptio Walliæ," containing most interesting particulars of the condition
of his native country in the twelfth century, are, in
their way, of equal value.   In studying any of these
works, the reader is conscious that his author is a
man who thoroughly understands the subject about
which he is treating.   Others may surpass him in
describing state pageantries and narrating minute
formalities of outside shows ; but in his pages we
see men free from the constraints of all pomps and
ceremonies.   With him we feel ourselves under the
guidance of one, who, to the learning of a monk, added
the knowledge and acute intelligence of a man of the
world, without being himself a worldling; of one who

had not dissipated his years in the retirement and amidst the routine of a monastery, but had made the grand tour, so to speak, and had personal knowledge of what he describes; a real clear-headed, observant, outspoken man; one of ardent and impetuous nature, it is true, but sensible withal; judicious; not too trustful; and, in everything he wrote, of the strictest veracity. On the occasion of his completing his " Topographia," Giraldus revived a practice pursued in our own day to excess. A great feast was given at Oxford, and the work was publicly read by its author. The enthusiasm on all sides was great, and among the numerous compliments paid to Giraldus, Robert Beaufoy, a canon of Salisbury, composed an " Encomium Topographiæ," and his friend and countryman, Walter Mape, addressed him in most eulogistic terms. Contemporary criticism, however, was not altogether of this pleasant nature. He had his detractors as well as his admirers, and their attacks, which he attributed to malignant jealousy, gave him much pain. As frequently happens, too, he appears to have suffered neglect as well as abuse; for he complains that his dedications of the "Topography" to King Henry II, and of the " Conquest," to his successor, were ungraciously received by both princes. In these two works the Irish were painted in colours that have endured. Giraldus describes them as being

utterly barbarous; ignorant of the rudest arts; un-
skilled in the commonest form of agriculture; idle
to an enormous degree; quarrelsome; and attached,
priests and people, to the excessive use of strong
drinks.   In attributing to physical causes their im-
provident habits, he anticipates the conclusion of our
own time, when men have begun to see that the
great **tide** of emigration, ebbing and flowing under
their eyes, is as much the effect of physical causes as
are the rise and fall **of** the Atlantic ocean itself, and
that no legislative enactments will enable **a** country,
suitable only for pasture, to maintain so large a
population as if it were subject to agriculture. **He was**
the first to disparage the Irish character, and give
the people that unsavoury repute among their fellow-
subjects, from which they have not been able, in six
hundred years, to free themselves.   He it **is** who
must **be credited with having** been the first to fashion
our current estimate of the nation; and for this he
will **never be** forgiven.   The "Topography" and
"Conquest" have been the objects of much abuse ever
since their appearance.   As early as 1603, when Cam-
den first printed them, they met with a storm of **dis-**
approbation, which has not yet altogether ceased.   An
Irishman, who styled himself Gratianus Lucius, but
who was in reality **a Dr.** Lynch, wrote a work, pub-
lished in 1662, in reply to what he terms the virulent

calumnies of Giraldus, and which, with singular modesty, he entitles "Cambrensis Eversus." This refutation has been issued in two volumes by the Celtic Society, and the reader who enjoys a treat of the sort, will find therein some of the most precious bits of abuse that were ever penned, even by a patriot. The doctor deals his blows with merciless severity. He gives no quarter and asks for none. Beginning with the title, he places Giraldus in a dilemma. If he knew not that topography means a description of any place whatsoever, and chorography, which is the term he should have employed, a description of an extensive region, he was an ignorant pretender to scholarship. If he did, and used the term designedly, he was malicious, and insulted Ireland by purposely and contemptuously classing her among gardens, meadows, parks, and other places of confined dimensions. But his dislike to the title of the work is mild in comparison with the disgust he avows for the work itself. He accuses Giraldus, "against whose "tongue heaven itself is no asylum," with being disqualified in every possible respect for writing on Ireland, and charges him with being ignorant of geography—" the first rule of which is to proceed from " west to north, and north to south." Besides, he was not a native, and, being an enemy to the natives, he was not the right man in the right place. He is, in a word, charged with every sin of commission and omission it is possible for an author to commit. When the doctor becomes explicit he is extremely severe and amusing. Every portion of the work under his review is industriously abused; but it is to the marvellous stories in the second " distinctio," or book, that he takes especial exception. Here he can speak from personal knowledge, and consequently has his enemy under disadvantage. When in the Munchausen vein Giraldus tells, among other strange stories, of an island in Connaught where dead bodies remained unburied and were exempt from putrefaction. At this the Irishman turns upon his adversary, shows that the present state of the island does not agree with the description, abuses him for his credulity, and concludes with the avowal of his own opinion that Giraldus had mistaken Aran for Inisgluair, in which latter place he candidly confesses bodies do not decay, " but even the hair and nails grow, so that one would " recognize his grandfather !" Again, Giraldus tells us it was reported that a controversy, whether Man belonged to Britain or Ireland, was decided in the following rather unusual way :—Venomous reptiles were brought there on trial, and these having been found to live, the island was unanimously adjudged to be the possession of Britain. Commenting on this story, the Irish critic seriously complains, not of the

credulity of Giraldus, but of his disingenuousness in
concealing the names of those who raised and concluded the controversy, and for neglecting to give the
date of their adjudication. " The brand of infamy,"
exclaims the doctor, " clings to him in his grave." He
considers the author's apology for introducing such
legends into his work equivalent to confession of guilt.
But what does Giraldus say? " I do not desire," he
remarks, " that everything I write should be readily
" believed, for except what came under my own obser-
" vation, or what could be easily ascertained, my own
" belief in my narrations is not fixed and unhesitating.
" I give them without myself pronouncing on their
" truth or falsehood." This candid confession is, one
would think, everything that could be expected from
the historian; but it was unavailing with his patriotic
adversary. The feud between Giraldus and the
Irish, which has prevented the nation not only from
treating our author's memory with ordinary respect,
but even from seeing the most transparent merits in
his great works, is, I suspect, doomed to be eternal.
The " History of the Conquest of Ireland" is criticised
and abused much in the same manner, the doctor assuming that Ireland never was conquered, and thus
at the very outset disposing of the value of a treatise
which concerns itself about an event which did not
actually occur.

These celebrated productions were frequently copied **by** the mediæval chroniclers, and were the earliest **of** our author's works to be reproduced by the printing press. Others, however, are perhaps read **with** greater interest by some classes of students. For the most part composed during a late period of his life, they **are of** a biographical nature, and derive their value from the true insight they give us into the **man,** and the **stirring** times in which he flourished. **That** entitled **" De Rebus a se gestis "** furnishing **an** account of the author's career to about the fif**tieth year** of his age ; the " Invectionum Libellus," undertaken by desire of Innocent III. as a reply by Giraldus to calumnies brought against him by his enemies in Rome ; the " Gemma Ecclesiastica," an **eloquent** address to his clergy ; **the** " Symbolum Electorum," containing his letters, poems, and speeches, together **with other** writings bearing on the great dispute between Canterbury and St. David's, **are all** characterized at once by sound scholarship and sound sense. In the composition of his works the author sat down resolved—and in this respect it were well if all authors would imitate him—to write about what he of the men then living knew best. He gives us an account of the life and opinions of one with whom **he was on** most intimate terms ; who was of **exalted station ;** who had **mixed on** equality with popes and princes; who was the bosom friend of some of the most eminent men of the age ; who had formed acquaintance with events, not by means of uncertain echoes reaching him through the doors of a remote monastery, but from opportunities that belonged only to one who was an active participator in the strife and fascinating excitements of the time ; who had visited court, camp, college, and cell, and who was able to describe with masterly touches what he had heard and seen and felt with unusual acuteness. Of the aims, and successes, and failures of this man, who, I need not say, was the writer himself, he presents us with an impartial account, detailing the thoughts and the events of his life without reservation, and with absolute frankness. It is for the quality of ingenuousness and for the freedom he displayed in his communications I most value him. Everything he has written is coloured by his own personality. He despised the petty courtesies prevalent during his time, and was not ashamed to assert himself in all his productions. He is the central figure of each. I know no more agreeable reading, even for those with whom reading is a mere habit, than is to be found in the various works of Giraldus. He practised every species of literature, and succeeded in all. His historical books combine the excellencies of Herodotus, Mandeville, Mr. Robert Curzon, and the "Arabian Nights;" and the personal revelations he has left us are as entertaining as those of Mr. Samuel Pepys. Many a Joe Miller may be traced to his pages, and many a clever story, attributed to the invention of the *Renaissance,* will be found to have been told by him three hundred years before. The language he employs in each of his works has the merit of being invariably suited to the subject, and shows its author not only to have mastered all the knowledge of his own time, but to have been intimately acquainted with the best models of antiquity. Mr. Brewer, a good authority, does not think his style purer than that of William Malmesbury, or so pure as that of John Salisbury—and there is no doubt that his writings are sometimes disfigured with quips, and cranks, and puns, and alliterations jarring on modern ears and repugnant to modern taste; but when the subject or the occasion requires elevation in the style, it is not absent. There is then a stateliness, a dignity, a conscious force of expression which is not surpassed, if indeed it is at all equalled, by any other of the post-classical writers.

The character and genius of Giraldus have never had full justice done them. The latest editor of his works, following in the steps of his predecessors, lays too much stress on the vanity exhibited by our author. To this one trait in the character of Giraldus he re-

peatedly invites the attention of the reader; he is
not satisfied with simple statement of the fact; he
reiterates it, and seems to delight in every opportunity that offers of indulging himself with a sly joke
or humorous remark on the subject. I do not here
wish to say that Giraldus was free from self-esteem
bordering upon vanity. There can be no doubt he had
an exalted opinion of himself, and was not indifferent
to the approbation of his fellow men. But who aims
at writing a poem, or painting a picture, or making a
statue, or composing a mass, solely for his own satisfaction and gratification? Why should not a man
work for love of praise as well as for love of bread
and cheese? Why not satisfy his mental appetite
as well as his digestive organs? The motive, whether
concealed or expressed, is in each instance gratification
of self through the applause of others. The old maxim,
γνῶθι σεαυτόν, however, seems no longer to hold good.
At the present day a man who does not desire to be
thought indecent, must know—not himself, not his
capabilities, not his capacity—but only his weaknesses
and shortcomings. Genius, we are told, is unconscious,
is modest, is self-depreciatory. If you are a genius
you must not know you are a genius—you must not,
at all events, say you are, or thenceforth you cease
to be regarded in that character. The world may
acknowledge your ability and pay court to you; but

the moment in **which** it perceives that **your** judgment
in the matter **agrees** with its **own,** and that, equally
with **itself, you are** able to appreciate **your** gifts or
attainments, it resents the coincidence of opinion, **and**
you subside **into** a man **of** inferior **parts.** But it is not
for accomplishing **great things, or for** regarding them
in their proper light, **that you are** thus condemned.
It is **for saying you see them,** and thereby arousing
the self love **of public opinion, which** delights **in the**
sole exercise of its power of praise and blame, and
does not **wish its** function **to be** shared **in by the**
recipient **of its favour, or** its award **to** be taken as a
matter **of course.** Self-depreciation by manner **or**
by direct assertion **is notoriously** the best method of
procuring from **others** favourable opinion of one's own
merits.   The most successful **performer** in any department, by avowing himself **a tyro in** his art, and
comparing himself to children **on the sea** shore, &c,
pays a tribute to others which will be returned a
thousand-fold **by** their exuberant esteem.   On the
contrary, if he should so far forget his interest as **to**
represent himself to be what they have **already ad-**
judged him **to be, he** is at once disadvantageously **com-**
pared with some superior imbecile, and dethroned from
the pinnacle upon which **he had perhaps** unwillingly
been exalted.   Giraldus, unfortunately, **as well for his**
success during life as for his reputation after death,

did not appreciate this fact. He declined to affect the humility he did not feel. Not content with silently knowing that his abilities were great, he allowed his contemporaries and posterity to perceive the estimation in which he himself held them. Are we altogether to condemn in a man the manifestation of this supreme self-consciousness? I think not. Horace boasted that his work would be *ære perennius*; Cicero, that he was the second founder of Rome. If either of these saw he was able to do what the whole world besides considered worth doing, and did it, I fail to perceive what impropriety there was in his confessing the achievement. All that a candid criticism can fairly require is proof that a man really is what he pretends to be, and possesses the gifts and attainments of which he boasts. If we test the life of Giraldus in this spirit, we shall find he had just cause for his self-assertion, and that he was one who really redeemed the pledges he gave.

His country was, in the 13th century, little removed from barbarism. The laity he represents as being governed by their passions; addicted to the worst immoralities; utterly uncivilized. The clergy, little better, were poor, and rude, and avaricious; neglectful of their duties, ignorant of the elements of theology and literature, and not free from some of the worst vices with which he charges their flocks.

Books well known in other countries were unknown among them; and he gives such instances of their amusing illiterateness as could not, I hope, have been, even in the 12th century, parallelled elsewhere. One priest, he tells us, went to his bishop and promised him in Latin two hundred eggs; he meant to have said *ducenta ova :* but from his ignorance of the language, he said *ducentas oves*—two hundred sheep. When the two hundred fresh eggs were brought to the bishop on the following day, his lordship peremptorily refused them, and, insisting on the literal fulfilment of the promise, extorted from the bad Latinist two hundred fat wethers. Another priest, in his sermon on St. Barnabas' day, informed his congregation that St. Barnabas was a good and holy man, *though* he was a robber, quoting, in support of his assertion, the passage, "now Barrabas was a robber." Of abbots and bishops, who were equally liable to similar blunders as those which characterized the inferior members of the hierarchy, he gives a very unflattering account. He complains that all the bishops transplanted in his days from England into Wales were overreaching, rapacious, always pretending the greatest poverty, begging at the abbey doors in England, haunting the Exchequer to obtain larger emoluments by augmentation or translation, and, in consequence, that their authority had completely fallen into con-

tempt. This state of things he was sincerely anxious
to correct. But it was impossible for him to effect
his reforms so long as St. David's was subject to
Canterbury, and Norman kings, to support their
rule, bestowed ecclesiastical preferment only on men
of their own race; men who were unable to speak
the language of the people, or to feel the slightest regard for their interests. This persistent determination to become bishop of St. David's has been severely
blamed by writers to whom his motives have not, I
think, been clearly understood. The ambition of
Giraldus, usually regarded as vulgar self-seeking,
seems to me to have taken its direction, less from a
desire of personal aggrandizement, than from a patriotic instinct to benefit his native land by the rectification of the grievous abuses to which it was subject.
Surely no ambition can be more justifiable or praise-
worthy than this. There was also another and, doubtless, a more personal influence at work in directing
his attention to St. David's—the desire, namely, of
occupying an influential position in the district where
he was born, and wherein he was best known. This
is a desire from which the healthiest minds have not
been free. Sir Walter Scott, we know, thought
less of the fame he had acquired by his writings than
of the reputation he derived from being considered
the laird of Abbotsford. To Stratford-on-Avon it

was that, having done his appointed work, Shakespeare—leaving behind him, as of little account, his reputation as playwright—repaired with the hope of being a man of consideration in the place which had given him birth. Nor is the feeling confined to churchmen and men of letters. Hastings, ruling with regal splendour millions of Asiatics, was, we are told, for ever thinking of the home of his fathers, and planning how he, too, should one day be Hastings of Daylesford, and exercise the limited but sweet authority possessed by his ancestors. In Wales and in Ireland this feeling is, perhaps, even more common and more intense than it is elsewhere. We daily see in these countries the son of humble parents, upon receiving ordination, almost invariably selecting for the scene of his ministration his native town or county, notwithstanding the slights and indignities he is sure to meet with from the squireens and diminutive local magnates; but the disappointments he experiences at one end of the social scale are, he thinks, compensated by the importance he exercises upon the other, and he resolves to accept the position with all its inconveniencies. In Giraldus this sentiment appears to have been more than usually strong. He was, moreover, of the highest rank; and, as has been explained, from his childhood had been looked upon as the future bishop of the diocese. To fail, therefore, was in his case to confess weakness as well as to experience disappointment. It is true he had opportunity of consoling himself by accepting several bishoprics that were successively offered him. But all these he resolutely and unhesitatingly refused. Just as Swift had set his heart upon an English bishopric, so did Giraldus yearn for the desolate see of St. David's. This was no caprice, but a life-long passion; the central essential aim of his existence; the hope to which his whole being had been attached from his earliest youth. And what was the bishopric for which this ambitious man rejected others of greater emolument? Here are his words, which are as applicable now as they were in his day:—" A stony " and barren headland, neither clothed with woods, " nor adorned by waters; visited only by storms and " winds." But although the place was not then more desirable than now as a residence, it is manifest that he cherished hopes of compensating these disadvantages by the satisfaction he would derive from elevating the see to its pristine dignity and power. Giraldus was the first to insist that the clergy should know the vernacular, and in this as well as in numerous other respects, proved himself to have been well acquainted with the principles on which all church reforms should be based. When he became the accepted champion of the Welsh section of his country who desired the independence of St. David's, he accepted the trust in all singleness of purpose, as is proved by his own confession, by his exhortation to the new bishop to evade the oath of subjection, as well as by constantly expressed solicitations for the interests of the see and its clergy. From the outset he avowed this to be his object, and that he intended to adhere to it through evil as well as good report. His failure, therefore, is not to be wondered at. Having enemies interested in opposing him, he neither cloaked his design, as a less conscientious man would have done; nor, as a more crafty man, having revealed it, did he attempt to appease his adversaries by a show of submission. He boldly avowed his object; so in the fierce struggle that ensued the civil power proved too strong for him, as in the case of Becket, and as in the ultimate issue it has always proved too strong for the champions of ecclesiasticism. There is no need to seek another cause for his defeat than that stated by himself—the king's fear that increased power would make him dangerous to English supremacy. For the notion currently entertained that he exaggerates the power and influence he was capable of exerting, I can find no ground, either in his own writings or in contemporary records.

Self-assertion is so distasteful to English readers,

and so unusual in English writers, that its presence is generally considered indicative of falsehood. But Giraldus is another example of the fallacy of the popular saying that boaster and liar are synonymous terms. He believed that diffidence was a hindrance to bold attempts, and that men of talent who give way to the disposition often grow old without knowing their powers. Avowing his admiration of those who, before their path in the future was yet plain, resolved on making it their chief aim to leave behind them some memorial whereby they might live in after times, he boldly expressed his determination to emulate them; and I think it will be conceded that he has achieved no equivocal success. In affairs his influence was even greater than he himself believed it to be. To insure a good reception for Prince John in Ireland it was he that was sent as his companion; when the Crusade was preached in Wales, his presence was considered essential to the success of the mission—ndeed so unsettled was the country, I doubt whether an English prelate and justiciary would have ventured through the land without his countenance and support—and afterwards, on the accession of Richard I, he was dispatched from France to his native land for the purpose of repressing the outbreak that was apprehended from the change. Nor was his influence less when exerted against the king than it was when employed in his favour.   During the great contest for the independence of St. David's, his partisans had become so numerous that the whole country was, as appears from the Patent Rolls, in a ferment ; *non solum pax partium vestrarum immo totius regni nostri tranquillitas turbaretur.* (5 JOHN, memb. 7. No. 32.)   Although, however, he cannot **justly be** censured for unduly exalting himself, it must be admitted that it would have been better, as well for his peace **of** mind as for **the** success of his schemes, if he had condescended to imitate the example of those around him, and exhibited more worldly prudence in his relations with the supreme powers.   Had he consented to debase himself, he would doubtless have been rewarded with ultimate exaltation.   **But** he **was no** sycophant.   Of all the eminent men of **his time, he** appears to have been the most sincere, and acted throughout in harmony **with his own nature.**   The presence of this great tall figure was a protest against the licentious court of Henry—crowded, according to **a** contemporary, with jesters, singers, gamesters, pastry cooks, bankrupts, mummers, barbers, spendthrifts, and **others of a** similar class, and in which, **if you** would learn the movements of the king, you must apply to vintners and loose women.   His very outspokenness, and the self-esteem **he** exhibited, were unmistakeable manifestations of a sincere nature. His fellow-countryman, the acute Walter Mape, saw, and satirized, the vices of churchmen and courtiers; but he looked upon them with the eye of one who did not much disapprove, and his satires, severe enough, leave an impression that, after all, they were produced more for the gratification of a facetious nature than for the profit of those who were the objects of his urbane censure. Some men possess that rare and desirable gift—a habit of supreme frankness—which lessens the effect of their shafts, and enables them to say unpleasant truths without being considered personally offensive. Men of this kind are either extremely artless, or masters of that consummate art which enables them effectually to cloak their animus, and renders it impossible for an ordinary bystander to determine whether annoyance is meant, or that the sally is ill-timed but unintentional. In the one case he is regarded as a cynic; in the other, as a well-meaning man, whose unfortunate manner must be pardoned on account of his well-known sincerity. Disagreeable criticism is in both cases unwelcome, but the object of the attack is unwilling to resent what comes from the latter, as if it had proceeded from the former. Nevertheless the disagreeable remark produces the same effect uttered by the one as by the other, just as unpalatable medicine is equally

efficacious when given in honey as if administered in
its native state, and has the advantage, moreover, of
not being succeeded by nausea in the patient. Giraldus was generally regarded as a well-meaning man,
and, in his bluff Welsh way, was permitted to say
things no one else would have dared to utter; things,
notwithstanding, which proved his moral courage to
have been as unbounded as his physical bravery.
He never failed to express his opinion manfully.
The Church of Rome was notoriously venal, and on
his first introduction to Innocent he did not fail to
let that prelate know he was acquainted with this
fact. "Others give you money," he said, " I offer
" you only books;" or, to quote his punning sentence, *Præsentant vobis alii Libras, sed nos Libros.*
And in his dedication to John of his " Conquest,"
he tells that monarch some home truths, under the
phrase, "permit me to offer you some advice," which
must have surprised his former pupil by his freedom
of speech.   In these cases no offence was meant, and
no offence could be taken. " My habit of outspoken-
" ness," he used to say, " is natural to Welshmen
" like myself; we can neither alter it, nor get rid
" of it."   But there were times (as in his early con-
tests with the sheriff of Pembroke and the bishop of
St. Asaph) when his bark was followed by a terrible
bite, and when he took care that there should be no

mistake as to his intention to wound. What chiefly characterized him, however, is his love of order, of precedent, of law. He was essentially the type of a mediæval churchman, even more than of a mediæval man of letters. The indications that manifested themselves on the white sands of Manorbeer at the first page of his life accompanied him to the close of his days. He loved the Church, and followed her precepts; requiring, at the same time, that others over whom he had control, should likewise do so. None more than he differed from some of her teachings. He doubted whether sins could be remitted by pontifical indulgence. Clear-sighted enough to see the inconveniencies from enforced celibacy of the clergy, he shows that neither in the Gospels nor in the apostolical writings is to be found any prohibition against their marriage; but so long as the restriction remained he would not permit his clergy to keep their *focariæ* in peace, but would extirpate them root and branch. 'Tis great pity to require in your ministers such a sacrifice; but no man is compelled to be a churchman, and if the vow is voluntarily made by the candidate for ordination, he must abide by it, and maintain the strictest observance of discipline. Keep your promise; be true to yourself: was the tenour of his whole life-teaching. Do you obey, for then only may you expect obedience from others. Look not upon the Church as designed for your convenience—if you are of it, you must be faithful to it and to its teachings. He was himself faithful, and he expected others to be as faithful as himself.

He was at once a genuine churchman and a genuine man of letters.

VIII.

MONTAIGNE.

THE fame of Montaigne is on the increase.
The "Essays" have been translated
into the languages of all civilized
nations, and edition after edition has
been called for and exhausted in each. They
have not in any country had for readers what
is known as the general public, but have obtained
only what Mr. Emerson calls a chosen circulation—
namely, among courtiers, soldiers, princes, men of
the world, and men of wit and generosity. There
are signs, however, that the appreciation is extending in the old world and the new; cheap editions of
his great work are issued, and the manner in which
they have been received may fairly be taken as indicative that the Essayist is becoming known to
readers who hitherto were acquainted only with his
name. In France there are men who make the
old Gascon the study of their lives, who devote

themselves to the elucidation of his writings, and
who quarrel over the interpretation of one of his
phrases with as much zest, if not with as much
acrimony, as scholars among ourselves quarrel over
the meaning of a passage in Shakespeare. Since the
revival of letters no French writer has exercised so
much influence upon our own literature. The Shakespeare Plays contain passages almost literally ex-
tracted from him,* and ever since the appearance of
the translation by Florio into English, all who have
made the study of man their theme exhibit in their
writings undoubted traces of familiarity with his
speculations. If he is not known at first hand so
well as he should be, he is well known at second.

---

* By the favour of the Head of the British Museum I have
examined the autograph, said to be of Shakespeare, in the copy
of Florio's Translation belonging to that Institution.   Sir
Frederick Madden, in *Archæologia*, vol. xxvii. p. 113, has
described this autograph, and given an interesting history of
the volume as far as it is known. It is now thirty years since
Sir Frederick made his communication to the Society of Anti-
quaries, and expressed his unhesitating belief in the authenticity of the signature, and he tells me he is still of the same
opinion.   There is no questioning the authority of so eminent
a Palæographer.   I must mention, however, that not a tittle of
external evidence exists to support the belief that the volume
was Shakespeare's, "and is the only book which we certainly
" know to have been in the poet's library."

Men who are ashamed to quote him, because he is reputed to be a sceptic, have no hesitation in appropriating his thoughts. I have heard a sermon by Montaigne from one of the most orthodox pulpits in London.

Montaigne was thirty-eight years old when, in 1571, tired of courts and public employments, but rich in twenty years' experience of the ways of men in court and camp, he retired to his château in Perigord. Neither by circumstances nor temperament was he fitted to make a great figure in the barbarous, cruel, and deceitful court he had abandoned; and it was without much regret at rising from the game he had left, that he sat down in quiet indifference to all things, to conclude the remainder of his life, already more than half past, in the agreeable and peaceful abode he had inherited from his ancestors. Here and now, then, with his wife and numerous retainers upon whom to vent his ill-humour when he should begin to pine for past pleasures, he really began to live. Hitherto he had been in school. The time for meditation had at length come, and the scholar, feeling desirous of ascertaining what progress he had made in his studies, seriously began to interrogate himself.

To the question *Que sçais-je ?* he was continually asking himself, we have for answer the three books which form the famous " Essays."

Most of his biographers pretend to see Montaigne
thinking in these " Essays," and fancy they come
upon a man in undress. They esteem him the
frankest of autobiographers—the most outspoken of
all philosophers and writers. But can you believe
them? Is he so ingenuous as they report? The
work is full of original and selected thoughts on innumerable subjects, but it can scarcely be said to
contain one predominant thought. He had no
theory to establish. In painting himself the writer
necessarily expounds his philosophy; but he is so
whimsical and inconsistent, and contradictory, that
the difficulty of ascertaining his central idea is insuperable. What was written in one mood has the appearance of sincerity, yet it is utterly different from
what, with equal sincerity, he sets down on the same
subject in another. His powers of observation were
of the highest order, and had been judiciously exercised; what he had seen clearly he could express
boldly; there is little opportunity for the dullest reader
to mistake his meaning; but his digressions are so
numerous, and occur so frequently, that the writer
himself often forgets, or pretends to forget, the text
from which he is preaching. When you begin a
chapter you do not know what is coming. The
" Essay on Lame People," for instance, is devoted
to an attack on miracles. He exaggerates, is para-

doxical, and despises the technicalities and accuracies
of any learning. It would be possible to string
together scores of his likes and dislikes, of his
opinions on men and things, and of curious personal
revelations, without getting a very accurate portrait
of the essayist himself. It is, therefore, useless
to attempt the discovery of his leading doctrine.
Indeed, I do not suppose he had any cut-and-dry
theory of morals or of man's destiny. He did not
set himself to satirize human nature; nor did he attempt to flatter the vanity of men by deriving their
descent from angels. To such questions he was indifferent. Sound philosophy, he thought, was that
which best insured sound health. " The most evi-
" dent token and apparent sign of true wisdom," says
he, " is a constant unconstrained rejoicing." He
could not, therefore, understand why a man should
fashion his belief to the customary, or conform to
what is suitable for another and not for himself.
Let every man's philosophy be in harmony with his
own nature, and then for him there will be unconstrained rejoicing. If he knows only by hearsay, let
him confess it, and not profess what he does not understand. As for himself, he shows in all he says
that he was influenced by some such consideration
as this. He was a brave doubter. Mrs. Grundy
does not seem to have had any terrors for him.

Through the fences Custom had set up he boldly trotted his horse; but he had no desire to widen the gaps he had made; certainly not to tear down the fences themselves. What Sir Thomas Browne calls "scenical and accidental differences," did not impress him. Kings and mountebanks are equally men, and one of his great pleasures was to teach those who in his time regarded the recovered classical authors as something more excellent than their contemporaries, that the great writers of antiquity were men of like passions with themselves; that they had natural wants like themselves; and like themselves would have acted under any given circumstance of life.

Montaigne is to be regarded as at once the product and representative of the *Renaissance.* Rabelais wrote as a mediæval monk would have written. He looked upon things from the same point of view as all acute minds had been looking upon them for ten centuries. In the productions of Walter Mape, whilst we miss the tedious buffoonery of the Frenchman, the same theme, the same spirit, the same fervid satire are to be detected as characterize *Pantagruel* and the *Gargantua,* and it will excite no surprise to say, that the author of these romances has become a modern more by reason of the licentious exuberancy of his vocabulary than by virtue of his inherent worth. Montaigne, on the other hand, was the first great exponent of the new classical spirit which had just reached France from beyond the Alps, and of which his predecessors knew nothing. The age of examination and doubt had replaced the ages of faith, and although in point of time he came a few years after the events from which we are accustomed to date the change, he was contemporary with the beginning of modern thought, popularized the new ideas, and became their chief representative. He was a Roman before he was a Frenchman. His queer old father, to make him a good Latinist, took care that he should not hear a word of his native tongue till he was able to speak in the language of Cicero. Influenced by peculiar views of education, he selected a tutor who was unable to speak French, and the domestics were strictly forbidden from uttering a syllable of the vernacular in the child's presence. Silence or Latin was the alternative he enjoined upon all. It would occasion no surprise if the future essayist had grown up to be a dolt, surfeited with the good things of which he had been forced to take too much; but Montaigne knew the value of the recovered learning, and he knew also the best things that had been produced in his own time. He knew, moreover, how to use both. Ben Jonson was not far wrong when he classed him among those wits that " turn over all books, and are equally searching in

" all papers, that write out of what they presently
" find or meet, without choice; by which means it
" happens, that what they have discredited and im-
" pugned in one week, they have before or after
" extolled the same in another. Such are all the
" essayists, even their master Montaigne. These,
" **in all** they write, confess still what books they
" have read last; and therein their own folly, so
" much, that they bring it to the stake raw and un-
" digested: not that the place did need it neither;
" **but** that they thought themselves furnished and
" would vent it." What he wanted, indeed, he took
without hesitation, and was never particular whence
he procured the straw, so that it was capable of being
made into good bricks. " If I wish to give an ap-
" pearance **of** reading to this ' Essay on Physiog-
" nomy,'" says he, " I have only to stretch out my
" **hand** and take **down a** dozen books consisting of
" extracts strung together. A single German pre-
" face would supply me with a store of learning."
And he has certainly availed himself of the plan,
for the reader will have difficulty in some of the
essays in discovering what is meant to be considered
original and what borrowed.

Towards the decline of his life—at a time of age,
however, when **with us** statesmen and lawyers are
considered **young men—the** little fellow, in

several of his essays, and notably in that on some
verses by Virgil, is solicitous to tell us that he is
going to be naughty. He is careful to warn us of
what is coming, and deprecates blame by giving us
examples of others before him who have been as
naughty as he intends to be. " Fallen into the ex-
" treme of severity, more peevish and more unto-
" ward," he purposely gave way to licentious allure-
ments, and, now and then, permitted his mind to in-
dulge " in wanton and youthful conceits," for the
purpose of recreating itself. He wishes us to understand that, hitherto, he had defended himself from
pleasure. Wisdom, however, has her excesses,
" and is not less in need of moderation than madness.
" Therefore, for fear I should dry, shrivel up, and be-
" come ponderous by prudence, in the intervals which
" my sufferings grant me, I gently turn aside and
" escape from the sight of that stormy and cloudy sky
" which spreads before me; which, thank God, I con-
" sider without affright, but not without application
" and study." So he wilfully turns away from serious
matters, and ceases for a time to contemplate the
tempestuous sky which constantly lowered before
him. He amused himself and the reader with re-
membrances of his youthful days; and youthful
tricks, long since forgotten, were brought up to
the session of sweet silent thought. " For my part,"

says he, " I am displeased with thoughts not to be
" published, and am resolved to dare speak whatso-
" ever I dare do ; and thoughts that cannot be pub-
" lished displease me. `The worst of my actions and
" conditions does not seem to me so ugly as the
" cowardice of not daring to confess it." We look for
great things after this avowal, but at last—and
this is to his praise—he is never very naughty ;
but only very coarse. If he is at fault, he is to be
blamed, not for calling a spade a spade, but for
making a spade the subject of his discourse. Those
who dislike to hear things called by their names
must not sit under our Gascon preacher. He does
not, however, excite the passions; this was not his aim.
He is writing about man as man, and will not abstract
that which belongs to him as member of a Religious
Tract Society from that which belongs to him in
common with the other animals. He hates a way-
ward and sad disposition that glideth over the
pleasures of his life and fastens and feeds on
the miseries. He will be no voluntary martyr. He
loved life and cultivated it, and lamented nothing
that gave pleasure. " I do not regret the necessity
" of eating and drinking, and should think myself
" wrong in desiring that necessity to be less." He
did not claim for us too high an origin. " We may
" mount upon stilts if we will, for on stilts we

" are still obliged to use our legs ; and on the highest
" throne in the world we place what we place on the
" lowest stool. The finest lives, to my mind, are those
" which do agree with the common and human model
" —with order, without miracle, without extra-
" vagance."

This is not contemptible philosophy.

Montaigne's personal confessions are as inaccurate
as those of Goethe ; but he has been so communica-
tive and so explicit in speaking of himself, that if we do
not know him we know more about him than we do of
most other men.

He has the credit of being the frankest of all
writers. He talks so much about himself that you
may be tempted to fancy he gives you a photo-
graph of his peculiarities. But do you believe in the
sincerity of his continual self-depreciation ? When
he takes you by the button, and, on tip-toe. jabbers
away in a loud, shrill voice, sometimes rather
too long-windedly, about his inability to dance,
or swim, or fence, or wrestle like other people, do
you believe he is despising himself for this?* When

---

* " Of addressing, dexteretie, and disposition, I never had
" any, yet am I the son of a well disposed father, and of so
" blithe and merry a disposition, that it continued with him
" even to his extreamest age. He seldome found any man of

he confesses his ignorance of the value of the coinage, and of the difference between barley and oats, or tells you he could not understand why leaven is put into bread, or how the apple gets into the dumpling, and therefore considers himself a lumber-headed old fool, do you take **him at** his word? Of **all** these things he was undoubtedly ignorant. But could not any of the retainers on his estate have enlightened him on these **heads, and do** you suppose Lord Michael de Montaigne, as Florio styles **him, of**

" **his condition, and that could** match him in all exercises of
" the **body; As I have** found few, that have not out-gon me,
" except **it were in** running, wherein I was of the middle sort.
" As **for** musicke, **were it** either in voice, which I have most
" harsh, and very unapt, or in instruments, **I** could never be
" taught any part **of it. As for dancing, playing** at tennis, **or**
" **wrestling; I** could never **attaine to any** indifferent sufficiencie;
" **but none at all in** swimming, **in fencing, in** vauting, or in
" leaping. **My hands are** so stiffe **and** nummie, that I can
" hardly write for myselfe, so that what **I** have once scribled,
" **I had** rather frame it **a new, than take** the paines to correct
" **it; and I reade but** little better. I perceive how **the audi-**
" **torie** censureth me : Otherwise **I am** no bad clarke, **I cannot**
" **very wel** close up a letter; nor could I ever make **a pen. I**
" **was never good carver at the** table. **I could** never make
" readie **nor arme a Horse: Nor handsomely array a Hawke**
" upon my fist, nor cast her off, or let her flie, nor could I ever
" speake to Dogges, to Birds, or **to Horses. The** conditions of
" **my body** are, in fine, **very well** agreeing with those of my
" **minde."—On** *Presumption.* Florio's Translation.

the noble order of St. Michael, and one of the Gentlemen in Ordinary of the French King's Chamber, could feel satisfaction in knowing what was fitted only to be known by them?

The literary worth of an author is, I think, to be estimated more by the extent than by the weight of his influence. There are writers who appeal only to a limited class, or fail to influence men except at a certain period of life. Wither and George Herbert, for instance, in poetry, and Sir Thomas Browne in prose, address but a very select class of minds. Their adherents, men of cultivated taste, admire them with an intensity that is never displayed towards writers who have become universal favourites; but to the general public they are scarcely known. It must not, however, be supposed, that because the common run of readers are unable to appreciate what men of higher intellectual rank admire that the fault is altogether with the former. The best books are those, which, appealing at once to the vulgar and the refined, are welcomed by both. Their authors have no partisans because all are on their side, and excite no enthusiasm because they are never slighted. They are the classics of all languages. Although it would be incorrect to say that Montaigne occupies a position among them, he differs from such writers as those I just now named in one very important particular. He numbers amongst his admirers the whole of the intellectual **class** in every civilized country, whilst admiration for them is confined to **men** with idiosyncrasies. He is the most catholic of all writers. His **views and** opinions are so varied **and** multifarious, that no man of culture can read **him** without finding himself reflected in the page. **An** odd **volume of** Cotton's translation of the " Essays" falling **into the** hands of Mr. Emerson, " newly escaped from **college,**" was the origin of that gentleman's admiration for the Essayist. " It seemed " **to me," he confesses, "** as if I had myself written " **the** book, in some former life, so sincerely it spoke " **to my** thought **and experience."**

---

* This appears **to be the case with others besides Mr.** Emerson. **The late Bayle St. John, in his** Biography of the Essayist, to which interesting work I acknowledge obligations, very correctly **remarks :—" The** Montaigne of Pascal and Malebranche is an " *esprit fort of* the seventeenth century ; the Montaigne of Bayle " is a gentlemanly sceptic ; the Montaigne of the Voltaireans **is a** " scoffer ; **the** Montaigne of the Abbé Laborderie **is a Capuchin** " **Friar ; the** Montaigne of Mr. Emerson is Mr. Emerson him- " self; **the** Montaigne of **Dr. Payen is the property** of Dr. " **Payen ;** and the Montaigne of **M. Grün is a** Préfet of the " Gironde."

In taking the measure **of Montaigne, his** biographers uncon-sciously furnish **us** with the means of taking their own.

Enough, however, is revealed to enable us to perceive not only his disposition and habits, but his religious and moral mood.   He was, I think, eminently religious; that is to say, he possessed in a high degree the religious sentiment from which all religions spring. His dissatisfaction with the various visible and formal manifestations of this sentiment was not active, but negative.   He could not conscientiously have subscribed to the articles of any Church, or assented even to the spirit of the popular religion.   Whilst, however, alienating himself, in a sense, from the Church of his fathers, and discrediting the dogmas preached by its ministers, much remained which he seems deeply to have cherished.   He cherished her ancient services; her solemn litanies and gorgeous masses were as dear to him as they were to others.   Had you accused him of hypocrisy in this you would have done him wrong.   He resembled men among ourselves, no longer members of the established religion, who confess themselves to be influentially and beneficially affected by its services, to whom church bells are " the " sound nearest heaven," and church prayers as balm of Gilead ; who, whilst unable to assent to the articles of membership, still term themselves sons of the Church, and would fight, if need were, in her behalf, against what they consider the bigotry and narrowmindedness of the sects.   It was dogmatism and not

devotion he resisted. By ordering the celebration
of mass in his chamber at the end, he cannot be said
to have contradicted the tenour of his life, which was
eminently pacific. He never broke with the Church,
but had so far sanctioned her practices as to have
spent fifty crowns at Loretto shrine, and upon
leaving, he presented a rich ex-voto. He disliked
Protestantism, because of its protests ; but he could
not understand martyrs on either side, willingness
to die being, in his eyes, no compensation for fanati-
cism. Religion he regarded as metaphysical specula-
tion, and to kill or maim a man because he dissents
from your conclusions as excess of folly. For that
self-assertion which manifested itself in striving after
converts, he had no patience; nor did he understand
how men could devote their lives to the attempt of
fashioning the world to their own ideas by painful
coercion. His convictions were not strong enough to
make him an active partisan in any cause ; he neither
wept at the follies, frailties, and vicissitudes of life
like Heraclitus, nor, on the other hand, did he think
too highly of man and his destiny. Even when he
did good he confesses to have been influenced by
no higher a motive than that of pleasing himself.
When they said a man must forget himself for his
neighbour he did not understand them, and considered
the precept was made more in favour of a man's neigh-

bour than of himself. He had **no wish to take sides.**
He avowed his readiness to **bring a candle to St.**
Michael and another to the **dragon. During the**
troublous **times** of the league he kept himself **square.**
There **are** people who will not understand that a man
may **constitute his own party.** They want him to
declare himself for **themselves or their opponents, and**
will not forgive him if in some matters he acts with
them, and in others on the **opposite side.** No doubt
Montaigne is liable **to** be termed what we now **call a**
trimmer. **Indeed, as** he confesses, during his lifetime some **called him Guelf** and others Ghibelline.
But he was indifferent to the distinctions that existed
between the parties, **and** was **most sincere in his in-**
difference. **To** the gospel **of** labour preached **of late**
he would have been **no convert. Labour for its own**
sake he thought a curse, **and he well** knew **the**
derivation of the word indolence. **What he did he**
accomplished by fits and starts. " Whosoever **will**
" **make use of me according to** myself let him **employ**
" me in affairs **that require vigour and** liberty ; **that**
" have a **short, a straight, and therewithal a hazardous**
" course. . . **If it be tedious, crafty, laborious,**
" artificial, and intricate, they shall **do better to ad-**
" dress themselves **to some** other man." **Fond of** his
own way, he would not be hurried in doing it ; **would**

M

not be bothered even for duty. Railways and punctual starting of express trains would have killed him.[*]

Montaigne is the **type of** every man of culture at a certain stage of his development. He looked upon mankind, **and chiefly upon** himself, diversely; and the conclusion **to which he came is the** same as that to which others **had come before. He** thought all is **vanity and vexation of spirit.** Everyone of us knows this; **but most of us desire to** forget it, or will not **choose to remember it. Montaigne does not deceive himself. He never gives** himself the air of **one who is** going to reveal secrets. You want to learn what **Is? He** cannot satisfy **you.** You must go to others; **he can, at the most, only tell you** what is not. It is **possible** that organization is tending to perfection; **but he does not know it. He is not sure** even of im**mortality, and carefully** abstains **from** saying that he **is. Indeed, with respect to this and** the other great **problems that interest us,** he had no view at all, and with

---

[*] " I am extreamele lazie and idle, and exceedingly **free,** " **both by** nature **and art. I** would as willingly lend **my** " **blood as my care.** I have a minde free and **altogether her** " **owne;** accustomed **to follow her owne humour.** And to this " **day never had** nor **commanding nor forced master.** I have " **gon as farre, and** kept what pace pleased **me best.** Which " hath **enfeebled and** made **me unprofitable to** serve others, " and made **me fit and apt but onely for my selfe."**—*On Presumption.* Florio's Translation.

unusual wisdom did not, I suspect, think it necessary
to have one. Many before and since his time have
troubled themselves with these questions, and for
certitude have experienced only doubts. Some there
are who eliminate these doubts by main force; or,
without having them resolved, consent for their peace
of mind to believe them soluble, and thenceforward
arrogantly assume that the opinions they have abandoned were unsound. This "bridging the gulf,"
as it is termed, confers on them, they suppose, the
right to believe they have performed a stage of
progress. A man who has once doubted, but doubts
no longer, gives himself a patronising air of superiority. "Ah! my dear friend," says he, " I once
" had doubts as you have; but happily they have
" disappeared. All the depths and shoals of modern
" thought are familiar to me, and now I feel sure
" footing. I have successfully bridged the gulf."
But does it follow that he who changes sides necessarily goes from darkness to light? If change of
opinion were in itself progress, the popularity and
influence of such a writer as Montaigne would
never be much. Before we can decide what is
truth, we must have an undisputed criterion. Montaigne will be perennial because his subject is perennial.

IX.

THE MAN OF LETTERS AS A STATESMAN.

ROGER WILLIAMS.

THE real meaning of the term religious liberty seems, even at the present day, to be but imperfectly understood. When Earl Russell and others refer to their exertions in the cause of civil *and* religious liberty, they doubtless consider these two terms as applying to two separate principles; and in this light they are very generally regarded. Little consideration, however, is needed to enable us to perceive that the connection between civil and religious liberty is of the most intimate nature; that the one is comprehended in the other; that the one is, in fact, a portion of the other. If a man is in possession of civil liberty—if, that is to say, he is free to think and act in *all* respects as he chooses, provided he thereby inflicts no wrong on the person or estate of another—it is manifest that he also enjoys religious liberty, which implies the right to think and act in *some* respects as he chooses. Hence, to talk of giving a man civil and religious liberty is much as if one were to speak of granting him a passport for all the countries of Europe and for Spain, or of permitting him to read all Shakespeare's plays and the *Merchant of Venice*. But although the term is thus misapprehended, the thing signified is not itself unknown or ill understood. In England at least, and wherever our race predominates, the state no longer uses the power at its disposal to repress or interfere with the religious opinions of its subjects; that portion of civil liberty known as "liberty " of conscience"—generally the last to be conceded— is now enjoyed by all; and the doctrine, that none is to be persecuted on account of his opinions on matters of religion, is happily universally entertained.

This noble doctrine is the growth of modern times and of our own land. In Christianity, it is true, the doctrine in question may be said to inhere; but from the moment when Christianity, in the person of Constantine, found itself in possession of power, the doctrine had not been asserted; it had not exhibited itself in the operative working of the religion; it lay latent; it had never been revealed. Many favourable opportunities for discovering it had presented themselves, and more than once did it seem about to be detected; but on each occasion it **was** over-looked.   It was overlooked even at that great upheav-ing of the nations at the beginning of the sixteenth century, when men, with minds unhinged, prepared for **almost any** change, went hither and thither—know-ing that something was wrong, **but** knowing not **what.   The** uneasy **feeling that** had been excited found rest **in** change **of** opinion without having lighted upon a change **of principles.**   Luther, Cal-vin, **Knox, and their** associates, whilst endeavouring **to acquire for themselves the right** to think and act **in matters of religion according to** the dictates **of their own** consciences, **all** regarded themselves as the sole depositaries of truth, and thought it their solemn duty **to** suppress, even **by force, if** necessary, what in their judgment was false **doctrine in others. They were, in** fact, guided by **the very** principle against **which they** contended **in others; and they** defended **conduct exhibited by men of** their party which they **were the first to condemn** in their opponents.   **In** England, **no sooner had the** Protestant party under Cranmer succeeded in establishing the right of pri-**vate judgment for itself as against the** Church **of Rome, than** it proceeded to **deny the right to** others; and, afterwards, the very **men who** had suffered severe persecution for their opinions **were amongst the most eager to inflict similarly severe persecutions** upon those from whom they dissented. The Scotch commissioners in London remonstrated in the name of their national Church against "sinful and ungodly " toleration in matters of religion;" the whole body of the English Presbyterian clergy protested against the schemes of Cromwell's party, and solemnly declared that " they detested and abhorred toleration;" Richard Baxter, the most eminent of nonconformist divines, avowed that he " abhorred unlimited liberty, " or toleration for all;" even John Milton's scheme of toleration was to have excluded Roman Catholics from its benefits; and in that of Lord Baltimore, lauded for the unusual liberality of its provisions, only persons professing belief in the Divinity of Christ were to share in the civil advantages of the colony he founded. Men contended ostensibly for free expression of opinion; it was in reality for the supremacy of their own opinion. The liberty at which they all aimed was to have been the privilege of themselves alone.

The honour of being the first advocate for full and absolute liberty of conscience belongs to Roger Williams—a man of heroic character, of catholic spirit, of inflexible principles; a man, moreover, who throughout a long life was himself guided by the principles he professed, wrote books in their defence, founded a state in accordance with them, and subse-

quently embodied them in the laws he framed.   Of
the early life of this very remarkable man few memorials exist.   Numerous lives and memoirs of him
have been written ; he has formed the subject of
academical discourses and review articles; poems
have been composed in his honour ; places have been
called after his name ; and his posthumous honours
have been many and great.   Till his arrival in America, however, only the scantiest information touching his life is to be gleaned.   After that event particulars are plentiful.   The Life by Dr. Romeo El-
ton (Providence, 1853), from which I abridge the
following particulars, may be recommended to those
who feel interested in the man.   The son of a Welsh
farmer, Williams was born in the year 1606, in Car-
marthenshire, at a place called Conwyl-Caio, where
for many generations his ancestors had resided.   At
an early age, he was removed to London, and was
there fortunate enough to attract the favourable notice of Sir Edward Coke, " who," says the daughter
of that eminent lawyer, " seeing so hopeful a youth,
" took such liking to him, that he sent him in to
" Sutton's Hospital."   Of this institution—now
known as the Charter House—he was elected a
scholar on the 25th of June, 1621, and three years
afterwards, having obtained an exhibition, he went
to Oxford, and entered at the Welsh College (Jesus).

This was on the 30th of April, 1624. How long he remained at the university is uncertain, since the records of his college furnish no evidence of his having taken a degree. Upon leaving, he was admitted to orders, and, as is presumed from a statement he makes in one of his works, he discharged the duties of the ministry somewhere in Lincolnshire.

The conflict that from the days of Elizabeth had existed between the prelatical party and the Puritans was at this period becoming more and more violent —the former being determined to enforce strict uniformity, and the latter being as equally determined to resist the enforcement. Roger Williams inclined in opinion to the side of the Puritans, and, moreover, had already advocated the doctrine which immortalises his name—*that the civil power hath no jurisdiction over the conscience.* In the clash of party strife, therefore, he could not hope to escape the unfriendly notice of those to whom such opinions and such a principle were obnoxious. Nor did he. Professing the tenets of the Puritans, he suffered the persecutions to which the expression of those tenets rendered him liable ; and finding it hopeless to expect to be suffered to preach in peace, he resolved to seek that liberty which was denied to him in the country of his birth amid the wilds of America, whither large numbers of his brethren had gone before.

The grief he felt at leaving may be learned from
a letter he addressed in after years to the daughter
of Sir Edward Coke. " Your dear father," he says,
" was often pleased to call me his son ; and truly it
" was as bitter **as death to me** when Bishop Laud
" pursued **me** out **of** the land, **and** my conscience
" was persuaded against the national church, and
" ceremonies, and bishops, **beyond** the conscience of
" **your** dear father—I say it was as bitter as death to me
" **when** I rode Windsor way to take **ship at Bristow,**
" **and** saw Stoke House, where the blessed man was;
" and **I then** durst not acquaint him with my con-
" science and my flight." **He** embarked with his
wife at Bristol in the *Lion*, Captain William Pierce,
and, after a tempestuous voyage of sixty-six days,
sailed **into Boston** harbour on **the** 5th day of **Feb-
ruary**, 1631.

His arrival in the New World is recorded in the
Journal of Governor Winthrop, and appears to have
occasioned much joy to the churches of the infant
colony. But he was soon to discover that the grand
idea he announced when he first trod the shores of
New England—that the civil magistrate had **no right**
to interfere in matters of conscience—would meet with
no echo in the hearts of the **Pilgrim** Fathers, and
that the " lords brethren" of Massachusetts were as
intolerant as the " lords bishops" of England. A

few weeks after his arrival, he accepted an invitation
to become assistant-pastor of the church of Salem,
and commenced his ministry there; but having declared his opinion that " the magistrate might not
" punish a breach of the Sabbath, nor any other
" offence that was a breach of the first table," the
civil authority immediately interfered to prevent his
settlement. The church, however, persisted; and
on the same day on which the magistrates at Boston
were assembled to express disapprobation of this,
and to desire the church to forbear any further proceeding, he was duly elected a minister at Salem.
But his residence there was destined to be of short
continuance. The church, in disregarding the wishes
and advice of the authorities, by calling him to be
their pastor, drew upon themselves the displeasure
of the magistrates; and so high rose the storm
of persecution, that before the close of the summer,
Williams was obliged to seek residence elsewhere.
He accordingly left Salem, and went to the colony
at Plymouth, " where," says Governor Bradford,
" he was freely entertained among us according to
" our poor ability." Two years afterwards, however, being invited to return, he complied with the
request, and resumed his ministerial labours in August, 1633. But the inflexibility of his principles,
and his determination to exhibit them when needed,

soon furnished the magistrates and ministers who
were opposed to him with many opportunities for renewed hostility. At one time they met to take into
consideration a treatise in which he had disputed
their **right** to **the** lands they possessed, because
they had not compounded with the natives; now
they charged him **with** having preached upon the
duty of females to wear veils **in** religious assemblies;
and now, again, complained that, **in** consequence of
his preaching, " **Mr.** Endicott **cut** the cross out **of**
" **the military** colours, as a relic of popish supersti-
" **tion.**"

The controversy between him and the civil and
ecclesiastical heads of the colony was clearly nearing
a crisis. Having expressed his opinion that the
taking of an oath **was an act of** worship, and that
" **no man** ought to be forced to perform this any
" more than any other act of worship," he was summoned in April, 1635, to appear at Boston. The
court on this occasion desisted from proceeding; but
in the following July he was again cited to answer
certain charges brought against him at the general
meeting then in session.

The most serious of these charges was of a frivolous nature. The accused was impeached for having
maintained **the** " dangerous " opinion, that " the ma-
" **gistrates ought not to** punish the breach of the first

" table, otherwise than in such cases as did disturb
" the civil peace." This doctrine was considered by
all present to be most pernicious; the ministers—
who had been invited to attend and give their advice
—thought the colony should rid itself of a man who
maintained that the civil magistrate might not inter-
meddle " even to stop a church from heresy and
" apostacy;" none agreed with the accused, whose
opinions were " adjudged by all, magistrates and
" ministers, to be erroneous and very dangerous."
" After long debate," says Governor Winthrop, who
wrote at the time, and recorded the proceedings in
his *Journal,* " time was given to him and the church
" at Salem to consider of these things till the next
" general court, and then, either to give satisfaction
" to the court, or else to expect the sentence." The
church of Salem obstinately adhered to their pastor,
and avowed their readiness to suffer the consequences
of their contumacy. The next general court was
held in October, when Roger Williams was again
summoned for the last time; " all the ministers in
" the Bay being desired to be present." " Mr.
" Hooker," Governor Winthrop says, " was chosen
" to dispute with him, but could not reduce him from
" any of his errors. So, the next morning, the court
" sentenced him to depart out of our jurisdiction
" within six weeks—all the ministers, save one, ap-

" proving the sentence." The health of Williams was greatly impaired by his severe trials and excessive labours, and he procured permission to remain at Salem till spring. But the court having meanwhile received information that he could not refrain *in his own house* from uttering his offensive opinions—to which, it seems, "he had drawn above twenty per-" sons "!—resolved to send him to England by a ship then lying in the harbour ready for sea. He refused to obey their summons to attend the court at Boston, but the magistrates were determined not to be defeated, and immediately despatched a small sloop to Salem, with a commission to the captain to apprehend, and carry him on board the ship that was about to sail for England.

When the officers came to his house, however, " they found he had gone three days before, but " whither they could not learn."

The principal Indian tribes occupying New England, when it was first settled by the English, were the Pokanokets, who inhabited the territory of the colony of Plymouth; the Narragansetts—most faithful to the English of all the New England tribes—who held dominion over nearly all the territory which afterwards formed the colony of Rhode Island, including the islands in the Bay, and a portion of Long Island; the Massachusetts, who dwelt chiefly about the bay which bears their name; and the Pequods and Mohicans—by far the fiercest and most warlike of the New England savages—who occupied the greater part of what is now the state of Connecticut. In the middle of January, 1636, in the coldest month of a New England winter, Roger Williams—forced to leave behind him his wife and young children, and escape in secresy and haste—fled from the tyranny of those men, who, under the name of Pilgrim Fathers, receive the undeserved sympathy of posterity, and sought refuge amidst primeval forests inhabited only by beasts of prey, and those savage tribes whose names I have just enumerated. Tradition has much to relate of this period of his life; but a letter of his, written thirty-five years after, furnishes authentic information of that time " when," says he, " I was " sorely tossed, for one fourteen weeks, in a bitter " winter season, not knowing what bread or bed did " mean." It appears that he made his way through the desolate wilderness to Massasoit, sachem of the Pokanokets, who dwelt at Mount Hope, near the spot on which the town of Bristol, Rhode Island, now stands, and who occupied the country northwards as far as Charles River. This famous Indian chieftain had known Williams at Plymouth, and on many occasions had received from him tokens of kindness. It was now his turn to confer benefit;

and the aged sachem **was** ready. He received Williams graciously, and granted him a tract of land on
the Seekonk river, which separates Massachusetts
from Rhode Island. Here, then, the friendless
exile, who was soon joined by several of the people
of Salem, began to build and plant.   But this terri-
tory was within the limits of the Plymouth colony,
and he **received** intelligence from his friend, Governor Winslow, **that he had** "**fallen** into the edge of
"**their** bounds." Thereupon, he **embarked**, with
five others, in a canoe, and proceeded down the river
in search of another resting-place, where the secular
arm should have no dictation in the concerns of religion.   Passing round the headlands now known as
India Point and Fox Point, he ascended the river that
runs **on** the west side of **the** peninsula, **to** a spot near
the **mouth of** the Mooshausic.   Here, in the spring-
time **of 1636,** Williams landed; **and** here, on the
slope of **the hill** that rises from the river, began the
first settlement **of** Rhode Island—a state which, in
the words of its founder, should surely be "a shelter
"to persons distressed for conscience." He called
the place Providence, in remembrance of God's providence to him in distress.

Through his intimacy with several of the Indian
chiefs, Williams was enabled to purchase the necessary lands for his new colony. His house and lands

at Salem he **was obliged** to mortgage, **in order to** make additional presents and gratuities **to the** sachems; and, consequently, **he** removed **his wife** and family immediately to the new **settlement.** He was the sole negotiator with the Indians, and the legal proprietor of the territory which they had ceded to him, and which, as he remarked, " was as much " his as any man's coat upon his back." He might have secured the proprietary of his colony by a patent from England, and thus have exercised a control over **its government,** and amassed wealth for himself and family ; but his views being eminently unselfish, he chose rather to found a state where all civil power should be exercised **by the people, and** where there might be " a shelter for persons dis- " tressed for conscience." The infant **community** prospered apace, and was rapidly increased **by the** arrival of persons from other colonies, **and from** Europe, who fled from persecution.

The banishment of Roger Williams, and the voluntary exile **of many of his** adherents, did not, it seems, put an end to the contentions in Massachusetts Bay.

The people were displeased **at the prosperity** of the settlements at **Providence and** on Rhode Island. **Incensed** at the reception accorded to the citizens **they had** expelled, they seized an opportunity to

order that if any one of the inhabitants of Providence
should be found within the jurisdiction of Massachusetts he should be brought before the magistrates.
This, however, was only the prelude of what was to
follow.   In 1642, shortly after Providence and Rhode
Island had regularly organized a government, and
had, true to the principles of their chief founder,
passed a special act, that " that law concerning liberty
" of conscience in point of doctrine be perpetuated,"
the colonists of New England, alarmed by reports of
hostile designs on the part of the Indians, adopted
vigorous measures of defence.   In the year following, the first confederacy of the colonies was formed,
and articles of union were signed at Boston by the
commissioners of the four colonies of Plymouth,
Massachusetts Bay, Connecticut, and New Haven,
under the name of " the United Colonies of New
" England."   Neither Providence (notwithstanding
that its founder had more than once, by his personal
influence, saved the English settlements from the
fury of the Indians), nor the neighbouring colony on
Rhode Island was invited to join ; and when afterwards they made application for admittance, it was
refused.   The reasons alleged were trivial, but they
were found to be insuperable.   The excluded colonies were therefore exposed to many inconveniences
and dangers, and left with no defence, except that of

their own citizens. Their increasing prosperity, their exclusion from the confederacy, and the declarations of enemies, that they had no legal authority for civil government, led the inhabitants to appoint a committee with instructions to procure a charter from the mother-country. The agency was accepted by Williams, who accordingly, in June, 1643, embarked at New York for his native land.

The state of affairs in this country was not unfavourable to the accomplishment of the mission with which he came intrusted. The nation was convulsed by the civil war; King Charles had fled from London; and the parliament, who were in possession of the legislative and executive authority, were disposed to strengthen themselves by conciliating the colonies of America. From the commissioners who had been appointed to regulate the affairs of the colonies, Roger Williams—aided by the influence of his early friend, Sir Harry Vane—obtained with little trouble, for the colony of Rhode Island, a charter, which conveyed to the inhabitants the most ample powers to adopt such a form of civil government as they should by free consent agree to. As soon as he had accomplished the object of his mission, Williams re-embarked for America. He landed at Boston, September 17, 1644, and the news of his arrival having preceded him, the inhabitants of Providence met

him at **Seekonk with a** fleet of canoes to welcome his
return, and to convey him home in triumph. The
form of government—eventually adopted, after con-
siderable delay and discussion, in a general assembly
of the people of the colony on the 19th May, 1647—
required the annual election **of a** president and four
assistants, in whom the executive power was vested.
The **code of laws was mainly** taken from those of
England, and concludes with these memorable words:
" **And otherwise than** thus, what is herein forbidden,
" **all men may walk as their** consciences persuade
" them—every **one** in the name of his God."

Williams, probably **to** conciliate the other towns,
cheerfully yielded his claims to the office of president,
and accepted the subordinate post of assistant for the
town of Providence. As might be anticipated, from
the various materials of which they were composed, the
several towns of the colony did not quietly coalesce in
one form of government, and Williams's skill and
delicacy were taxed to their utmost extent in har-
monizing **the** discordant elements. **One of the**
chief causes of his disquietude at this time **were the**
proceedings of William Coddington, the principal inhabitant **of the settlement** on Rhode Island, who,
being attached to the party **of the king, was** disposed
to promote Royal authority in the colony. Coddington having persuaded a faction **to unite** with him,

first attempted to obtain admission for the island settlements into the league of the New England colonies; but having failed in that effort, he went off
to England, and succeeded in procuring from the
council of state a commission, constituting him governor for life of the islands of Rhode Island and
Canonicut. When he returned in 1651, bringing
with him his new charter, great excitement was produced in the settlements. Other troubles, moreover,
arose in addition to these internal dissensions. Massachusetts, Plymouth, and Connecticut—all of whom
were opposed to the heroic state that persisted in proclaiming liberty of conscience for all men, irrespec-
tive of creed—asserted claims to portions of the
colony; the Indians, too, now began to commit depre-
dations, and to offer insults which the individual
settlements were too feeble to punish, and which the
commissioners of the United Colonies refused to
redress. In this crisis, when it was apparent that
their safety lay only in a union of all the towns, John
Clarke, a man of liberal education, courteous manners,
and the original projector of the settlement on the
island, was induced to proceed to England to procure the repeal of Coddington's commission, and the
confirmation of Williams's charter. From reluctance
to leave his large family, as well as from his inability
to sustain the necessary expense, Williams, who was

urgently importuned to accompany Clarke, and cooperate in the accomplishment of this important
object, at first declined to accept the trust, but in the
end he was prevailed on, and accordingly once more
crossed the Atlantic.

Williams on this occasion remained in England for
nearly three years. Since he had last visited the
kingdom, great events had occurred; an ancient
monarchy had been subverted, and the supreme
authority was now vested in a Council of State.
The application made by the two commissioners met
with opposition from many quarters; but an order
was at length passed to annul Coddington's commission, and to confirm the former charter.

Leaving Clarke behind, Williams returned to his
colony in the summer of 1654. During his absence,
the general assembly which met at Providence addressed to him a letter, in which they " humbly con-
" ceived that, if it be the pleasure of our protectors
" to renew our charter, it might be the pleasure of
" that honourable state to invest, appoint, and em-
" power yourself to come over as Governor of this
" colony, for the space of one year, and so the go-
" vernment to be honourably put upon this place,
" which might seem to add weight for ever hereafter
" in the constant and successive derivation of the
" same." Roger Williams took no steps to procure

his election; but on the first general election, held on the 12th of September, he was chosen President of the colony. During the term of his office, he made efforts to establish more friendly relations with the neighbouring colonies, especially with Massachusetts, and succeeded in obtaining some of the privileges for which he had long contended. Upon his retirement from office, he declined being a candidate for re-election. He did not, however, neglect any opportunity to promote the interests of his fellow-citizens, honourable mention of his name frequently appears in the records both of the town and colony. His death occurred in May, 1683, in his seventy-eighth year; and "he was buried," says Callender, "with all the "solemnity the colony was able to show." There is no portrait of him extant.

During his last visit to England official duties brought him into frequent intercourse with the eminent individuals who then wielded the power of the state. He renewed his friendship with Sir Harry Vane, and enjoyed the hospitality of that statesman at his country seat; he secured the powerful influence of Cromwell for his colony; and, what is of more interest for us, he often passed his hours of leisure with John Milton, "who," he says, "for my Dutch I "read him, read me many more languages." It was during this visit a curious episode occurred. He was acquainted with Mrs. Sadlier, the daughter of his early patron, **Sir** Edward **Coke.** The letters that passed between them are preserved in the library of Trinity College, Cambridge, **and** exhibit Williams's **character and** tone **of** mind **in a** very favourable light. The lady, who was opposed **to** the existing order of things, and was not backward in confessing her disapprobation, **would** not so much **as** look at one of Williams's works which he **sent to** her; and, **upon** being desired **to read** a book by another author, she wrote **a** remarkable letter to Williams, from which **I quote** what follows, as it gives us her opinion **of one of** the most remarkable men of the time: " For " Milton's book, that you desire I should read, if I be " not mistaken, that is he that has wrote a book of " **the lawfulness of divorce ;** and, if report says true, " he **had at** that time **two or** three **wives** living (!). " **This, perhaps, were good** doctrine in New England, " **but it is most** abominable in Old England. For his " **book that he wrote against the** late king, you should " have taken **notice of God's** judgment upon him, " who stroke him **with blindness;** and, **as I have** " heard, he was fain to have the help of one Andrew " **Marvell, or** else he could not have finished that " most accursed libel. God has begun his judgment " upon him here—his punishment will **be** hereafter in " hell. But have you seen the answer to it? If

" you can get it, I assure you it is worth your
" reading."

It was during this visit of three years that Williams
gave to the press those works in which he has clearly
expounded the noble principle for which he suffered,
and which is the most endurable memorial of his
name. The views he himself professed of theological affairs are not very attractive ; may, indeed, be
characterized as almost repulsive in their nature.
His writings are amongst the dreariest of the dreary
productions that appeared during the commonwealth.
Everything he wrote, if we except his philological
work, " A Vocabulary of the Narraganset Language,"
designed to facilitate intercourse between the Indian
tribes and their white neighbours—is occupied with
considerations of minute and unimportant points of
controversy, which, let it be hoped, have now
altogether ceased to be of interest to intelligent men.
He hated popery and prelacy ; was an interpreter of
prophecy ; and saw in the events of the day fulfilment of some of the most abstruse problems of the
Apocalypse. Thoroughly convinced of the soundness
of his own views, and unable to see how others could
reasonably dissent from his favourite notions, he was
ever ready " to discuss, debate, dispute, either by word
" or writing, with whom, or before whomsoever the
" present debate concerns, with all Christian meek-

" ness, and due submission." He must have been one of the most troublesome and irrepressible disputants that figured in the controversial battles of the day. His merit, however, does not lie in this direction, but consists exclusively of the consistency with which through life he advocated the important doctrine we associate with his name. Not only in " The Bloody " Tenent of Persecution," where he has discussed it at length; but in season and out of season, in every-thing he wrote, did he avow his belief that the opinions of one man do not concern another, and that the state has no right to interfere with the religious views of its subjects. I have before me a quarto publication of thirty-six pages, printed at London, " in the second Moneth, 1652," and entitled, " The " Hireling Ministry None of Christ's, or A Discourse " touching the Propagating the Gospel of CHRIST " JESUS. Humbly Presented to such Pious and " Honourable Hands, whom the present Debate " thereof concerns. By Roger Williams, of Provi-" dence, in New England." In the Epistle Dedi-catory, the author informs his readers, that having been engaged in several points of the same nature " in my former and later endeavours against that " Bloody Tenent of Persecution for cause of con-" science; and also having been forced to observe " the goings of God, and the spirits of men, both in

" Old and New England, as touching the Church,
" the ministry and ordinances of Jesus Christ, I did
" humbly apprehend my call from Heaven not to
" hide my candle under a bed of ease and pleasure,
" or a bushel of gain and profit; but to set it on a
" candlestick of this publike profession, for the bene-
" fit of others, and the praise of the father of all
" lights and Godliness."

The pertinacity of the man in this respect is, indeed, surprising, and it is worthy of remark, that
although he believed himself to have had a call from
heaven, he never, in the least degree, exhibited a
disposition to coerce others, or forcibly bring them to
profess the views he himself entertained on any subject. Men who have " a call" usually act otherwise.
They become persecutors, being just as ready to inflict martyrdom as to suffer it. To me it has always
been a matter of wonder that a man of Williams's
way of thinking should have been in advance of the
age in which he lived, inasmuch as his nature, as far
as I have been able to discover it from his life and
works, appears to have been composed of all the
elements that go to form a bigot. He thoroughly
believed in himself, and could not conceive that
others, when they differed from him, could be in the
right; he possessed that eager, restless, obtrusive
disposition, which suffers no opposition, and will

acknowledge no defeat. **He had,** moreover, the power in his newly-founded state to enforce, with **some degree** of success, uniformity of opinion. But there is no evidence that he ever made the attempt. **He** consistently abode by the principles for which he contended from the day when he first en-**tered** the ministry.

If the **man who reveals to us a** new and beneficent moral principle occupies **a** higher place in our regard **than he who discovers a** new universe in Lyra, **or tells us** what are **the** constituent elements of the moon, Roger Williams **is** entitled **to** a very exalted position. The doctrine he announced was the want of his age. The spirit of compromise had prevented its propagation at the Reformation, and down to **his day no one had been able to** make the **great discovery. He was the first to** proclaim it, **and,** being a man **of** one idea, like all men of one **idea who devote their lives to a** cause, he had im-mense influence in his generation. That one member of the community should legally be roasted to death **for** holding **opinions at** variance with the rest was to him **as** horrible as it is to ourselves. There are at least **two sides to every question. He knew** too much of human nature to suppose all **men** in a nation think alike on religious matters, **and** was well **aware that** constraint **and restraint** effected by the

civil power could result only in outward manifestations of conformity.   All attempts to place limita-
tions to liberty of conscience, whether made by his
opponents, or by his co-religionists, he strenuously
denounced.   He would have no sliding-scale of
toleration, but contended for free and absolute
liberty.   He never lost sight of a great principle.
His own opinions may be ill founded; his doctrines
in religious matters may shock people of refinement;
his style of argumentation may put at defiance all
the rules of elegant composition; but he does not
desire to impose his views upon others, or force them
to read the books in which he has enunciated them.
All are free to choose for themselves.   They may
worship Baal if they please—he would not interfere
with the rites—he desired that every man should
worship his Gods without molestation.   He was our
first advocate for unlimited toleration.   The ancients,
it is true, permitted liberty of religious worship to
its fullest extent.   To the Greek the same truth was
discoverable under all forms of worship,* and the

---

* I am reminded of the condemnation of Socrates.   There is
little doubt that the philosopher was attacked chiefly on political
grounds.   His connection with the oligarchy was sufficient
cause for his arraignment by Anytus who had been their chief
opponent, and the prime agent in the revolution by which they
were overthrown.   The charge of impugning the state religion,

Romans, from political motives, recognized every religion that was held by their subjects, or had been introduced into the metropolis. Christians formed an exception to their usual toleration, because, from the nature of their faith, they would not and could not suffer ways of thinking different from their own. In self-defence, therefore, other religionists were forced to attempt the extinction of the creed, not because *nova,* but because *malefica,* as Suetonius puts it. From the time when Theodosius made penal laws against the Manicheans, to the time of Roger Williams, every sect that sprung up and demanded

---

and corrupting the youths—a crime not referring to the minds of these youths, but to a capital offence then as now—was brought forward to strengthen the case of the prosecution. The indictment was well framed. The opinions of the philosopher on religion could not have been so heinous an offence as to warrant death in a state which permitted the free discussion of men who explained away the Gods and their providence, and investigated the origin of the ideas they represented with a licence that is not tolerated in our day in England. One has great difficulty in understanding the sympathy that, from the time of Plato to that of the latest writer who has made the famous supper the subject of his discourse, has been bestowed upon Socrates. If Socrates believed himself to have been unjustly condemned, as he professed, he should unhesitatingly have taken advantage of the means provided by his friend Crito for escape, and evaded his doom. By submitting to the execution of an unjust sentence he was himself a party to injustice.

the adhesion of mankind had threatened those who declined to comply with its invitation. " Believe or " perish," was the motto of each. The founder of Rhode Island was the first to preach the old doctrine to the new civilization; and it is for this that his name and memory should be held in grateful remembrance by all generations.

X.

STEELE.*

HE author of the latest memoir of Steele, who thinks, and thinks justly, that Thackeray, in his " Esmond," has caricatured him, and, " for the sake of being " graphic and dramatic," has given the reader the general impression of his being a sort of Captain Costigan, is an apologist and advocate of the worthy knight. His work is an attempt to reproduce the age of Queen Anne " through the medium of a life of " Steele." The animus is undoubtedly good; but we fear the attempt must be considered unsuccessful, inasmuch as it has resulted in very unsatisfactory performance. It will furnish those who are altogether unacquainted with the history of England and its literature during the period treated with a large number of facts relating to eminent persons and great affairs which

---

* Sir Richard Steele, Memoir of the Life and Writings of. By H. R. Montgomery.

cannot fail to be of value. It is a collection of very useful materials, that in a second edition may be turned to good account. But to the student of the period—to him who is already familiar with so important and critical a period in our annals as the reign of Queen Anne—it can in its present form have but the slightest interest. He will find in its pages nothing that will be new; and what is old will lose all interest, by reason of the inefficient treatment it has received.

What is above all things required in a biographer is the power of forcibly bringing before the reader the individual whose life he has undertaken to write. He must abstract that which belongs to him in common with others, and present only the result. There must be no generalities, no stringing together of ill-selected epithets, no incongruities in the presentment; but the portrait must preserve all the characteristics of the original. Few men are able successfully to do this. Mr. Carlyle, in his "History of the " French Revolution," has proved himself to be one of the great masters of the art. Some of his portraits are marvellous for the vigour with which they are conceived and represented; they have all the distinguishing marks of having been drawn from the life; and although, we believe, several of them, in very important particulars, bear but the faintest resemblance to the particular personages with whose names they are labelled, each of them seems to have **the** merit of being a real portrait of somebody. We feel there are real men and women before us, and are ready to be convinced that we see the texture of their skin, and **hear the** sound of their voices, and **know** the phraseology in which they are about to address us. The reader will be disappointed if he expects to **find in this** work manifestations of so **desirable a power as that possessed** by Mr. Carlyle. And it has **another defect.** It is now usually agreed that a biography should confine itself to the actions and fortunes of the individual; everything that does not bear upon the development of his character or course of life should be excluded, and the successive events should be so narrated **as to** enable the reader to have a true portraiture of the **man.** In these **memoirs,** however, there is no individuality. From the seven hundred pages which form the two volumes, he will not derive so distinct a notion of Steele, or **any** of his contemporaries, as he now possesses of **the** fictitious De Coverley from the few papers devoted to that hero in *The Spectator.* The work is a made-up work. It contains too much **and** too little. As a whole it is sadly deficient in the unity essential to such a work as this.

Not only have we biographies of the persons who

wrote for the several publications with which Steele
was connected —"a group of sketches around the
" central figure "—but, " in accordance with the ex-
" pressed aim of the design," we are presented with
sketches of those to whom the several volumes of
the works were dedicated.   Nor is there the least
art displayed in the grouping or presentment of the
figures that pass before us.   The people who are introduced are introduced on the slightest pretext.   A
casual allusion to a name, or its occurrence in correspondence, will evoke its former owner and trot him
through a dozen pages.   The author has failed to
give us an intelligible picture of the age, or a striking
portrait of the man, but instead thereof offers discon-
nected memoirs and world-famous anecdotes.   We
have the old story of the loves of Swift, and are told,
in the words often employed before, how one day,
entering the room where Vanessa was sitting, " with
" that terrible look which he assumed when angry,
" he flung down a packet on the table and strode
" out without uttering a word; " how a bullying
lawyer, provoked by the great Dean's keen satire,
called at the Deanery to revenge himself, and having
sent up his name as Serjeant Bettesworth, was met
by the Dean, who calmly demanded the name of the
regiment to which he belonged; that when " Gulli-
" ver's Travels " appeared, a master of a vessel said

" he knew Gulliver well, but that **he lived** at Wap-
" ping, and not at Rotherhithe ;" **how** King William
taught **the** famous Irish parson **to** cut asparagus.
Once again, we read in these volumes the fate of the
unfortunate Budgell, and have Pope's stinging lines
on the event; of the quarrel between Pope and Lady
Mary Wortley Montagu ; of Wycherley making
acquaintance **with the** Duchess of Cleveland, and of
his marriage with the **Countess** of Drogheda ; of
Congreve's friendship with the Duchess of Marlbo-
rough, and the fantastic **way** in which **her Grace,**
after the death of the poet, is said to have preserved
his memory by inviting to her table, as a constant
guest, " an automaton model of **him** in ivory "—and
of scores of similar stories, as well known to ordinary
readers **as** the Nelson Column **to the** porter at
Northumberland House. **The author's** insight into
character may be learned **from the** expression of his
belief that when Steele **left** the University without
a degree, and enlisted in the Horse Guards, " great
" admiration of **the** character **of** King William **had**
" something to do with it ; " and his taste and fairness **from the** regret he avows that **Steele** was not
equally wise in his generation with " **the** Reverend
" Dr. Swift, who had gone such lengths in doing the
" **foul work** of party, **to earn the wages of** mercenary
" **apostacy."** Our **author's** opinion of the Dean may

be right; but surely he is here doing in the case of Swift what he complains of others doing in the case of Steele.

In addition to the fundamental faults we have indicated, the work contains minor defects, too numerous to be mentioned, the nature of which may be inferred from what has been already said. Incorporated with the text, however, and by far the most useful portion of the work, are the letters reprinted from " Steele's Correspondence," published in 1809, by Nichols, from the originals in the British Museum. These are invaluable records. Some of them are addressed to Swift, Pope, and other literary friends; but by far the greater number are to Lady Steele. They are the shortest epistles in existence, and all of a character.* The writer was always in a hurry, and always excusing his delay in returning home. " The coach is passing, and I can say no " more ;" " I am drinking a pint of wine, and will " come home forthwith ;" " I put myself to the " pain of absence from you at dinner by waiting to " speak to Salkeild ;" " I have received money, but

---

* There is great variation in the style and caligraphy of the original letters. Some were evidently composed with the most deliberate neatness, whilst others bear unmistakable signs of having been written in great haste, and probably after the writer had seen the third bottle brought on the table.

" cannot come home till about four o'clock"—such
is the tenor of them all. We suspect, however,
from numerous indications, that it was not always
solicitude for his wife and dread of her prolonged
anxiety that induced him to write so frequently.
We fear Lady Steele was in the habit, like a foolish
wife, of seeking her husband when in company.
More than once he writes, " Do not send after me ;"
" I shall be ridiculous," and he complains that he
must always be giving her an account of every
minute of his time. His eternal want of money was
a great misery to him, and, to judge from these letters, we cannot help thinking, in opposition to most
men, that the seemingly cheerful demeanour of our
saucy-faced Captain too frequently concealed trouble
and dimness of anguish. " If the man who has my
" shoemaker's bill calls, let him be answered that I
" shall call on him as I come home. I stay here,"
he adds, " to get Johnson to discount a bill for me,
" and shall dine with him for that end. He is ex-
" pected at home every minute." When his wife
went to Carmarthen, to her native place, leaving
him in charge of the daughter afflicted with small-
pox, he writes : " We had not when you left us an
" inch of candle, a pound of coal, or a bit of meat
" left in the house ; but we do not want now." And
she, with her Welsh ways, and her Welsh advisers,

was perpetually worldlying, complaining of what he owed her, and urging him to get money. He, poor fellow, felt the reproach keenly. His little notes are a series of promises to mend his means. " I do as " you advise," he says; " court and converse with " men able and willing to serve me;" and, again, upon being reminded by her of the ingratitude he had experienced : " I have as quick a sense of the " ill-treatment I have received as is consistent with " keeping up my own spirit and good humour." He reproached her at first by innuendo ; but once or twice he fairly lost temper, and wrote in rage. " In " the name of God," he exclaims, " have done with " talk of money !" But his rage was of short duration, and in his next note he was on his knees, a doating husband, writing to his wife to put on her mask and come to Somerset stairs, or desiring her to take a coach and " come to this lodgings," or feeling such interest in her appearance as to request her to " look a little dressed, or everybody will be enter- " tained but the entertainer."

He was ever most sanguine, and had, withal, a knack of hoping rarely equalled. He tells his wife, in one letter, that she, her servants, and children, shall be better provided for than any family in England; and in another—in high spirits at the anticipated success of a scheme for bringing live fish

to the London market—that he hoped in " a post or
" two to give an account of a thing that will bring a
" great sum of money." " I shall soon be a clear man,"
and, " I am in a fair way to be a great man," was the
burden of his daily song. Do we need more than
these brief notes furnish to know the man Steele?
What occasion is there for a list of his debts, of the
offices he held, of the comedies he wrote, of the bottles
he drank, of the houses he inhabited?

To institute comparison between famous personages
is a favourite employment as well with impulsive
critics as with the general public. The comparisons
are in most instances provokingly puerile. Accurate
thinkers regard each man as good of his sort, and
with them, therefore, there could arise no dispute
as to which is the greater. For the advocate of
the one to dispute the claims of the other would
manifestly be absurd; they wisely content themselves with crediting each with being what he is.
English readers, however, and intelligent English
writers, are not satisfied with this. They pit one
man against another, with whom, in reality, he has
no points of similarity, or, if he has, they are due to
circumstance, and not to nature.

Steele and his coadjutor, Addison, are thus
usually classed together to be compared, and are
seldom compared without being classed. Each has

his advocates and partisans, among whom are to be numbered well-known authors, some favouring Steele to the disadvantage of Addison, and some depreciating Steele and obscuring his reputation for the sake of glorifying Addison. Thackeray and Lord Macaulay are the most eminent who have declared in favour of the Right-honourable gentleman; while, Coleridge, Hazlitt, Leigh Hunt, Charles Lamb, and, more recently, Mr. Forster, seem, on the other hand, to incline to the side of the knight.

But Steele's backers are not very resolute in support of their champion. The majority of readers and writers find it difficult to conceive a "great" man made of such stuff as he. They look for strong character in their heroes; and this disposition influences the idea they form of a man's writings. Dignity of attitude, gravity of countenance, and, in some degree, conformity between opinion and action, are indispensable for securing their applause. If Mr. Ketch's arguments for the abolition of capital punishments are ever so unassailable, they discredit them, because the preacher's mission makes it occasionally necessary for him to act contrary to his opinion. Like Hermotimus, an interlocutor in one of Lucian's Dialogues, who became a convert to the Stoic philosophy solely because he observed its professors were serious in demeanour, they regard levity in manner

as indicative of shallowness in intellect. It is not
surprising, then, that the reckless and irresolute
Steele, whose career was a solecism in morals, does
not obtain the praise he merits. From the time of
his leaving college without a degree, to the day of
his death on the banks of the Towy, at the age of 58,
an old man before his time, he was the victim of his
own temperament. He was completely incapable of
restraining himself. **He was** genial, good-natured to
excess, **fond of good** society, and, to use the words of
Lady Mary W. Montagu, like Fielding, so made
for happiness, that **it is** a pity he was not immortal.
But happiness never came. In politics and in the
business of life he was equally unsuccessful. Even in
affairs of the heart, in which, as might be supposed,
he had his share, he does not seem to have prospered.
The " perverse " widow (**widows,** as De Coverley and
more of us have experienced, are too often " per-
verse") left a wound **in** his heart that, we suspect,
was never quite healed. Indeed, as Charter-house
boy, collegian, soldier, lover, pamphleteer, gazetteer,
Parliament man, patentee, inventor of fish machines,
and father of a family, poor Sir Richard failed to
reach the personal success he promised himself. He
was a brave adventurer, but **he** never had the luck
to secure a great prize; or, having secured it, he
was unable to **retain it. And** the reason is plain.

He failed, as all others have failed who attempted to eat the grape and drink the wine.

But to abstract the author from the man—and, logically, this is the only way to judge him whose sole claim to notice is a literary claim—Steele must take high rank as an English man of letters. Neither he nor Addison was, it is true, a man of the highest culture. Neither took a commanding view of literature or of life. Both were inferior in range to Swift, whose vision, blurred and bleared as it was, included humanity itself, whilst their horizon was very contracted, the aim of both being avowedly limited to satirizing the conventions by which they were surrounded, and to framing characters of domestic life. They held the mirror up to Fashion and not to Nature. At best they were tea-table moralists, and in their homilies we miss the force we look for in sermons addressed to more stormy audiences. For his share in the work, Addison—partly from grace of style, and partly, no doubt, by reason of his greater specific gravity—has undoubtedly secured the larger share of credit, and although their polish has a tendency to make his writings appear weak, the underlying thought, or semi-thought, is for the most part more vigorous than what appears in his friend's essays. The one derived his insight from direct experience; the other considered our nature by aid of reflected experience, and, paradoxical as the assertion may sound, saw deeper, and further, and clearer. But the praise of Steele is far higher than that of Addison. He was one of those whose writings are said to be greater than the writers. He planted a seed of revolution in our literature, thereafter, as we all know, to bear abundant fruit. " Bickerstaff" must be credited with the honour due to an inventor. He gave a new form to our literature; or, as it is quaintly put by one of his contemporaries, " his " writings have set all our wits and men of letters " upon a new way of thinking."

STERNE.

LTHOUGH much has been written on Humour, and very many acute observations have been made on its nature and functions, every formal attempt to define what it is has proved to be signally unsuccessful. Each definition has the demerit either of excluding men who are admittedly entitled to be ranked among the humourists, or of being so comprehensive as by its terms to embrace not only writers distinguished for their humour, but others whose claims to the honour will be generally disallowed. The difficulty of determining the true nature of humour and of discriminating it from the other kinds of literary production to which it is germane, is, indeed, very great. Addison, whilst treating the subject in one of the "Spectators," expressed his opinion that it is much easier to describe what it is not, than to say what it is. He had before him Cowley's well-known defini-

tion of wit. But, declining to adopt the method he approved, he was bolder than Cowley, and proceeded to give his own notions on the subject, "after Plato's "manner, in a kind of allegory." Without pronouncing on Addison's success, and having no desire myself to hazard a new definition, I may, I think, venture to express my belief that, however much they differ in manner, the great masters of humour must be divided, with respect to their matter, into two well-defined classes. The one, making the conventionalities his subject, deals with the affairs of every-day life. The minor morals form his topics. He has to do with what is incidental in human affairs; the fashions, the foibles of individuals, the eccentricities of society are the theme of his discourse. He is concerned with what is transient, and his influence ceases with the phase of civilization of which he has been the exponent. The other is the humourist of nature. He deals by choice with the old Adam that leavens us. The beggarly elements in our composition are his favourite topic. His attention is not confined to what is dependent upon fashion for its interest, but is directed to our natural and permanent passions. He is tolerant; does not satirize folly (indeed, he believes nothing human can justly be considered folly); and his sympathy is so wide-embracing that he is lenient even with what we term the vicious propensities of our nature. It is in the latter class that Sterne must undoubtedly be placed.

There is a reigning idea concerning this incomparable humourist of which the late Mr. Thackeray may be taken as the most eminent exponent. That writer, who in this instance seems to have judged men and things from a no higher point of view than that of a shrewd Charter-house boy, believed to the night of his death that Laurence Sterne was a great jester and not a great humourist—a charlatan, who brought out his bit of carpet, spread it, and tumbled on it for the amusement of bystanders, without himself sharing in the mirth he created, and without caring much whether it was mirth or sorrow he produced, so long as halfpence, in the shape of applause, came tumbling in upon the performer. And not only in this explicit portraiture he has left us of Sterne, but in every story the great novelist produced, did he manifest inability to appreciate—or even, I think, to apprehend—a character like that of Yorick. He could not—and this, to me, appears to be his cardinal defect as a novelist—bring himself to believe it possible for a man to be double-minded in a good sense as well as in a bad; and whenever he conceived or attempted to delineate an individual of the order to which Sterne belonged his representation is glaringly unreal and unartistic. Such defec-

tive representation, **whenever** produced, is partly
owing, of course, to want of intellectual insight in the
critic; **but in** a greater degree is it due to moral
obliquity—to a deficiency of tolerance for what is
beyond **the area of his own** experience and customary **horizon.** **A man who exhibits** himself, either
in literature or in society, in two obviously antago-
nistic relations, is thoughtlessly condemned for insin-
cerity. **His critics** conclude that one or other phase
of his character must necessarily be fictitious. They
do not conceive that it is possible for both **to be**
genuine, **and** for the man in each case to be true **to**
his own nature.

For one **who is not** always the same, as well in
letters as in **life,** men avow their aversion. Cor-
diality to-day **and coldness to-morrow** they cannot
understand, and will not suffer. They require a man
to be " genuine **;" and how can he** be genuine who is
at one time cordial and at another indifferent, or
worse? The censure resulting from this conviction
is levelled against a whole class of writers; but
Sterne, perhaps more **than any** other, suffers from
this defective way of judging. Is he pathetic in the
presence of suffering in the brute creation and at the
same time guilty of ill-treating his nearest relatives?
His pathos is obviously assumed. **Does he** weep at
the recital of **woe** by the lips **of a stranger** whilst his

imprudence is the occasion of **deeper misfortune**
among members of his own family ? **Be** assured that
his tears are crocodile tears, springing from no
genuine feeling, but mechanically produced as a bit
of harlequinade for the delectation of the gentle
reader. To this view of Sterne I cannot **bring**
myself to assent; and prolonged acquaintance with
his productions serves only to confirm me **in the**
belief of his absolute sincerity. Sterne, however, is
in some degree **liable to the** implied censure. **Men**
of sensitive nature **like his find** relief in making
their feelings **objective** and contemplating them at **a**
distance. **In this process there is** for them refined
happiness akin to **that felt by people who derive**
comfort from the act of confession—only **in their case
the** confession is made **openly to the public and not**
confided to the ears of a priest. **His critic would have**
us believe that Sterne, finding his tears infectious, and
that they **brought him a** great popularity, designedly
exercised **the** lucrative gift of weeping, utilised it,
and cried **on every occasion. I** know **no** reason why
a man should **not** utilise his sensations as well as his
reflections, and publish " Sentimental Journies " as
well as " Snob Papers ;" nor can I **see why he**
should be abused for the one more than for the other.
Let us be thankful **for** both. Sterne was not a whole
man. He was an " episodical " character ; one of those

whose "component parts" are so ill-assorted that they never come to fit well together. The very temperament, however, that made him sympathize with a distressed and unknown wayfarer would make him suffer acutely and resent warmly the want of a sympathetic and conciliatory spirit in a cold-hearted wife. The sympathy and the resentment were connate. But people talk of him as if affection could be excited at will, and its direction and force regulated with as much precision as it is possible to regulate the direction and force of a jet of New River water. With peremptory solicitude they make out a list of those whom you must love and those whom it is improper for you to love. Sterne, by first disregarding their list, and then by disregarding them, had the misfortune to acquire their permanent ill-will. He went his own way. What was congruous with his nature alone affected him; and he too had the courage to seem to be in his works what he was in his life.

There are men, such as Johnson, who are not affected by another's mental grief, and are unable to understand why any healthy, well-fed man can ever be miserable. An unfortunate woman who is hungry even Johnson could carry home and feed in his chambers: but for the heart suffering from unrequited love, or sick with hope deferred, it was impossible to have aroused his active sympathy.

Sterne, on the other hand, was so susceptible as to be more sensibly affected by ideal sorrow than by material misfortune. In disclosing his nature, however, he made no pretence of being regulated by principles of philanthropy. Distant misery did not disturb his equanimity. He confessed that the figuring to himself millions of his fellow-creatures in slavery did not influence him. But the sight of one solitary captive in his prison was ever enough to arouse his sympathy and make his heart bleed. Even the mechanical notes of a starling, attempting its deliverance, was enough to awaken his affection —for "they were true in tune to nature." The generosity that " endowed not the arts and sciences " but gave to the decayed artist," was what he practised with admirable consistency.

Insincerity, however, is not his only crime. Two other vices, shamelessness of life, and want of delicacy in his writings, are charged against our incomparable humourist. He was, they say, at once a bad man and an immoral author. There is obviously something to support the accusations; but there is also much to be said in mitigation of them. A good deal of Sterne's character was unconsciously derived from the circumstances of his early life and training, and to these we must refer most of what we condemn. The facts of his career—if we except his being swept under a mill water-wheel, and shot out on the other side unharmed—are not of a very eventful nature. Nevertheless, when at the age of eleven he was entered at the Halifax grammar-school, he had undoubtedly experienced more of life's buffetings and had seen more of its vicissitudes than any of his young companions. Born in a barrack, the son of a poor marching lieutenant, he was carried by his mother after the regiment—from native Clonmel to York; from York to Dublin; thence to Exeter; then a second time to Dublin; back to Bristol; once more to Ireland; tossed about in the Channel; in danger more than once of the miserable packet going down with her freight; suffering all kinds of privations and misery for years. In all these journeys, voyagings, marches, the poor mother and her children had hard times of it. When young Laurence's enforced wanderings ceased he was eleven years of age. His cousin, a Yorkshire squire, placed him first at school, and afterwards at Jesus College, Cambridge, where he remained till his ordination; his uncle obtained for him the living of Sutton and a prebendal stall in York; and so he was set up in the world. When he became a famous author, further advancement was afterwards expected, but none came. He lived and died a country parson. He was always Yorick.

There can be no doubt his life was not in strict

keeping with the character of a clergyman as we now conceive it to be. But parsons in the eighteenth century were not generally exemplars of all the virtues. I find they gambled, hunted, drank port wine, ate to repletion, and had red noses; but, notwithstanding this habit, they were not supposed to forfeit their position as respectable members of society. Sterne, by his temperament, was preserved from the orthodox virtues of his cloth. His delicate organization was always on the verge of coming to an end. Blood-vessels in the lungs were periodically giving way and bringing him to death's door. His existence was a struggle with disease. He had to fly more than once for life; but, cheerful even with death at his heels, he could not abstain from enjoying himself in his own way. When the first volumes of " Tristram " had converted the obscure Sutton incumbent into the famous author, what a pleasure it must have been for the poor, lean, hectic, invalid to escape for a while from the atmosphere of York, loaded with local pretensions, and to receive his triumph here in London. Bond Street was a happy promotion from the York coteries, and the incense burnt for him by the best in the land compensated the personal disputes and pompous formalities of the county families. The town circles into which he was intro-

duced must have seemed paradise when he compared them with those he had left, wherein " repu-
" tations are sent out of the world by distant hints,
" nodded away, and cruelly winked into suspicion."
His sojournings in London were the occasion of
much scandal. With his frail frame he could not
stand what his robust friends were able to endure
with impunity. Strong men who could draw, and
did draw, upon their constitutions for six times the
amount poor Yorick ever ventured upon, were
not ashamed to reproach Yorick with excess. Our
author's delicate relations with women especially
have subjected him to much censure. But for the
most part. I believe the charge undeserved. He
possessed that frankness of manner which never fails
to ingratiate its possessor, and was one of those who
are able to form an acquaintance of seven years'
strength at the first introduction. Life, he contended, was too short to be long about the forms of it.
In one respect he resembled his own La Fleur, who
carried a passport in his looks; and, although lean
and haggard, he possessed that insinuant presence
which makes a man successful no less among women
than among men. He was indiscreet; but to judge
him by strictest canons of morality, he will not be
found guilty of active wrong. It was a necessity,
however, of his nature always to have in his head

some Dulcinea. " It has ever been one of the sin-
" gular blessings of my life," he writes, partly in
play and partly perhaps unconsciously avowing his
real feeling, " to be almost every hour of it miserably
" in love with some one." This was true. And he
pretended to think that a man who had not a sort of
affection for the whole sex was incapable of loving a
single one as he ought. To arouse his sensibility it
was necessary that he should have an object at hand;
and he generally took the nearest, believing himself,
by some special grace, to be recognized on the lady's
side, privileged to make his court to any woman he
pleased. Is it to be wondered at when he could pay
such compliments to the sex? * But it must not be

---

* " There are three epochs in the empire of a French woman.
She is coquette—then deist—then devotee. The empire during
these is never lost—she only changes her subjects. When
thirty-five years and more have unpeopled her dominion of the
slaves of love, she re-peoples it with the slaves of infidelity,
and then with the slaves of the Church.

" Madame de V—— was vibrating betwixt the first of these
epochs; the bloom of the rose was fading fast away; she ought
to have been a deist five years before the time I had the
honour to pay my first visit.

" She placed me upon the same sofa with her, for the sake
of disputing the point of religion more closely. In short,
Madame de V—— told me she believed nothing.

" I told Madame de V—— it might be her principle, but I
was sure it could not be her interest to level the outworks,

inferred that his love makings were very serious, or had criminal result. There is, at least, no evidence to convict him of ever having abused the agreeable privilege he claimed for himself; for although some of his actions were equivocal, and some of the letters he sent to his fair friends such as none of us would now think of writing to female acquaintances, they are certainly not the actions or the letters of a man who is guilty of having betrayed the confidence he had evoked. It is quite possible to account for his conduct, reprehensible it may be, without conceding that in his intercourse with the sex he ever deli-

---

without which I could not conceive how such a citadel as hers could be defended—that there was not a more dangerous thing in the world than for a beauty to be a deist—that it was a debt I owed to my creed not to conceal it from her—that I had not been five minutes sat upon the sofa beside her but I had begun to form designs; and what is it but the sentiments of religion and the persuasion they had existed in her breast which could have checked them as they rose up? We are not adamant, said I, taking hold of her hand, and there is need of all restraint, till age in her own time steals in and lays them on us—but, my dear lady, said I, kissing her hand—it is too—too soon—

"I declare I had the credit all over Paris of imperverting Madame de V——. She affirmed to Monsieur D—— and the Abbé M——, that in one half hour I had said more for revealed religion than all their encyclopædias had said against it. I was listed directly into Madame de V——'s *coterie*—and she put off the epoch of deism for two years."—*A Sentimental Journey.*

berately transcended due bounds. I cannot value
that man's judgment or knowledge of women who
would deduce a different conclusion from the notes
he sent to " Eliza," and which, above all, are thought
to bear unmistakeable evidences of his baseness.
The famous passage in one of his letters to this lady
proposing that, in the event of his wife's death, Eliza
should take her place, is evidently a bit of pleasantry
on the part of the writer, meant and accepted as such.
He well knew that in all probability his wife would
survive him; and that there was little opportunity of
seeing his fair Indian friend again. The truth
seems to be, as he tells us, that he, like many more,
derived comfort from the attentions and delicate flat-
teries of the other sex; and being, as others have
been, not strong enough to renounce them, he over-
indulged himself in the exquisite luxury he derived
from contemplating his happy situation.

A worthless man, as severe moralists term him,
could never have obtained the good will of so many
of his contemporaries as Sterne did. He was valued
by all his acquaintances, and his circle included the
best in the land. He was able to boast that he
never lost a friend. Nor was he without a more
valuable reward than public applause. Everybody
whose society is courted in fashionable circles, who is
fortunate enough or unfortunate enough to be treated

as a lion in society, must desire some retreat where
he is no longer regarded as the illustrious author, or
statesman, or soldier, but as a close friend whose
defects are observed as well as his merits; where his
true dimensions are taken, and where he is at home
without ceremony, and on terms of close intimacy
with every member of the household. Such a treasure Sterne was so fortunate as to have possessed in
the Jameses of Gerrard Street, a family by whom he
was esteemed as much as he was courted by others.
In their circle he used to eat his Sunday dinner
during his stay in town; to them he used, like a spoiled
boy, to confide his innermost secrets; and from
them he took advice that would have been unpalatable coming from others. They had great regard
for him, and it was to them he looked for protection
of his child when he was gone. In every emergency,
present and prospective, we find from his letters he
put trust in their generous and disinterested kindness. To inspire the good will of such people as his
friends appear to have been, is in itself, one would
think, sufficient proof that he deserved it.

The coolness that existed between him and his
wife has been adduced as a proof of his want of true
sensibility; but even here there is little to warrant
the adverse view of his character. It was better for
both that they should live apart. Their tempers

were incompatible, and there is much to excuse his
want of ardent love for the lady. He was, however,
always solicitous for her ease and comfort; always
considerate of her happiness; and when they lived
apart he must often have pinched himself to provide
means for her separate establishment. On her side
I can find no conciliatory attempt ever made by the
lady; no desire to make her husband feel that any
effort of his to please her had been successful: but,
on the contrary, she seems to have been one of those
women, specimens of which existed till very recently,
who derive gratification from the feeling that they have
reason for regarding themselves as martyrs. As for
his daughter Lydia, who accompanied her mother in
all her wanderings, no one pretends that Sterne did
not love the girl with intense fondness. The letters that
he sent her are among the most delicate and charming I have ever read; full of the tenderest affection;
of most playful humour, (and of the same kind, too,
as that he produced for the readers of his works, notwithstanding he never dreamed of having them
printed), and bearing obvious proof of the deep
interest he took in everything that related to her
interest and happiness. Indeed, I know nothing
more affecting than these letters, — except it be the
fact, that the poor girl was forced, after her father's
death, to dispose of his correspondence by reason of her

poverty. These letters, **none of** which the writer ever thought **would see the** light, but upon which rests most of the abuse to which his memory has been subjected, if they prove Sterne to have been neither " fat **nor** modest," cannot **be** accepted as evidence that he **had** a corrupt heart, or was a sorry jester. On the contrary, they afford irrefragable evidence of the reverse.

Sterne's aim in **writing, or, as he puts it, the** ends **he** proposed **to** himself **in** commencing author were, **not to be fed,** but **to be** famous, and the hope **of** doing the world good by ridiculing what he thought deserving **of** ridicule or of disservice to sound learning. The aim is undoubtedly good. As we all know, he attained the former object—has he not also succeeded in the **latter?** **On the** appearance of the first volumes of " Tristram," his too sensitive friends, influenced not so much, **I think,** by their tone as by the personalities **they contain,** remonstrated with **him. A medical friend writing** from London— **Yorick** had the same contempt for doctors **as** Montaigne and Molière—lets him know that " the general " opinion of the best judges, without exception," was that " it cannot **be** put into **the hands of any** woman " of character;" and this charge of indelicacy—started simultaneously with the appearance **of the** works— **has ever since been brought against them. I confess**

I would not put the book into a lady's hands any more than I would recommend Lempriere ; and yet Lempriere is not a bad book. The exploits of gods and goddesses, of demi-gods and heroes, were a little coarse in their nature, and are given with a freedom that makes them not the fittest reading for our wives and sisters. Sterne is not mean ; is not ungenerous; he does not cease to excite pity for everything that has life and suffers : but we in England are a peculiar people, and are presumed to be so combustible a society that the tender passion must not be mentioned except in so far as it leads its votaries to St. George's, Hanover Square. It alone of all human wickedness is to be tabooed in literature. We may place in the hands of women of character tales wherein murder is scientifically performed ; wherein the exact processes of thieving are revealed ; wherein backbiting and reviling one's neighbour are exhibited as fine arts : but anything like an allusion to the amorous propensity of our nature—except the economic issue to which I have adverted is clearly and obtrusively kept before the constant attention of the reader— is visited with critical disapprobation. That Sterne did not *think* his writings had an immoral tendency is sufficiently proved by his making confidants of his wife, of his beloved child, and submitting what he wrote to some of his intimate female acquaintances whom he most respected. He even had thoughts of submitting them to the Archbishop, whereby he hoped to close the mouths of his clerical revilers at York. He doubtless discovered he was improper; but he persisted in the belief he was just, and his critics wrong; influenced by the same spirit as that which tempts us to tease a known prude or puritan. He knew, moreover, that nothing he wrote was capable of exciting unhallowed passion in the other sex. His most subtle innuendoes are for men; any latent meaning could be discovered only by those who had experienced what it aims to disclose. His books are essentially men's books. But people in their censure are like the Paris landlord who gave Yorick notice to quit because Madame de R.'s young woman had visited him in the evening, and thus overthrew the credit of his house. This practical censor would not have minded had twenty girls visited his lodger, provided only it had been—in the morning.

This capital charge of grossness made against Sterne has, however, some kind of foundation; for it must be confessed his was not the chastest pen. But there is much to be said for him. When he wrote, only a few years had elapsed since ladies visited theatres in masks; and even in circles he was familiar with, a freedom of manners prevailed of

which the general reader has little notion. True it
is, Addison had already written, and Goldsmith was
his contemporary. He did not form himself upon
such models, nor upon the new literature which
reached Yorkshire, but upon preceding writers. He
was bred in past fashions of thought, and, like Montaigne, dared to write what he dared to think. This
can happen only to few writers. Some men refuse
to be moulded by surrounding ideas, or rather, they
are moulded by ideas derived from their favourite
authors, and remain uninfluenced by those current
among their intimate associates. These occasional
natures, adhering to past manners and past modes of
thought, may be compared to the old bucks of the
last generation, whom we sometimes see in our
streets, strutting about in the costume of their youth,
and descanting on the superiority of the manners
that distinguished the Regency. Sterne, by force of
circumstances, by the life he led as an impression-
able boy in barracks, by the queer companionship
into which he was forced in after-life, became satu-
rated with a mode of thought from which he could
not free himself, and, being a Humourist, he was
able to reproduce himself in his works. We profit
by his gift. The gentler moods and the tenderest
passions of humanity have had in him their appropriate and best interpreter, his divining rod having

revealed treasure so recondite as to have remained unobserved by others.

In " Tristram Shandy," in the " Sentimental " Journey," in his Sermons, in his Letters, we see the revelations of an exceptional nature, fed upon proper nutriment, and manifesting itself with genuine and triumphant delight. **What a** novel is " Tristram " Shandy !" It is **true we** have something more than the conventional proprieties. No such gallery of worthies, however, had ever before been painted; and **none such will** ever again be presented to our notice. Other writers concoct their situations, and then ingeniously adapt their puppets to the predetermined scheme, as if there were a regularly constructed plot in every Shandy family. They erect a house, **and** then provide suitable furniture for the building. Sterne worked with a different aim. He had furniture of quaint but rarest fashion, and was indifferent as to where he should house it so long as he was able **to fix it** somewhere in the edifice. A **set** of gentler human creatures was never before collected under one roof. Nothing, it is true, was well **hung;** the creaking **door, always** unswung, **was** never repaired; the dispute begun was never ended. **It was** a queer family, in which things were apt to take a sinister turn; but **every** member of it becomes an especial **favourite with all** who have passed an hour under their roof, and, once known, none is ever again forgotten. The family resemblance is amazing; all are Shandean: but to each has been assigned a well-defined individuality by which he is recognized. With inimitable strokes, Toby, the well-beloved, is discriminated from his brother, the elder Shandy. Different in every respect, and yet how like! The one is single-minded; the other, " who " accounted for nothing like anybody else," of an acrid humour. The one had such " a stabbing way " with him in his disputations that in less than half- " an-hour he invariably had the whole party against " him;" the other, patient of injuries, was of a peaceful, placid nature; had scarce heart enough to retaliate upon a fly that had annoyed him, and answered an argument by whistling half-a-dozen bars of " Lillebullero." Is there any character in our literature better delineated, stronger in the elements of particularity, more loveable, more worthy of love than Uncle Toby? Mr. Fitzgerald, to whom all admirers of Sterne are much indebted for his recent volumes, incidentally compares him with Sir Roger de Coverley, and Parson Adams; but neither of these worthies is comparable with him, inasmuch as their creators in the several delineations deliberately station themselves on a moral elevation which necessarily prevents them from exhi-

biting that complete sympathy with their characters
which is apparent in every line of Sterne's inimitable
creation.   He who tells us the heart out of which
sprang "Tristram Shandy" was a vain, shallow, canting
heart, is not a critic in whom we ought to feel ourselves disposed to put explicit trust.   Then there is
Trim, the model of a faithful servant and friend,
whose devotion is so great that he would willingly
hammer out his last half-crown to gratify a single
wish of his master; Slop, who always " evaded the
" question;" Yorick, Susanna, the Widow Wad-
man—all are conceived and developed with a pathos
that now for a hundred years has made them dear
friends of the public, and will continue to make
them favourites with our grandchildren in the next
century.   And do you seek a moral in this wonderful
story ?   Learn, then, that all of us have eccentricities; that all of us are afflicted with hobbies, and
that it is unwise for one man to laugh at his neighbour's folly, seeing that his own is just as ridiculous.

Sterne was conscious of his genius.   What they
said of his works losing their popularity he disregarded.   Nor did he doubt of immortality.   In his
dedication to Pitt, he tells the great commoner how
he is to behave, " by taking this book (not under
" your protection—it must protect itself; but) into
" the country with you."   " As my life and opinions

" are likely to make some noise in the world," says he, in another place, " and, if I conjecture right, " will be no less read than the Pilgrim's Progress " itself, I find it necessary to consult every one a " little in his turn." The idea of going down to posterity in company with Bunyan is one of the most characteristic in his works, and is to be matched for quiet irony only by himself in that passage in the Preface to his Sermons where he acquaints the reader that " the sermon which gave rise to the " publication of these, having been offered to the " public as one of Yorick's, he hopes the most serious " reader will find nothing to offend him in his contin- " uing these volumes under the same title. Lest it " should be otherwise," he proceeds, " I have added " a second title-page with the real name of the " author. The first will serve the bookseller's pur- " pose—as Yorick's name is possibly of the two " the more known—and the second will ease the " minds of those who see a jest and the danger " which lurks under it, where no jest was meant."

A Dr. Ferriar has written a book to show up Sterne. He has proved by addition and subtraction that Yorick's wit was borrowed from his predecessors, and his learning filched from sources long since for- gotten. I have not read the doctor's book, but there doubtless is much truth in what he says. Few men

are born with an intuitive knowledge of the ancients
and their works. One must get all one knows from
somewhere, and a **quotation** is equally effective when
taken from Burton as from Horace. A thorough
examination will triumphantly **show**, that, although
his treasury **may** contain some base foreign coin, all
the genuine pieces are from his own mint, and un-
mistakably bear **the** image and superscription of him
by whom they were issued. But his great success is
due less to wit and learning than **to his** power of
exciting the reader's sympathy. This may in some
measure be seen in the Sermons, which are among the
best **in our** language; but more especially is it to be
seen in **the** " Sentimental Journey," where he had
full scope **for** the exercise of his peculiar powers.
His was the **loving eye** that could see where all was
darkness to others. The learned Smelfungus pronounced everything barren from Dan to Beersheba,
" **for every** object he **passed was** discoloured or dis-
" torted." **He, on the** contrary, interesting his heart
in everything, would have found in a desert some
object to call forth his affections. The compass of his
observation was **wide, and he had a** penetration with
which he **is** not usually credited. **The** French, who
have made this work their own, **and several** editions
have appeared among them, **say he is** the only
Englishman who **has ever** understood them. It will

be found, moreover, that this **sympathy** has a different source from what is produced by the exhibition of suffering on the stage, or in the works of most other humourists. There the spectator, or reader, is moved because he is made to contemplate himself in the situation represented. When, for instance, Don Quixote suffers indignities, when his bones are broken and his teeth knocked down his throat, our sympathies are excited in a greater degree, perhaps, than for any other hero of fiction. We feel the strokes of his assailant; every blow that falls upon him falls also upon us, and we are kept in a constant state of apprehension for the safety of the unfortunate knight. But why are we indignant at the treatment he receives? Is it not because our experience being superior to his we are able to anticipate the desperate issues that will come? Even Falstaff, whose transcendent social qualities must receive our admiration, occasions in us no spontaneous affection, no unconscious sympathy. We feel what we feel, and we know why. Our pity is largely interfused with a sense of our own superiority. We are never entirely *en rapport* with him. He bears the same relation to Uncle Toby as the man at whom you laugh bears to the man with whom you cannot help laughing. In company with Sir John you feel much as Prince Hal and his rollicking companions felt; in presence of Uncle Toby you yourself become Shandean.   Sterne's **magic art** is superior to that of all his predecessors.   He does not excite emotions in us.   We suffer them in company with him; we feel merely because he himself feels.   Although his literary merits in other directions are great, in this particular excellence he has no equal.   He is the greatest and most genuine of our humourists.

XII.

THE LITERARY MAN AS SATIRIST.

SWIFT.

E are first introduced to Swift at the famous coffee-house in Covent Garden kept by Button, and frequented by the gentlemen who were termed " the wits." These wits, one of them tells us, had for several successive days observed in the coffee-house a strange clergyman, who seemed utterly unacquainted with any of them, and whose custom it was to lay his hat down on a table, and " walk backward and forward " at a good pace for half an hour, or an hour, without " speaking to any mortal, or seeming in the least to " attend to anything that was going forward there. " He then used to take up his hat, pay his money at " the bar, and walk away without opening his lips." The wits, as may be supposed, were greatly fluttered by the apparition; for, having observed this sin-

gular behaviour for some time, continues the nar-
rator, " they concluded him to be out of his senses,
" and the name that he went by among them was
" that of ' The mad parson.' "   One evening as Mr.
Addison and the rest of the wits were observing this
strange character, they saw him cast his eyes several
times on " a gentleman in boots, who seemed to
" be just come out of the country;" and at last, " in
" a very abrupt manner, without any previous sa-
" lute,"—for Swift even then did not fashion himself to the decorums—" asked him if he remembered
" any good weather in the world."   The gentleman
in boots, who seemed to be just come out of the
country, after staring a little at the oddity of the
question, answered that he " remembered a great
" deal."   " That is more than I can say," rejoined
the questioner.   " I never remember any that was
" not too hot or too cold; too wet or too dry.   But,
" however God Almighty contrives it, at the end of
" the year it is all very well."   The spectators of
this scene, who had quitted their seats to get nearer
the interlocutors, were, we are told, more than ever
confirmed in their opinion of the strange parson's
madness.

Such was the first appearance of Jonathan Swift
on the scene where afterwards he was to be the
moving spirit.   He lived from 1667 to 1745, having

for contemporaries six English sovereigns. But though the days of his existence exceeded three-score years and ten, he cannot be said to have flourished during the whole period. At the height of his career, however, he was the most important figure of the time. Although he never held office, he was so powerful as a statesman that the sovereign with her friends conspired against him; and so high a notion was entertained by the people of his power that they believed, had he chosen, he could have brought in the Pretender and placed the crown upon his head. At one time grand juries ignored bills at his dictation, and a whole nation would have risen as one man to defend him from the assaults of his enemies. In the literary world he exercised as much influence as in the political; and so highly was he esteemed that the leader of the wits who had named him " the " mad parson" afterwards pronounced him to be " the greatest genius of the age." Nor is his posthumous reputation inferior to what he enjoyed during his lifetime. All men of education are acquainted with his works; and anecdotes are recorded of him by people who have never read a line he wrote, and are ignorant whether he flourished in the time of George IV. or of Boadicea. Alas! is there anything in history more sad than the end of this imperious intellect? The closing years of his life were passed

under the shadow of superhuman misery.*　" Good
" bye; God bless you, and I hope I shall never see
" you again," were the terms of his parting bene-
diction. For three years he was dumb, and deaf, and
mad. Then came that release he had longed for.

Notwithstanding all the fame and power he acquired, and all the volumes that have been written
about him, the occurrences best known in the lives
of most of us are in Swift's case disputed. His
life is still a mysterious problem. Where was he
born? who was his father? did he marry? who was
his wife? were questions not answered during his
life, and are only half-answered at the present day.
That he was born in Dublin and educated in Dublin
University; that he came to England in Revolution
year, and lived—except for a short time, when he
returned to his native land for ordination—as secretary with Sir William Temple; that after the death
of that nobleman he went over to Ireland with Lord
Berkeley in the capacity of chaplain and private
secretary, and, being superseded in the latter post,
accepted as compensation the rectory of Agher and the

---

* His food had to be cut up for him, and he would not eat
in the presence of others. Body and mind were decaying. One
of his eyes swelled to the size of an egg, and at times it was
with difficulty that five attendants could prevent him tearing
it out.

vicarages of Laracor and Rathbeggan; and that he
afterwards became Dean of St. Patrick's, in the possession of which preferment he died—is all well known.
We know, too, that he wrote famous books, and that
the influence he exercised over the political events of
his time was unparalleled. But with his domestic
history we cannot pretend to be acquainted. There
are theories to account for the *sæva indignatio* he
exhibited through life, theories to explain his madness, theories to clear up the relationship that sub-
sisted between himself and those gentle women
whose names he has made immortal. But can we
regard any of them as satisfactory? Does not the
explanation itself require explaining?

Swift's view of the literary calling was not a very
high one. He had no desire to be classed among
men of letters, but used literature as a means to an
end. Like Shakespeare, he exhibited little interest
in the success of his most important works, but
allowed them to take their course, satisfied if they
were effective, and served the purpose of the hour.
The most original, facile, and versatile writer of the
period, he had no literary jealousies. He was even
without the ordinary vanity of the author regarding
his productions, and seldom looked at a work after
he had sent it to the printer. To Pope he gave permission to correct, burn, or blot what he liked; and,

at Addison's suggestion, forty lines of " Baucis and Philemon" were altered, **forty were** added, and forty entirely erased. For the applause of the public, whom he regarded as his inferiors, he cared not in the least. He wrote for the immediate ends he had in view—to turn out a Ministry and replace them by his friends, or to shelter his own party when in office from the assaults of their opponents. Of his transcendent merit as a man of letters we need not here speak. His prose has received commendation from all sides; and if we cannot admit he was a great poet, we must agree with Scott that he possessed the highest gift of a poet—imagination. His intellect was the richest in England; he could rhyme with the best of them; he had imagination beyond them all. With the chief requisites for the successful cultivation of the art, he ought to have been a great poet. How comes it, then, that he has left us nothing that we can place beside the accredited masterpieces of poesy? I believe the true reason is, that he was too proud to exercise the gift he possessed. If others chose to talk in metaphor, to use similes, to say what they do not mean, or mean more than they say, they were welcome to follow the bent of their inclination, as is their duty. For himself, his pride would not suffer him to attempt the sublime or the beautiful, and perhaps in his heart he despised what we call sublimity and beauty. I suspect he would have been ashamed had he been regarded by his friends as " Dr. " Swift, the great poet." "Cousin Swift," said Dryden to him, " you will never be a poet;" and he was right. Swift's appropriate vehicle was prose, and his power herein was so great that every line he wrote told materially in favour of any cause he espoused. The side to which he gave the weight of his pen was almost sure of being victorious. Johnson truly says that for a time he dictated the political opinion of England. But it must not be supposed that he was a hireling. One of the ministers having once ventured to offer him pecuniary remuneration for his services, he regarded the proposal as an insult, and was deaf to all entreaties to be reconciled till he had received from the offender the utmost satisfaction. " If we let these great ministers pretend too much," he writes in the Journal to Stella, " there will be no " governing them. He promises to make me easy, if " I would but come and see him; but I won't, and " he shall do it by message, or I will cast him off." Afterwards the same statesman proposed to him to become his chaplain; but the appointment was declined. " I will be no man's chaplain alive," he said. There was a prize, however, which it seems he coveted. He would have liked to have been an English bishop. Strange how terribly high is the

value placed on official rank in a settled country like
ours! We see Swift running backward and forward
from Ireland to England to earn a bishopric. He
could pacify a nation, or rouse it to the verge of rebellion; he could procure the appointment of others
to the ecclesiastical bench, but he was unable to seat
himself thereon. Mitres were not for such as he,
but were reserved for men of more accommodating
nature. An insatiable soul like Swift's would not
have been satisfied with a bishopric had he obtained
it; but he regarded professional promotion as the
outward sign given by society of its formal recognition of a man's merits and approval of his work; and
so he was indignant at being passed over for men
whose claims he considered to be far inferior to his.

He has been enrolled among the humourists. If
the playfulness of the cat with a mouse between her
teeth can be termed humour, then was he rightly so
classed. In the time before fancy and imagination
were desynonymized such a vague description might
have been allowable; but now, we, who pride ourselves upon our greater accuracy, decline to bestow
upon the fierce genius who painted for us the terrible picture of the Yahoos the title of humourist.
His theme is identical with that of the humourist,
only he regards it in a different light, uses it in a
different way, and for a different purpose. The

materials, too, that he employs are the same, but the
fabric he turns out is totally different from what is
produced by the other. That tenderness which with
the ludicrous is the element that forms what we call
humour, is altogether missing in Swift. We find
no trace in him of the quality. He was essentially
a satirist. He was never an adept at being sprightly.
In making the town laugh, he was himself serious;
and I fancy the last reader who amused himself with
the hideous fun in Gulliver laughed under restraint,
much as a traveller would laugh at a joke from the
highwayman who presented a pistol at his head
through the carriage window. He is the greatest
master of satire that has appeared on the earth, and
no humourist. For the way in which he employed
his great abilities in this line he has been severely
blamed; but when we consider that an epigram from
him could kill a man's fortune, it is greatly to his
honour that he so seldom employed his tremendous
power upon individuals. One of his critics calls his
striking when he had an opportunity, " striking in
" the dark," as if, forsooth, he ought to have struck
when no opportunity offered. If a man takes offence,
but does not think it worth while to remember it,
what is the use of his taking offence? With Swift
the offence lasted till it was expiated or avenged;
but the notion that the reason he struck in the dark

was because he feared to strike in the light is not
warranted by fact. To call Swift coward and sneak
—" if you had met him like a man he would have
" quailed before you," says his critic, " and years
" after written a foul epigram about you "—is pretty
much like saying that water does not wet, or fire
burn. Why, Swift was the bravest man of his
time. A hundred instances of his courage are on
record. He was not intimidated by threats of personal violence, nor did he quail when a reward was
offered for his head by a Government not indisposed
to have caused his ruin. Upon the appearance of
the Drapier's fourth letter, the printer was thrown
into prison, and proclamation was issued promising
£300 for the discovery of the author. Even then
the Dean was not appalled, but acted as a kind, considerate, and brave gentleman would have done.*

---

* " He went to the levée of the Lord-Lieutenant, burst
through the circle with which he was surrounded, and, in a
firm and stern voice, demanded of Lord Carteret the meaning
of these ' severities against a poor industrious tradesman, who
had published two or three papers, designed for the good of
his country.' . . . Two other anecdotes occurred, which
served to show the bold, stern, and uncompromising temper of
the Dean. The first is well known. A servant, named Robert
Blakeley, whom he entrusted to copy out and convey to the
press the Drapier's Letters, chanced one evening to absent
himself without leave. His master charged him with treachery,

What are we to say to the personal character of
the man? are we to admire that? For myself, I
think I can detect in Swift great goodness of nature,
and kindness more than in most men usually reputed kind. He never exhibited meannesses like
those reported of Pope and Addison. He could
confer favours by a word, and it was always gratifying to him to be able to oblige men of letters
without distinction of rank or party. Money and
influence were equally at their service. The recorded
instances of his kindnesses are, indeed, numberless.
All his friends benefited by his favour. Thackeray
thought he must be a bad man if you would not like
to live with him. Even if this criterion of a man's
worth were admitted, Swift will not hold a low place
in our esteem.

His agreeable qualities are notorious to readers
of the memoirs of the time. His friends concurred in
believing that his goodness was equalled only by his

---

and, upon his exculpation, insisted that at least he neglected
his duties as a servant, because he conceived his master was in
his power. 'Strip your livery,' he commanded, 'begone from
the Deanery instantly, and do the worst to revenge yourself
that you dare do.' The man retired, more grieved that his
master doubted his fidelity than moved by this harsh treatment. He was replaced at the intercession of Stella; and
Swift afterwards rewarded his fidelity by the office of verger
in the cathedral of St. Patrick's."—Scott's *Life of Swift*.

genius.* In the quarrel between **him and** Steele he displayed, in a letter **to** Addison, unapproachable greatness. He there propounds **a** view of friendship as chivalrous as that of the lover who, in deference to the wishes of his mistress, avowed his disbelief that she had kissed a rival whom he himself had seen her kiss. " **What if I did not** [do the mean action of which he had been accused] ? **Steele,**" he says, " should not have thought I did **it, if he could** possibly think I did not," is the tenor of the communication. **He never** denied the charge brought against **him,** disdaining to do that although he was innocent. Throughout the whole **dispute he showed** magnanimity and tender-

---

* " He relieved the necessitous, **he** supported the dependent, **and insisted that more** distinguished genius should receive from **his powerful friends that kindness and** distinction to which **it is so well entitled. Congreve, a** Whig in politics, and who apprehended being **deprived of** his office under government, **was** treated **by Harley, at** Swift's request, with such marked regard and assurance of protection, as excited his astonishment, while it allayed his apprehensions. . . . He obtained also for the amiable Parnell **that** prompt attention which is most flattering to the modesty of merit. At courts he contrived that the lord-treasurer should make the first advances to the man of letters, and thus, **as he boasts to Stella,** made the minister desire to be acquainted with **Parnell, not** Parnell with the minister. Pope, who was now labouring on his Homer, experienced that warm **and effectual support which** is acknowledged in the preface to the Iliad. . . . **It was by Swift's**

ness of the very highest order. **It was impossible**
for him, the most influential politician of the time, to
treat Steele always with that kindness he would willingly have exhibited towards him in literary matters.
In the only work to which he ever put his name he
did speak in very complimentary terms of his friend.
But when Steele entered the political arena, his toes
necessarily came in Swift's way. Indeed, neither he
nor the great Mr. Addison was intended by nature
to be kings of men. They were not unworthy men
of letters. **The one** was a sort of inventor in literature, and the other was, at once, a bright exemplar
and a good performer. Both had benefited morals

---

interest that Gay was **made known** to Lord Bolingbroke, and
obtained his patronage. Arbuthnot, although **he needed not**
our author's recommendation, having **established himself by**
his professional merit, enjoyed, in the most intimate **degree, the**
pleasure and advantage which were afforded by his society.
Berkeley, afterwards the celebrated Bishop of Cloyne, **owed to**
Swift those introductions which placed him in the way **of pro-**
motion. . . . **In like manner he recommended** Rowe to a
post under **government, and** although Prior, **with whom he**
lived in strict **intimacy, had** no occasion for his services **during**
the reign in which he flourished as a political character of eminence, yet, in that which followed, **he received,** during his dis-
tresses, the **most effectual support from Swift's** experienced
friendship. . . . **In short, as he** expresses it in his Journal
to Stella, he found himself able to forward the interest of **every**
one, excepting only his own."—Scott's *Life of Swift.*

as well as letters. But what did they in politics? It is not surprising that when either of them went out of his way and met a lion in the path, that the inevitable consequences followed. In literature, which was their proper field of action, the great Dean would have helped them—given them hints (and the authors of the " Tatler" and the " Beggar's Opera" were not the only men who knew how valuable were hints from him), written for them for nothing—handed over to them the profits of his own works, have done any acceptable service for their benefit,—but let them not square themselves against him in the political ring, or they must not complain of the bruises they receive in the fray.

The men who knew him best—and they were the most eminent of the day,—loved him best, and we know that beautiful and accomplished women sacrificed their lives to be near him. All who have heard of Swift have heard of Stella and Vanessa, so there is no need for me to repeat their story, and I refer to the subject only for the purpose of mentioning that as there is no proof (or likelihood, indeed!) that Stella was married to Swift, the charge frequently made against the Dean of having indulged himself in the society of the one whilst he was irrevocably bound to the other must fall to the ground. This haughty intellect could not, however, suffer the conditions of ordinary friendships. He claimed to impose his own. This he has clearly expressed, where we should least expect to find it, in a letter to his early love, "Varina," in reply to a notification that *she* at least would not dislike to live with him. He there demands to know, before promising to wed her, whether she would engage to follow the method he should point out for the improvement of her mind; whether she could bend all her affections to the same direction which he should give his own, and so govern her passions, however justly provoked, as at all times to resume her good humour at his approach; and whether she could account the place where he resided more welcome than courts and cities without him. He certainly sometimes exacted too much. We are told how at Lord Burlington's her ladyship, to whom he had not been introduced, having refused to sing, he said she should sing, or he would make her; how, to try a man's temper, he bade him drink the lees of a bottle of wine; and how he introduced himself to a curate as his new "master." A thousand and one such anecdotes are related of him by Mrs. Grundy, who shrugs her wrinkled old shoulders at the shocking effrontery of the Irish parson, who showed no respect for the forms and ceremonies of conventional life. His manners were, in truth, not always of the most amiable description, and it is not to be denied that he could never have been improved even by the best society, inasmuch as he would not take its impress, but gave to it the seal of his own personality. Not of an affirmative nature, he was invariably found with the " noes," and never strove to imitate the fashion. Some called his behaviour eccentric; others, who thought they saw deeper, were disposed to attribute it to affectation; but they agreed that his conduct was offensive.

It is, however, satisfactory to find the whole of his biographers and critics concur in one matter. They all admit that he was ever ready to make amends by his civilities for any rudeness of which he had been guilty. The author of " The English Humourists," in referring to his rough manners and kind deeds, asks,—" If you were in a strait, would you like such " a benefactor?" and confesses he thought he would rather have had " a potato and a friendly word from " Goldsmith than have been beholden to the Dean " for a guinea and a dinner." I do not know if the reader is of the same mind, but it is reasonable to suppose that a man in distressed circumstances would appeal to one who could succour him. Swift knew how " those devils of Grub Street authors" spent their earnings, and he never omitted to take advantage of an opportunity that offered to lecture them for their spendthrift ways. But he relieved them though he bullied them. And hadn't he the right to bully them for their imprudence? What was the good, then, of their slinking off for sympathy and a potato? A potato would not pay the rent for which they were pressed; would not put a shawl on their wives' shoulders, or provide shoes for the naked feet of their little ones. No! the great Dean knew better than that, and acted from his superior knowledge.

Much abuse has been heaped on him for the arrogance of putting himself on equality with men of exalted rank or office. The accusation shows, I think, inherent weakness in the nature of those who make the charge. If they did not feel it was a great honour to be on terms of intimacy with a duke, or a minister of state, they would not make so much of it. Many readers will have observed the effect in a circle if one of the company happens to repeat anything he had heard from one of higher rank than that of which the party is composed. All resent the mention of the circumstance; they really are hurt, and feel it to be a rebuke upon themselves that the speaker should have been more fortunate than they in his invitations. Their self-love is wounded, and in retaliation they attempt to heal it by accusing the author of their smart of being unduly impressed by

rank. There is a story told of a literary gentleman who, returning from some nobleman's house where there had **been** no fish for dinner, remarked upon the omission to a party of whom Jerrold was one. That **wit** thereupon administered what is regarded as an apt **and** deserved reproof to the guest who had ventured to complain, **by** suggesting that probably they had eaten all **the fish** *upstairs.* **If** a man dates his letters from Windsor Castle during his stay there he is sneered **at**; but **if he speaks of** his **residence** in **Islington** he escapes animadversion. Why should men of letters, whose importance is derived neither from **wealth** nor **rank,** censure one who really despised what they themselves profess to undervalue; who appraised the diamond star on a peer's breast no more than a horse-shoe, **and** who did not esteem an acquaintance because he **was** wealthy **any** more than **he did because he was** healthy? Indeed, this arrogance **in his treatment of** the great partly arose from dread lest men should suppose that *he* was given **to** flattery. **The Lord** Treasurer heard ill with the **left ear** and so did Swift, but the latter " dared not " tell him that I am so, for fear he should think that " **I counterfeited** to make my court;" **and** this, too, it **was** that **made** him when at court "affect to turn " **from a lord to the meanest** of his acquaintances." **Not** by inheritance did he derive his rank, so he knew

that men who are unacquainted with such a nature as
his would accuse him of giving undue importance to
fictitious distinctions if they had seen him deferential.
He was aware that although a duke might dress in
shabby habiliments without losing his position, a man
of his rank is expected to observe the conventionalities. So he must have been *aut Cæsar aut nullus,*
and as he could not afford to be *nullus,* he did not
understand why he should not be Cæsar and send
for the Lord Treasurer as well as the Lord Treasurer send for him. He would make the reputation of wit and great learning do the office of a blue
riband or a coach and six. Are we to blame him?

Our chief concern, however, is with his philosophy.
What are we to think of that? Those whom he benefited by his countenance or injured by his scorn
and bitterness are gone. The influence of his personal character has long ceased to be felt. But his
books—what of them? Are they such as we can
honestly commend? Is humanity the better because
they were written and are immortal?

It is well sometimes to be taught our true place in
the economy of the universe. There are plenty of
writers ready to flatter our vanity, by insisting that we
are only a little lower than angels. For more than
a thousand years it had been reported and believed
that all things were created for our especial benefit.

Sun and stars, moon and planets, were designed with a view to serve us; every flower that sheds its perfume grows and brightens for our gratification; and the inferior animals were sent expressly for our use. Against this view of the matter Swift lifted up his voice. He proclaimed to mankind that they are as these animals, these insects, this lichen—as the lowest thing that has life; liable to the same conditions, subject to the same end. People, mistaking the artificial and accidental for the real and permanent, had misnamed our functions and instincts. What is the result of culture and experience they confounded with what is essential to our nature, and had come to regard the uncustomary as identical with the unnatural. They had begun to forget themselves. The mission of Swift was to remind men of their origin and end. He stripped them of their artificial trappings as effectually as the storm strips the drowned sailor, and ruthlessly showed them to themselves in all the deformity of their necessitous nakedness. The Foplings and Chloes and Lady Bettys of the time were shocked, of course. Beaux and oglers discredited his views, not because they believed them false, but because they felt them to be degrading, and Society ever since has treated their propagator as a bold, impious, and distempered madman.

Shakespeare and Swift may be classed together as

the two who of all men of letters obtained clearest insight into the intricacies as well as the artificialities of our nature. Both knew the full extent of its weaknesses and imperfections, and neither cared to withhold his knowledge from the world. But how differently this experience affected the two men. In all he wrote it is clear that "The Dance of Death" in Stratford Church left deep and permanent impression on Shakespeare's mind, and that the Skeleton was ever present, disquieting his imagination. By virtue of a happy temperament, however, he was able to suppress the disgust he felt, and he loved our nature with all its imperfections, and partly, perhaps, because of its imperfections. To him there was " some soul of goodness in things evil." But the other would not or could not forget that evil is an ingredient even of good, and to him the uses of this world seemed " weary, stale, flat and unprofitable." Finding men ashamed of their infirmities he was indignant, and felt pleasure in reminding them of what things they least desired to remember. He would not take the estimate they had formed of themselves, and refused to admit that by subduing other animals they had thereby taken themselves out of the category, or that their boasted intellect is acted on by a higher force than that which makes fire burn or a tree propagate its kind. He was the hardest hitter that ever penned a line. **Is** it wonderful, then, that his views, and the manner in which he presented them, are unpalatable, and that **men** should decline to accept his theory ? People applaud **a play** that exposes the **worst features of** their character, if in the end virtue **is rewarded and vice punished.** Indeed, they **prefer a drama of that sort to** another in which there **is** nothing but virtue served **up for** their entertainment. Show **them their nature vicious if you** will, **only let the vice be** occasional **and** accidental, **not permanent and radical, and they are** satisfied.

If the aim of satire is rightly defined to be the **correction,** by exposure, of vice and folly, it must **be admitted** that Swift, the most powerful of all satirists, fails, because he satirized what **it** is impossible to **correct.**

" *Qui vitia odit homines odit,*"

was the conclusion at which he **had** arrived, and he **boldly** satirized **our nature itself. Yet,** in spite of **this** limitation, **he has** performed **a vast** and permanent **service by** making people **behold** themselves **in a light wherein they seldom care to** regard themselves, **but in which it is well they should** sometimes **be seen.**

XIII.

THE LITERARY MAN AS PATRIOT.

MAZZINI.

OVE for one's native soil, and desire for personal consideration in the place of one's birth, are sentiments which — though proveably not innate—have been found to exist very extensively in every race that has hitherto attained to the dignity and advantages of a settled mode of life. Moreover, they are not confined to vulgar minds, but have exercised a predominating influence over some of the noblest men that ever lived. The privilege of triumphal entry into one city has been held sufficient reward for the conquest of great countries, and the huzzas of an enthusiastic multitude have effectually drowned the echo of the innumerable groans of slaughtered foreigners. To such minds as are thus influenced, exile, whether voluntary or enforced, is a misfortune to be evaded at any cost. Their happiness is centred in their country. In the twelfth century, as we have seen, Giraldus Cambrensis, the most eminent man of his age, roamed up and down Europe venting his rage, and bearding kings and popes for keeping him from the see of St. David. He had been offered an archbishopric, and the choice of more than one bishopric; but he would accept nothing whilst the throne of the miserable little city in which he had been bred was withheld. Prolonged absence from Florence poisoned the life of Dante, and undoubtedly shortened the great poet's existence. These men were influenced by the feelings that influenced Jacob when he charged his sons to bury him in the field of the Hittite. " There they buried Abraham and " Sarah his wife; there they buried Isaac and Re- " becca his wife; and there I buried Leah."

This attachment to locality — this belief that Abana and Pharpar are better than all the waters of Israel—is not in itself Patriotism; but it is obviously the source whence it springs, and on which it feeds. The sentiment is repeated on a large scale; men mass their feelings; and the result is what has been termed "greatest of virtues" by the ancients, and is even now highly esteemed. After all, what does this sentiment mean? By chance, or agreement, or compulsion, an imaginary cordon is thrown around a

certain district, whereupon all within the circle are
regarded as compatriots, while those who remain
without are treated as enemies. The history of our
own country affords us an eminent instance of the
ill effect of such an arrangement. There were once
seven Englands. The England which had its head-
quarters at Winchester did not consider itself unpatriotic when it made war upon the England represented by Canterbury, or that at Canterbury while
it acted similarly towards those whose capital was at
York. At length, however, a persistent course of
unpatriotic attempts at fusion was successful, and
these seven Englands eventually became one. From
that time it was no longer regarded patriotic in the
Englishman at Durham to make aggression upon the
Englishman at Dorchester; the attempt would have
been civil war then. But there was consolation for
him. Across the northernmost river was the land
of an enemy from whom he might still honestly steal,
and whom he might still conscientiously kill. In
time that land, too, became an integral part of England, and consequently legitimate patriotism could
no more discharge itself within the four seas; it
must thenceforth exercise itself only against distant
countries.

The tendency of events is indefinitely to enlarge
the area enclosed by the cordon to which we have

alluded. **The** tendency of patriotism, ancient and **modern, has, on** the contrary, been invariably to maintain it as it is, or to restore it to the limits it occupied at some former time. The attitude of Belgium in view of French invasion is a manifestation by that country of its desire to accomplish the one. Polish insurrections, Irish conspiracies, and the recent action of the American slave States, are conspicuous instances of attempts at effecting the other.

It frequently happens that a man disposed to be **patriotic,** and willing to take upon himself responsible action, **finds** it impossible to determine **his** course by the current maxims of patriotism. This may arise from either of two causes—he may have doubts as to where his country is, or he may be un**able** to determine what it is. A well-known instance of doubt, arising from the former, is presented in the case of " Stonewall " Jackson, at the outbreak of the **late** contest in America. Jackson was by profession **a** soldier, owing allegiance to a country that stretched across a vast continent. He had no inclination to be **false** to this country. **One** day, however, he found that the inhabitants of an **area** of 70,000 miles had resolved to sever themselves from the rest of the community ; and he, having been born in the district, considered it his duty as a patriot to join them, notwithstanding his disapproval of the course they had adopted. Were we to carry the principle from which he acted to its legitimate and logical conclusion, its absurdity would be apparent. If, now, instead of an area of 70,000 miles, one of 35,000 only were to disengage itself, he would consider himself morally bound to partake of its secession; and if his native county afterwards desired to withdraw itself from the diminished area, he would still conceive it to be his duty to offer her his services. Such an idea of patriotism would inevitably lead to political annihilation.

Of the difficulty of discovering what is your country, an example is to be found at the period of the French Revolution. Chateaubriand, returning from his American travels, found France distracted. The King had been sacrificed, and "the patriots" were in possession of supreme power. Princes, nobles, and ecclesiastics had been forced to fly. Chateaubriand could not remain inactive; he hastened to consult Malesherbes. Old France, to whom he owed fealty, and with whom were his affections, was beyond the Rhine. Should he join his friends and relatives who had congregated at Coblentz? This was the question. After much consultation they decided it in the negative, assigning as their reason that to act otherwise would be to act unpatriotically! If one's country consists of rocks and

rivers only, they would have been undoubtedly right.
But if, as we believe, a man's country is made up of
his associations, of his personal liberty, and of the
constitution under which he was born and had lived,
Chateaubriand was wrong in considering those who
retained possession of the soil and of the temporary
direction of affairs as the representatives of his native
land. His France was no longer in her accustomed
place. **He** carried his **country in** his knapsack.

At one time these old-fashioned notions of patriot-
ism, the notions which drill-sergeants and so-called
patriotic **songs** have made familiar, were of service.
The consciousness of belonging to a nation that had
achieved great things cast a sort of reflected greatness upon each citizen, and may have had the effect
of inciting him to emulate his predecessors. But
divisions of mountains **and rivers and** frontier garri-
sons are no longer so effective **as** formerly, and will
in time be altogether dispensed with. Improved
means of intercommunication, **a** more diffused knowledge of foreign languages, and more extensive busi-
ness transactions with men of other lands, are gradually preparing the **way** for the total suppression
of nationalities. **We** shall feel less regret at the
ultimate disappearance of patriotic feelings when we
are able to bring **ourselves to consider** they are
merely the effect of cultivated prejudices ; that they

are customary, not rational; and that in desiring their extinction we are in strict accord with the spirit of modern civilization.

This spirit aims at homogeneity and centralization, through the absorption of the weaker by the more powerful. It is manifested in social life by the increasing number of joint-stock companies, trade unions, associations, and by the organization of opinion and of labour. It is equally apparent in politics. On the other side of the Atlantic it developes itself with greater rapidity than on this. The failure to effect a disruption of the States in union was inherent in the attempt, and there seems to be no well-grounded fear that the effort now being made to confederate those provinces that possess independent governments will be unsuccessful. In Europe, which in ancient times was united under one government by the Romans, and more than once in the middle ages partially united by intermarriage of sovereigns, the tendency would seem at the present moment to have been checked, except so far as regards Italy. Greece was made independent of Turkey; Belgium separated, to its great loss, from Holland; and under the pretext of furnishing them with independence, Austria and Prussia have wrested Schleswig and Holstein from Denmark. Germany itself still remains a comical triacontarchy, split up into as many states as there are days in the month; but it is very probable her late action will hereafter have the effect of diminishing the number of her petty rulers in a way they little expect.

We believe, however, this halt to be only temporary. The smaller states, which dread the loss of their nationalities, should therefore learn in time to look with complacency upon what is inevitable, and to see good in the coming evil. Scotland, Ireland, and Wales once patriotically resisted union with England. They have long since seen, however, that the loss of independent government is amply compensated by the greater benefit they derive from participating in the enlarged and more vigorous action of a more powerful state. Local self-government is less important to a people than good government—all required is, that the worse should give way to the better. What difference does it make to a people whether the centre of ministerial action is here, a mile off, or in St. Petersburg, 2,000 leagues away, if only that action is wholesome and efficacious? For Russia, however, to annex England would be a retrograde step, and should be resisted. But who will say that it would not be a benefit for Turkey to be placed under the control of one of the great European powers, or that the Mexicans would not be more prosperous if their country were formally annexed to the United States, or quietly submitted to the protection of France?

The aim of Christianity is identical with the tendency of civilization. Its endeavour has been to make the world one fold under one Shepherd; the convert to Christianity was to become completely denationalised. Some are of opinion that in this respect it has failed to accomplish its mission, just as Rome failed permanently to effect it by conquest. Philosophy, we are told, has now set itself the task of directing and regulating the feeling from which it is to flow, and it remains to be seen how swift and complete will be its preparation for " the Parliament " of Man, the Federation of the World."

One of the most important agents at the present day in effecting the coming change being necessarily the man of letters, it becomes a matter of universal interest how he views the situation. What and where is the goal to which he would direct and hasten society, and what and where are the means he would employ for reaching it, are, therefore, questions of paramount importance. Of those who, for several years past, have offered themselves as leaders of the new thought, Mr. Mazzini, being a man of action and of letters, is at once one of the most eminent, and most influential; and his utterances are consequently entitled to a higher degree of consideration than we should be disposed to pay to one of meaner rank and lower aspirations.

Mr. Mazzini is probably the most maligned man in all Christendom. He has been persistently traduced by those who have not taken the trouble to make themselves acquainted with the principles of which he is the apostle ; and has had the misfortune more than once to be misinterpreted even by those who incline to favour his cause. His career has been vicissitudinous in the highest degree. He began life, at an early age, as a man of letters, and it is to literature, we believe, he chiefly devotes himself still. But between the year 1828,—in which, full of high hopes, he established the *Indicatore Genovese*,—and the present time, when he confesses his soul to be dead to happiness, and withered by sorrows, delusions, and ingratitude, he has more than most men experienced sundry and manifold changes of fortune. Driven from his native land on account of his opinions, he takes up his abode at Marseilles ; ordered to quit French territory, he seeks and finds refuge in Switzerland ; returning thence into Italy, he is thrown into prison ; escaping, he is again at Marseilles ; then in London ; then, upon the outburst of the last French Revolution, in Paris ; then once more in Italy ; then, a second time, obliged to fly to Switzerland. At length, Rome having declared herself a Republic,

we find him in the Eternal City—Triumvir, ruler,
dictator; organizing the army of the State; re-ar-
ranging its finances; establishing its foreign relations;
and seeking to settle its disordered domestic affairs.
But his season of power was of short duration. After
ninety days the city was crushed by the cannon of a
foreign nation, and the Triumvir is once more an
exile. During the whole of this time, however—
sorely tried as he must have been in the furnace of
affliction—Mazzini is not known to have misdemeaned
himself. According to the testimony of those most
competent to speak, he has remained pure-minded,
faithful, unselfish, truthful in the highest degree.

Why this man—enthusiastic, and possessing surprising vigilance,—is a terror to the Courts of Europe, by whom he is not unjustly regarded as the
petrel of revolution, is not difficult to be understood.
Why he continues to be depreciated and defamed in
England is less clear. His unpopularity in this
country cannot arise from dislike of his opinions; or
his lieutenant, Garibaldi, who shares them, would
not have experienced the treatment he received from
us during his visit. This general—this hand which
had come to rejoin its head—was honoured during
his stay in England with unprecedented attentions.
Professional men, men of letters, Parliament men and
noblemen attended his *levées*; Cabinet Ministers un-

dertook the charge of his health; and even the heir
to the throne, representing Majesty itself, did not
think it indecorous to pay him court. The streets
through which he made his entry were thronged by
an enthusiastic people; his outgoings and ingoings
whilst amongst us were minutely chronicled by newspapers; and terms were employed in reference to
him that would be too eulogistic if applied to the
most famous heroes of antiquity. And yet this
general obtained the success which brought him such
unexampled honours by no eminent display of political sagacity or military ability. The enemy against
whom he went out proved to be a secret friend; and
he entered the capital of the kingdom he invaded,
as an English tourist would enter it, in a carriage
and pair. He was victorious solely because he was
regarded by the Italians as the representative of the
doctrines professed and preached by Mazzini.

How comes it, then, that the master is disparaged
whilst the pupil is caressed? That Joseph Garibaldi
is esteemed whilst Joseph Mazzini is abhorred?
We believe there are two reasons for this inconsis-
tency. In the first place, apart from the disavowed
and disproved charge of being a patron of assassina-
tion, Englishmen accuse the triumvir of habitually
inciting others to undertake dangers in which he declines to participate. The accusation is undeniably

true ; but the inference sought to be drawn from the
fact is as invalid as would be an imputation of cowardice against our War Minister for sending a regiment into action whilst he inhumanly smoked his
cigar in Pall Mall. Mr. Mazzini, like the Minister
of War, is a civilian ; and, like him, probably believes
that for thirteenpence-halfpenny a-day a thousand
men may be found better qualified than himself to
shoulder a rifle and endure the fatigues of a cam-
paign ; whilst, without much vanity, he may conscientiously suppose that neither of the thousand
could serve his country so effectually as he by counsel
and direction. In the second place, and chiefly,
Englishmen are unable to appreciate Mazzini, from
their inability to perceive a principle until it becomes
embodied. They must have a personal representative of the qualities they admire, and must see an
idea applied before they venture to approve it. Our
press is never more happy than when it has the opportunity of ridiculing a nation that can be so silly
as to go to war for " an idea ; " and our House of
Commons, generally regarded as an intelligent assembly, is never more unanimous than when it votes
against " abstract questions." Honourable members
are not indisposed to entertain " questions ;" indeed,
they rather like " questions," and flatter themselves
they understand " The Mexican Question," or " The

" Eastern Question," or " The Timbuctoo Question."
But the principle that covers any of these, that com-
prehends it and all similar questions, they resolutely
refuse to discuss and entertain. They regard abstract
resolutions with deeper abhorrence than that with
which a Jew is said to regard pork.

Mr. Mazzini, on the other hand, claims notice as
the originator and champion of certain principles,
which he carries to their extremest consequences.
He has no wish to be considered a statesman in our
sense of the term.   Unlike his countryman Paolo
Sarpi, who preferred waiting for events, and " drawing
" from them the greatest possible profit *for* his ideas,
" to all attempts to determine their course and create
" facts *through* ideas," he aspires to be something more.
He desires to be an Initiator; to be classed, not
among those who, " taking in at one glance all the
" elements, all the forces, actually in operation,
" know how to bring them into play, and to put them
" in a favourable position for drawing from them
" the grandest results which they are capable of
" yielding "—but with them " to whom enthusiasm
" and the energy of conviction communicate the
" power of setting in motion that unused activity,
" that surplus of hidden strength, which exists in the
" men of every age."   In a word, he would create
the future by the force of Ideas.

We respect the men who bring us **principles more than** those who confine themselves to the **consideration of** " questions." **They take** higher **rank in the** hierarchy of benefactors. **But to** ensure **our esteem it** is **necessary their** principles **should be sound. We do not believe those** entertained **by Mr. Maz-** zini **on politics,** literature, **and** art **to be sound. We** agree with **the current notion of** Englishmen **re-** specting their merits; we do so, however, not **because,** like them, we **dislike broad principles, but because** we conceive **the principles to be false. The most** important deduction **Mr. Mazzini makes from his** well-known **tenets is the necessity for the unifi-** cation of **Italy, with Rome as its capital, and the** establishment **of a Republican form of government.** This is the mastering **idea of his life. Herein he has** ever been consistent. **The views indicated in his** earliest publication, **under the pretence of literary** discussion, **he has continued to enunciate ever since—** through **evil report and good; in the press; in con-** versation; in preparing **insurrections; in the day of** his success; **in exile. The triumph of this idea** would, he conceives, **make his** country **once more** great, glorious, and **free. We do not believe this. We** believe **the freedom and** happiness **of a people are not** the result of **their political** institutions, **but that their political** institutions are, in **great degree, the** result of their own temper and aspirations. The Government of no people, left to themselves, can remain, for any length of time, out of harmony with the sum of the wishes and requirements, and deserts, of the governed. Mr. Mazzini cannot be unaware that Rome was once the capital of Italy as well as of the world, and that even then the Peninsular was not united. During the Middle Ages again, at the end of the thirteenth century, the country was split up into independent governments; yet the several States possessed power and enterprise which all Europe could not match. Pisa, Genoa, Venice, Florence were rivals; but they were each great. During the twelfth and thirteenth centuries, as Mr. Mazzini must well know, European commerce was almost entirely in the hands of the Italians. His countrymen were the bankers of Europe, and the great carrying-people between the East and West. The shores of the Mediterranean were lined with their vessels and war-galleys, and the influence of their counsels was felt throughout Christendom. Yet the country was then less united than it is now. The truth is, Italy was formerly great from causes, moral and physical, which no longer exist within her limits. The elements of success are now wanting in her, and all attempts to make her equal her former exalted state by any political changes that can be devised will inevitably result in failure.

Nor does Mr. Mazzini confine his principles to action; he applies them equally to literature and art. In his writings, now in course of publication, his method of application is clearly seen. Literature, with him, is the means to an end, and that end " an " appeal to the youth of Italy to create a country for " themselves by force of arms." He complains that previous to his time writers of the Romantic School devoted themselves to objective art, and not to what he avers to be his sole merit, " declaring themselves " for liberty against oppression." His notions of art, too, are similarly vicious. He is of opinion that the special aim of art is " to excite mankind to reduce " thought to action." Just as English critics would make Art the handmaid of Religion and Morality, he would make her the handmaid of Revolution. Two errors, he tells us, threaten art—the theory that it is an imitation of Nature, and the theory that has created the formula of " Art for art's sake." " The first would deprive it of all spontaneous indi- " vidual life ; the second break the link that binds it " to the universe."

It is scarcely necessary for us to say we differ from Mr. Mazzini's notions of art and literature as widely as we differ from his political principles. He surely mistakes the function of literature, if he would make it a vehicle for direct political action. We hold that to do this would be to degrade literature. During the War of Independence in Germany, people were constantly in the habit of blaming Goethe for not raising his voice against Napoleon, just as the Italian now blames the *literati* of his country for not interrogating " the thought of the epoch in the nation." In opposition to this view, we commend to the attention of Mr. Mazzini, and such as would make literature the vehicle for direct political action, the reply of Goethe, than whom no one in this century better understood the function of literature.* The same eminent writer's observations on the functions of art also may be studied by them with advantage at the same time. Goethe contended, as we do, that art would no longer be art if deprived of an aim and object of its own, and that to deprive it of these would be to deprive it of its legitimate influence and power.

---

* " How could I write songs of hatred without hating ! How could I, to whom culture and barbarism are alone of importance, hate a nation which is among the most cultivated of the earth, and to which I owe so great a part of my own cultivation ? Altogether, national hatred is something peculiar. You will always find it strongest and most violent when there is the lowest degree of culture. But there is a degree where *it vanishes altogether*, and where one stands, to a certain extent, *above* nations, and feels the weal or woe of a neighbouring people, as if it had happened to one's own."—Eckermann's *Conversations with Goethe*, Vol. II., *Oxenford's Translation*.

XIV.

DESCRIPTIVE LITERATURE.

 OFTEN wonder who first left his home for change of scene, or migrated to the seaside; not *on* business,—but *from* business; not for the purpose of residing there,—but as a *bonâ fide* visitor. What were his belongings? Was he a bachelor or a married man? Did he carry his carpet bag, or was he himself carried in a coach, and accompanied by a train of attendants? Was he able to dine upon eight hundred a year, or did he require twice that amount to do so satisfactorily? Whoever and whatever he was, none can justly deny to him the title of great social reformer, or refuse to his now numberless followers the right— when his name shall have been discovered—of erecting an appropriate statue to his memory.

Before his time people resided constantly at home,

and had no desire to leave it. Life with them passed
away without the worry and turmoil of our day, and
change of scene was not so much as thought of for
its own sake. Such is not now the case. There
certainly are men to be found who, like Dr. Johnson,
from choice reside in London all the year, and who
think green lanes to be all very well in their way,
but would consider them greatly improved were they
paved. These, however, are the exceptions. The
vast majority have long since become disciples of our
great social reformer, and cheap and expeditious
travelling is daily increasing their number. All
who have means, and can make opportunity, now
habituate themselves to their annual " run"—spend
a portion of the year away from their every-day occupations—and feel aggrieved if they are prevented
from doing so. All who are able to go, do go.
Some seek the sea-side, some settle amidst the rural
scenery of our home-land, and some wander in foreign countries. Now I do not underrate foreign
travel. On the contrary, I value it very highly ;
agreeing with Bacon, that in the younger sort it is
a part of education; in the elder, a part of experience. But I think its advantages are usually over-
estimated. Home travel, however, is too often
thought commonplace ; and, with the vulgar, an
object is interesting in proportion to its distance or

the difficulty of its attainment. " 'You have *been*
" in France?' said my gentleman, turning quick
" upon me with the most civil triumph in the world.
" So," says the author of " Tristram Shandy," " I
" went straight to my lodgings, put up half a dozen
" shirts and a pair of black silk breeches, and—"
and the " Sentimental Journey" is the result. For
" France" read " North Pole," " Interior of Africa,"
or " Chimborazzo,"—and the scene is taking place
to-day. People crave to see what others have not
seen, to visit where others have not visited. A bewildering desire, which is extending itself amongst
all classes, possesses them to pass by the ordinary
in search of the extraordinary; and many suppose
they find it when they arrive at the uncommon.
By them

" *Omne ignotum* **pro** *magnifico est.*"

Hence they climb the loftiest and most arduous
mountains—penetrate the most impenetrable deserts
—explore the sources of unknown rivers—and then
" turn quick upon you with the most civil triumph
" in the world."

This activity seems to arise from two causes;—
love of scenery, and veneration for the past. For
the exercise of both sentiments England furnishes
abundant scope. She possesses scenes of beauty

matchless in other lands; hills of admirable proportions—smiling pastures—smooth streams—rivers of
sweetest beauty. In *largeness* of scale the scenery
of these islands is admittedly inferior to what is to be
found elsewhere. It can boast no Himalaya Mountains, no Mississippi river, no Niagara Falls. But
it abounds in qualities of which the intellect and
senses never tire; and in the elements of rural beauty
is incomparable. There is, moreover, infinite variety. Britain is not only a country of lawns and
parks and stately avenues. She has wild moorlands
of vast extent, heaths of melancholy aspect, track-
less hills as desolate as can be found elsewhere.
Then, what a coast! Here, lined with cliffs of im-
posing grandeur—bare, rugged, precipitous; there,
masses of blown sand, extending inland for great
distances, form themselves into an endless number of
hills and valleys, whose inner slopes are covered
with luxuriant vegetation. In one direction sub-
merged forests, attesting the power of volcanic forces
in former times; in another, green meadows, or
cornfields, smiling with golden harvests, run down to
the very water's edge—Ceres, as fabled of old, unable to escape the importunities of Neptune. Lack-
ing mountains that crush the senses, and plains that
bewilder, it still possesses the agreeable, happy medium in which alone can be found that feature which

has been named the Picturesque. And yet scores of
persons go abroad for what lies at their very doors,
and is to be found with but very little seeking.
The other day I met, at Ghent, a Londoner who had
distinguished himself by " making a hole in £100,"
and by penetrating as far as Vienna and Prague,
without the knowledge of any continental language.
He was a licensed victualler in search of the picturesque, and had determined upon visiting Prague
because his wife, who accompanied him, had so willed
it. Her only knowledge of that town was derived
from a piece of music termed " **The Battle of Prague;** "
and from some odd association of ideas she had become firmly convinced that Prague was the most
picturesque city in the world. The gentleman " did
" not care much for the mounseers," but with the
scenery everywhere, after he had left these shores,
he expressed himself as being delighted—" nothing
" like it in England, sir !" This was his opinion of
the England he had never seen. As with him, so
with the majority. The view borrows enchantment
from distance, and strangeness in character, customs,
and costume, adds largely to the enjoyment.

The other source of preference for travelling on
the Continent is the belief very generally entertained
of the vast superiority to our own land of other
countries in interesting associations. But historical

and poetical associations are not wanting in England. Where can an Englishman find a country so full of them as his own? The land is pregnant with stirring memories, and nowhere can more striking suggestions be presented to his mind. He may, if he choose, inspect and examine the religious and sepulchral monuments of those who preceded him in the land 1800 years ago—may enter the very caves and holes of the earth which were their homes. He may tread the ground—now, perhaps, waving with cornfields,—under which are engulphed cities which were built, long centuries ago, by Roman hands, inhabited by Roman citizens, and called after Roman names. He may find numberless memorials of his far-off Saxon ancestors, and traces of that invasion which gave them foreign masters. He may wander without impediment through grim fortresses, now slowly crumbling into decay, but which at one time were the habitations of those who pursued

> " —— the good old plan,
> " That they should take who have the power,
> " And they should keep who can."

He cannot fail to be frequently reminded, too, of that bloody contest, which we name Roses War, and which was characterized by as much treachery and shocking barbarity as any that the Continent can boast. Then, again, he will frequently come upon the scene of one or other of those conflicts which took place when **Naseby, Worcester, and** Marston Moor were names as often on **men's lips** as Alma, Inkermann, or Balaclava have been of late. There remain **to** this country more perhaps of **these** monuments than to any other. **We have castles, abbeys,** priories, crosses, and cathedrals in **abund-** ance; each a reminder of other days, each **possessing** its traditional story. In one place will be **pointed** out the room in which **was born** the first **Tudor ;** in another **the royal chamber** " in which is King " Charles's window." Here are the **remains of that** splendid **pile which was erected and richly** endowed **by** William the Conqueror, **in commemoration of the** battle which delivered **over** to him a kingdom ; **there,** those of that other in which the last Stuart **came to** the resolution of flying from **his** indignant subjects. This is the spot where, **for** the last time, stood a **knight** proclaiming himself ready **to** " answer all " **comers** " at tilt and tourney ; **on this,** for the first **time, was the** printing-press set **going on** its errand in England. **These ruins** are the **cast** aurelia shells out of which the nation emerged into her modern existence. Whilst inhabiting these, **her energies** were concentrated upon the nutritive functions, econo- mising her **resources for future use ;** now, her power of active movement is illimitable **and** irresistible.

Some one has said that were all written records of our history destroyed, the chief incidents could yet be ascertained from our language.   In like manner, were we to interpret aright the teachings of one of **these broken walls,** we should have a most instructive lesson, and such a one as is seldom to be found **in books.** Each is a type of the struggle between Old England and **New.   When we** enter it we are conscious that our tread **is on a system,** and that we are surrounded **by an** epoch in stone.   Its situa-**tion is, in** most instances, in harmony with its fallen **condition.**   It is out of the vulgar gaze.   Silence surrounds **it, and to** reach it we have to pick our steps through a thorny path, brushing aside the underwood that has completely choked up the moat **of former times—a solemn** contrast **with** the time **when every** road, for miles around, **led** hitherward **to** the baron's **residence.   Then all was** bustle and activity ; **now, the sound of the** armourer is dumb ; **the inner and outer ward are both** deserted ; the **donjon-keep** has not **been** tenanted for centuries ; " the **voice of the people is heard no more.   The** " stream of Clutha is removed from **its place** by the " **fall of the** walls ; **the thistle** shakes there its lonely " head ; the moss **whistles to the wind.**   Desolate is " the dwelling of Moina."

Washington Irving has recorded the delight ex-

perienced by an American upon beholding, for the
first time, the mouldering ruin of an abbey overrun
with ivy. He was from a land to which time had
left no such legacies. What would not America
give in exchange for these heirlooms of the race? for
what is birth without its proper pedigree? Even a
horse, with ever so valuable qualities, has infinitely
more worth to most eyes when his pedigree is trace-
able to illustrious ancestors. You treat the descendant of " Hero " or " Flying Childers," though degraded to the plough, with greater regard than his
work-mate, notwithstanding his inferior qualities.
And that picture you have in your gallery, and on
which you set great store, would it be worth so much
by half—nay, faded and dimmed as it is, would you
even give it house-room—did you not possess in
your *escritoire* convincing proof of its being the production of a master? Or, to ask a more pertinent
question, would you, my lord, set so high a value
upon yourself as you do, were you not encouraged
by that curious *tree* that hangs against the wall of
your library? Well, these ruins of Old England,
scattered over the land, are the genealogical tree of
our race. Not the truest pedigree, for that is to be
looked for elsewhere, but symbols of splendid reality.
The origin of the sentiment is not obscure.

There is, it would appear, in the mind of man, a

principle which prompts him to regard, with some
degree of pleasure and veneration, these relics of
departed days, or the scene of any remarkable by-
gone transaction.   And this principle, whether natural or inherited, or to whatever cause due, is
found to be so prevalent as to be esteemed universal.
It is named the sentiment of Veneration.   Its birth
has been traced to a lofty source, and many an
encomium has, at different times, been bestowed
upon it by writers not unknown to fame.   But an
examination of the claims upon which their eulogies
are based will indubitably lead to the discovery that
its descent is not to be boasted of—its parentage by
no means so honourable as is represented.   At the
best, Veneration is but the daughter of Wonder and
Fear.   The savage, we are told, when first he beheld
the steam-ship doing battle with the winds of heaven,
and overcoming, as appeared to him, the laws of the
Great Spirit, was filled with wonder, and bent the
knee in reverence.   Afterwards, however, when the
novelty of the spectacle had worn itself out—when
ignorance had given place to knowledge—he con-
templated the same object with the utmost uncon-
cern.   Wonder vanishes at the approach of knowledge; when there is no longer any fear, veneration
also takes its departure.   But although the sentiment
springs from no such high lineage as is mostly

claimed for it, it yet forms an important element in human nature, and is extremely beneficial in human affairs. This it is which makes men conservative of the past, and cautious of change in the future ; forms the basis of chivalrous loyalty ; and is a prime source of all religious feeling. It is seen in democratic states equally with aristocratic, and if in the former the objects upon which it is exercised differ, it is not for that the less visible there. Things are mutable, and those now reverenced will one day disappear, but only to be succeeded by others. Reverence itself is seldom lost.

To this sentiment, love of fame is the complement. There have never been wanting a few select minds who have declined subjecting themselves to either of these influences, and have proved themselves superior to both. But the majority of mankind have, in all ages, shown themselves not otherwise than solicitous to set apart certain opinions and objects as suitable for their veneration ; and to supply the demand created by this exigency, there has been no lack of candidates. Ambition, that infirmity of noble minds, is ever as ready to offer " something that the world " will not readily let die," as the world is to receive what is offered for its acceptance. Thus, we see, men have perpetually striven to transmit their names to times far distant from their own. With toil and

care they have erected monuments which they imagined are to endure through all ages. In every case
the end in view is the same—the having themselves
in remembrance hereafter.

To England the times gone by have bequeathed a
prodigious number of such legacies, and in no nation
has reverence for the past taken deeper root than in
ours. The feeling manifests itself in a vast variety
of ways. We call our country " Old" England, and
are proud of her age. When we typify the Englishman, do we not delight to do so by picturing him as
a gentleman somewhat advanced in years? Are we
not predisposed to bestow a larger share of support
upon an old-established " institution " than upon its
newly-started competitor, however favourable the
auspices under which the latter sprang into existence,
however satisfactory its guaranty of success may be?
Our houses of business which have been " established
" for upwards of a century," take care to advertise
that fact, and they find their account therein. The
bar parlour of the Old Three Crowns is much more
likely to be found filled on an evening than the
smoking-room of the New Inn on the opposite side
of the way, notwithstanding the fact of the bever-
ages to be obtained at the latter being, in all respects,
equal to those of its rival.

Old age with us is allowed to count honours,
where youth is not permitted the privilege.

The same sentiment has a demonstrative influence on Modern Art, where it shows itself in a tendency to look upon Age and Decay as a legitimate field for the display of artistic skill, and to regard them as types of the beautiful, or at least as useful accessories to Beauty. Hence a man in rags is thought to be a much more interesting subject for the pencil than another in goodly raiment; a rude thatched cottage, with children, dirty and in tatters, playing in the adjoining kennel, is chosen for representation in preference to a decent dwelling-house; a narrow, sombre street, composed of gable-ends, tottering, irregular, and many-coloured by the hand of Time, is held in greater esteem than ever so stately a terrace of modern mansions—although this is built without an architectural blemish, and with an elegance to which that has no pretensions. Especially in regard of mediæval ruins, those glorious examples of grandeur in decay, does this tendency display itself. To light upon "a really fine old ruin" will an artist travel many a league, over highway and byway, through unfrequented parts, enduring much fatigue; and when at length he reaches the object of his search, the pleasure he experiences compensates every toil. He "jots down the really fine old ruin," carries it away in his portfolio, and, if he is a master in his art, will find a purchaser as ready to buy as he to sell.

This disposition to rank decay as a type of the beautiful is, I presume, a peculiarity of modern Art. We do not find it to have existed in ancient Greece. She, too, looked back with reverence to the Past, and saw there much to admire. But it was courage, strength, and length of days—never decay. To be beautiful was with her to be young, fresh, joyous— above all, to be young. And in modern Art it has been developed only in late years. The ruin has not always been considered an object of beauty, and certainly at the beginning of its decline not even an object of interest.

A not uninteresting subject for inquiry would be, when did it first of all come to be regarded as such?

The ordinary mind is disposed to look upon the time of the origination of any social change which is destined seriously to affect posterity as one of tumult, anxiety, and confusion. It overlooks the fact that those who were spectators of the event in its birth had not the same means of seeing its magnitude as we who are witnesses of it in its results. It would be an error to suppose that the western voyage of Columbus, which gave his age a new world —or the Renaissance of Art and Religion—or the invention of printing—affected men in the manner, and to the extent, we are liable to imagine, and think it ought to have affected them. The actors

are ever too near their action to see its effect. Besides, things are gradual in their processes; men, in
time, get used to all exceptional conditions, and
forget to consider them exceptional. It is only the
Partingtons of society who wonder how it was possible for the ancients to " carry on," seeing they had
no bread and butter, no tea and coffee, no gas, no
tobacco and seltzer water, no railways and electric
telegraphs, no lucifer matches and penny newspapers.

Thus it fares with our representative old ruins.
When the castles were dismantled by order of Parliament, " lest they might be held by disaffected per-
" sons," the event excited, in the contemporary
mind, ideas and emotions by no means kin to those
we are apt to imagine. To us, at this distance of
time, that would appear to have been a period of
melancholy and universal excitement, when the tenants of the strong fortress migrated to the modern
dwelling-house; and equally so that other, when the
time-honoured old abbey was abandoned, when the
performance of matins was rudely interrupted, when
the monk had to abandon his teaching, and the lay-
brother his gardening operations, all because the
king's grace had seen fit to change his wife and his
religious opinions. But even these events were soon
regarded as matters of course, and men went on their
way to follow, as usual, their several avocations.

Castle and abbey, widowed of their grandeur, lay unheeded, their chief importance consisting in their capacity to furnish material for the erection of other and meaner buildings.

A long time elapsed before they were looked upon in any other light. Scott, it undoubtedly was, who elevated them to rank as objects of veneration. He it was who, by giving the general mind a turn in the direction of mediæval antiquities, first secured for these souvenirs of Old England the interest which they now inspire. Others before him may have felt an archæological concern in them, but he it was who popularized the feeling, and gave it additional stimulus, by endowing them with poetic beauty. Thenceforth they became sanctified relics of chivalric and monastic glories. At the same time it was that the pursuit of scenery as a diversion, and the description of scenery as a form of literary activity, first became fashionable in England.

So universal among us has view-hunting now become, and, as a consequence, so numerous are the interpreters of Nature, that the present generation has difficulty in believing that little more than half a century has elapsed since descriptive literature began to be in vogue. A correspondent of a literary journal, in giving an account of a curious duodecimo volume upon which he had lighted, supplies us almost with the very year. The work consisted of two letters, which had been privately reprinted by Wordsworth from " The Morning Post," and the blank leaf contained, in the poet's handwriting, the following passage :—" A relative of mine, about thirty years " older than myself, being congratulated on the great " advantage she must have had in being brought up in " the romantic county of Cumberland, said, ' Don't " ' think about it ; when I was young there were no " ' lakes and mountains.' " The date on the flyleaf is " Rydal Mount, August 18, 1845." Wordsworth was born in 1770. His youth may therefore be considered as having been spent in 1790 ; so that if we take thirty from that year, we shall have 1760 as the proximate date at which the picturesque was unknown in this country. People of education and culture, presumably occupying the same rank in life as those who now go into ecstasies in the presence of fine scenery, had then not begun to regard lakes and mountains otherwise than they are now regarded by untutored rustics. Sensibility to the external forms of nature is, indeed, of modern growth. Among the ancients that people who of all nations were endued with perceptions of beauty the most intense have left us in their literature no descriptions of scenery, except by way of simile, intended to heighten our interest in human action and events. Although they deified

Nature, they had no sense of what we now term the picturesque: the feeling manifested by the moderns towards scenery being by them transferred to the " spirit " which they imagined presided in mountain, wood, and stream.*   It has been thought that the founders of their cities could not have been without a sense of beauty in the selection they made of the several sites.   But although the ruins are now in perfect harmony with the scenery amidst which they are situate, the original builders were influenced in their choice by no considerations of beauty, but were guided solely by considerations of strength.   They had no more notion of being picturesque than the Dutch had whilst forming their canals.   The authors of republican Rome, too, who were perfectly ignorant that the representation of external nature, either by painting or by narrative, would give pleasure or be of interest to others, have left us nothing whereby we are able to discover what sort of impression was made upon them by the scenery with which they were surrounded.   To them, as to their Greek predecessors, the work of man's hand was more interesting than the bend of a river, the bosom of a lake, or the snow-capped head of a mountain.

---

* " *Pinea brachia cum trepidant audio canticulum Zephyri.*"— Martianus Capella, quoting some unknown writer.

Representation of scenery first came into fashion in a civilization similar to our own, landscape painting, according to Pliny, having been invented in the time of Augustus by S. Tadius.* It will be remarked that, among the Romans as among ourselves, almost simultaneously with this desire for the representation of external nature arose the taste for antiquities. Just as people began to see beauty in Gothic art and Gothic architecture, hitherto despised, at the time when they first felt pleasure in landscape, so in Rome, within similar circumstances, there sprang up a race of collectors, among whom, we are told, was C. J. Cæsar, who bought up paintings, of old masters (*tabulas operis antiqui*), bronzes, engraved gems, &c. with as much avidity as the most enthusiastic connoisseur of our own day. The taste fell, however, with the Empire. During the middle ages what we may call the sense of scenery was lost; and in our elder writers, at the period of

---

* " S. Tadio, divi Augusti ætate qui *primus* instituit amœnissimam parietum picturam; villas, et porticus, et topiaria opera, lucos, nemora, collis, piscinas, euripos, amnis, littora, qualia quis optaret; varias ibi obambulantium species aut navigantium, terra que villas adeuntium asellis aut vehiculis: jam piscantis, aucupantis aut venantis aut etiam vindemiantis."—Pliny., H. N., xxxv. 10 (Jan's Edition). The old reading for S. Tadius was *Ludius.*

U

the Renaissance, there is no trace of its having been recovered. **Shakespeare** has been praised for the beauty **of his** descriptive passages, and the absence **of stage** scenery in his time has been given as the reason for his excellence in this respect. References **to the** plays, however, will clearly show that even **he has** never attempted a sustained description of the outer **world.** **The** famous passage in "Lear," **with reference to** Dover cliff, may be taken as an example and **a proof.** **Here we find the** allusions entirely subjective, **having** reference to sensations naturally produced **in** the mind by vast height.   If we come nearer our own time, we shall find the same lack of the feeling.   The "great" people who performed the Grand Tour never thought of putting their heads out of the carriage **window** to admire **scenes that have since** become famous for their beauty **or** grandeur.   They went to see man and **his ways, and it did not** occur to them to record **their** impressions of the country through which they travelled **to** find him.

Mr. Carlyle, who deprecates description of scenery **for its own sake,** and disapproves **of** "euphuistic "gallantries with **nature,"** **supposes that** first in the "Sorrows **of Werter" the practice came** decisively into use.   **A writer in the "North** British Review," on the **other hand, claims for** Patrick Graham, author of " Sketches of Picturesque Scenery on the " Southern Confines of Perthshire," 1806, the honour of having been the founder of our British school of professional tourists and describers of Nature. There can be no doubt, indeed, that view-hunting had its origin somewhere at the end of the last century, for it must have been rampant at the time when Dr. Syntax's tour appeared to burlesque it. The Waverley Novels undoubtedly increased the mania, and the love of out-door life and the spirit of adventure which distinguish the English seem likely to perpetuate it among us. Since the time of Scott, the number of descriptive books, in poetry and prose, is almost too great for calculation. I might give chapters of " euphuistic gallantries " (which, for any value they possess, may well have been put into a page), and so make a little book a big one; but what need is there of examples? Every modern reader is well acquainted with the school.

View-hunting has been named a vice; and in no way, except by rantings on female loveliness, has more vain admiration been thrown away than in speaking of the beauties of Nature. It has been said with truth that this over-admiration both of nature and woman is derived from the young;— that is, it is founded, not on facts, but on a conjecture of facts, before the facts have been ascertained.

When the conjecture is discovered to be wrong, the sentiments which have been based on it ought properly to be corrected; but, unfortunately, this is not done, and the false idea is kept, cherished, and transmitted. View-hunting and view-describing, however, are useful—in a measure even necessary—just as literary criticism is useful. Since you have not the good fortune to be possessed of that Eastern carpet, seated on which you might, by a wish, transport yourself whither you desire, and thus judge of each scene for yourself, you must suffer yourself to be guided or directed by others. It is to be hoped, however, that the view-describer will, in his rhapsodies, strictly confine himself within proper limits, and not pretend to derive from his pursuit more than it is obviously capable of yielding. He should be careful not to discredit by his extravagancies the only form of literature the moderns can claim as their own invention.

THE END.

CHISWICK PRESS:—PRINTED BY WHITTINGHAM AND WILKINS, TOOKS COURT, CHANCERY LANE.

LECTURES ON POETRY

DOYLE

DELIVERED

BEFORE THE UNIVERSITY OF OXFORD

1868

BY

SIR F. H. DOYLE, Bart., M.A., B.C.L.

Late Fellow of All Souls'

PROFESSOR OF POETRY

𝕷𝖔𝖓𝖉𝖔𝖓

MACMILLAN AND CO.

1869

OXFORD:

BY T. COMBE, M.A., E. B. GARDNER, E. P. HALL, AND H. LATHAM, M.A.,

PRINTERS TO THE UNIVERSITY.

PREFACE.

In giving these Lectures to the world, I believe I am only taking a usual step, and one that is expected of Oxford Professors, more or less, by that University. I need only then ask my readers to bear in mind that they are lectures, to be heard, as ancient Pistol says, 'with ears'—not subtle disquisitions to be meditated upon in a quiet study. They have therefore been thrown into a key more rhetorical and familiar than I should otherwise have adopted, and are rather, to use Aristotle's phrase, epideictic orations than argumentative essays. I must add that for five-and-twenty years and more, I have done nothing as an orator, except to mumble now and then a few words, against my will, at a wedding breakfast. It follows that these compositions must be, in point of tone and style, necessarily tentative. Indeed, one reason for not putting off publication till a greater number of them had heaped themselves up, is, that the sooner any corrigible defects and mistakes are pointed out to me (and

I dare say I shall find critics obliging enough to meet
my wishes in that respect), the less delay will there be, on
my part, in reconsidering the whole subject, and in mend-
ing, so far as I can, the error of my ways.

INAUGURAL LECTURE.

LECTURE I.

INAUGURAL LECTURE.

W<small>HEN</small> any one steps into the place of a poet and critic such as Mr. Arnold, he naturally feels somewhat awkward in undertaking his new functions. 'If it had not been,' he fancies his hearers saying to themselves, 'for the inconvenient restrictions by which this Professorship is hampered, we might have kept, with all the tact and power superadded which arises out of a long experience, our man of genius. Now, however, he is forced, for us at least, into an unnecessary silence, in order that another may speak—another, who has, no doubt, much of his business yet to learn, and who, even when he has learnt it, is not likely to give out anything half so good as that to which his predecessor has accustomed us.'

And yet, perhaps, if we suppose the founder of this Chair to have been actuated, in limiting its tenure, by reason and not by caprice; there is something, even

B

though it may involve temporary failures and occasional disappointments, to be said for such a limitation.   Criticism, to speak roughly, for I am not aiming
at any logical division, is of two kinds—the criticism of
knowledge, and the criticism of sympathy.   The critics
who know, of whom Aristotle may be taken as the type
and representative, judge mainly by the intellect; and
any great leader of that school, if he be, in his degree,
worthy to follow in the steps of his master, throws,
like the noon-day sun, a broad and equal illumina-
tion over all the departments of his subject alike.
But as the lovelier tints of colouring, and the more
pathetic lights, are due to those narrowing rays which
fasten upon their own domain, so is there a criticism
of the sympathies specially worth having, wherever
those sympathies are specially interested.   It therefore
might be not unreasonably hoped, and not unwisely
attempted, to accumulate the most delicate insights,
and the liveliest sensibilities of different minds, so
that, converging from opposite quarters, they should
coalesce into a perfect whole.   For an unbroken succession of Aristotles it is vain to hope.   But thus,
it might be possible to build up, limb by limb, a
great body of doctrine—of doctrine, keen with that
intensity, which the wide critic is apt to want, and

all-embracing in that width, which no passionate critic is likely to attain to, unless he be one of those rare men, whom the world waits for through centuries of expectation. In this manner it ought to result, that the poetry of thought and the poetry of passion—that which belongs to the present and that which is reflected from the past, that which is of home growth, and that which rises up among other habits of thought, and takes its shape from a different national character—should, in their turns, be adequately interpreted and discussed.

If this way of looking at the office of Poetry Professor, and at the objects which he has to set before himself, be, under ordinary circumstances I mean, a right and convenient one, he should, I think, take the earliest opportunity (as I hope to do on the present occasion) of opening himself frankly and freely to his audience. It seems to me therefore desirable, before I enter into any details of criticism, before I praise one poet or disparage another, that my general view as to the nature of the poetical imagination, as to its uses and its dangers, as to the manner in which it acts for itself, and reacts upon the character at large, should be known to those for whom such criticisms of detail are intended. All this I believe to be desirable, not only for you who hear, but also for me who speak. These questions go so deep into the roots of life, they have been so often disputed about, and still remain so incompletely solved, that I, for one, am not going to dogmatize thereon. I can but state plainly, and without affectation, what I think and feel. I can but promise that, being at least as anxious to learn as I am willing to teach, the objections which will rise up against any theories of mine, as they have risen up against the theories of men to whom I should not dream of comparing myself, shall be examined (if I know my own mind) with an attention unvexed by prejudice, and only eager for the truth.

So complete, indeed, is the discordance of sentiment, as to all these matters, between rival instructors, who alike claim the highest authority, that even before entering upon the actual subject of this address, I have to go a step back, and to fight, as it seems, for my very existence here, by undertaking the defence of Poetry itself. Against whom you will say, *Quis vituperavit?* Ay, that is the question; not against men up to their necks in business—stockbrokers, bankers, and the like—not against the family of that typical clerk—

'Foredoomed his father's soul to cross,
  Who pens a stanza when he should engross,'

but against writers of the highest genius, who could, as far as we can judge, equip, out of their rich and powerful imaginations, an ordinary poet or so, without much feeling the loss. Against such high authorities, in a word, as Mr. Carlyle and Mr. Ruskin. I am not clear at this moment whether Mr. Carlyle has ever put his hatred of verse-making on record, in any formal shape; but it may be gathered from any one of his writings. Everybody knows how he confides, at uncertain intervals, to the eternities and immensities—his bitter regret, that men of noble faculties, like Tennyson and Browning, should have become entangled, under some evil star, in the meshes of rhyme, instead of devoting themselves to —I do not exactly know what—but to something or anything else. Mr. Ruskin, however, in one of his most characteristic passages, announces himself to the universe as admitting but two orders of poets. Both of these, according to him, must be first-rate in their range, though their range be different, and with poetry second-rate in quality no one ought to be allowed to trouble mankind. 'There is quite enough of the best,' says he, 'much more than we can read or enjoy,

in the length of a single life, and it is a literal wrong
or sin to encumber us with inferior work.' 'I have
no patience,' he now proceeds (by way of encourag-
ing and inspiring the bards of the future), 'with the
apologies made by young pseudo-poets, that they believe that there is some good in what they have
written; some good—if there is not all good, there is
no good. If they ever hoped to do better, why do
they trouble us now?' If these views were correct,
the first thing to strike me in this place, would be
that a conscientious Poetry Professor must have a
dreadful time of it. His mission he must look upon
as wholly negative; his motto could only be, 'Preven-
tion is better than cure.' His duty would summon
him to rise up early and late take rest, to run hither
and thither, saying to this undergraduate, 'Writing
for the Newdegate? Have you no principles?' To
that bachelor of arts, 'What! at your age contend-
ing for the triennial Religious Poem? Do you not
know that you are guilty of a literal sin?' He must
consider himself, in short, elected for the purpose of
proctorizing generally the haunts of song, and of hunting up meditated stanzas, in the act of concoction, like
an Irish exciseman on the track of an illicit still.

Happily for me, I do not feel bound to incur any

such onerous responsibilities. I differ entirely from every one of the sentences quoted above, and the very last position, which I should think of taking up, would be that of a critical Canute, who plants his foot upon the brink of the advancing age, and says to the rising tide of genius, as it rolls shoreward under an irresistible impulse from within, 'You know you should not come here.'

I have said that Mr. Carlyle and Mr. Ruskin are possessed of rich, I might have added of almost inexhaustible, imaginations; I suspect, however—and it makes them all the greater if I am right in my conjecture—that for neither of their minds is it absolutely the dominant or master faculty. Now I think we shall find, that whenever this is the case, whenever other gifts and talents (equally admirable, perhaps,) have the power, and, indeed, in some sort, the right to struggle against the rule of the formative imagination, the result is not a genuine poet, at least not a genuine poet of the normal type; but a thinker, or a rhetorician, or a critic in verse. One test of this I believe to be, that when such a man has recourse to poetry, that he may embody and communicate what he thinks and feels; he finds himself moving, no matter with what degree of vigour and energy, in

an element which is not his most natural one; his
thoughts do not flow as freely as they should; his
metaphors do not kindle and rush upon him with their
usual affluence and splendour. He differs, in short,
from the real singers by this, that for him the pressure
of rhythm and the law of measured words weighs down
like a fetter, instead of uplifting as a wing. Hence a
certain distrust of poetry itself; hence, unconsciously,
I dare say, something like a contemptuous bitterness
against smaller men, who, amid the stumbling-blocks
and intricacies which have half baffled their superiors,
go twittering about, more comfortable, and more at
home, than, in the opinion of the giants, they have any
business to be.

Setting, however, all this aside, and taking Mr.
Ruskin's utterances for what they are worth, without
attempting to explain their origin, let us examine them
in turn, and endeavour to ascertain their real value.

First, Mr. Ruskin admits only two orders of poets.
Of the higher order, he names Homer, Dante, Shakespeare; of the lower, Wordsworth, Tennyson, Keats.
Nothing can be better; but how is he to get his
chosen ones? It seems to me that what he desires
is to gather the perfect fruit without any blossoms
competing beforehand; without any previous rise or

struggle of the sap. He may have been somehow
or other clothed by Apollo with a special mission
to move about among undeveloped rhymesters, and to
pronounce at once, by the help of some diviner instinct, 'This poet-grub is a pseudo-grub, be careful
that his wings are cut hereafter. This one again is of
royal spirit, let him be put into a royal cell; feed
him upon honey-dew; make him drink the milk of
Paradise, and train him up, without any disturbance
from importunate rivals, into a bard proper.' But
unless something of this kind can be done (as bees in a
difficulty, under the impulse of their unerring instinct,
fix upon the very one they want, out of a multitude of
seemingly undistinguishable little creatures, and feed
it up into an unexceptionable queen), we must, I fear,
be content to take our poets as they arise, according
to the methods in which nature usually supplies them.

Now, we all know the story of Brummel's valet coming
down-stairs with an unshapely mass of crumpled neck-
cloths under his arm; and how, on being asked what
on earth he was about? he replied, not without a
tincture of becoming pride, 'These are our failures.'
Meanwhile, the successful tie above was, I may say,
the poet of muslin, a consummation and a flower which
had emerged out of some thirty dishevelled existences.

Or, to take another illustration, if you go into a
china manufactory, you may see the workman carefully
shaping, out of the same raw material, bowls, and jugs,
and vases, but the form of this one is not perfect, the
paste of that other is too thin to stand the trial of
fire.   But come, here is a third; surely that will do?
No, not quite yet.   There is a half imperceptible flaw
somewhere, which renders it unfit to bear the required
stress and strain.   And thus they are all of them
mercilessly kneaded up again into chaos, till the eye
and hand of the artist have taught themselves to work
in harmony together, and the structure, sufficient at
last, receives that delicate texture, and imbibes those
glowing colours, which often last on without a blemish,
when bulkier and stronger, and apparently more important productions have rotted, or crumbled, or rusted
into ruin.   I recollect standing at Worcester long
ago, amid work that was thus going on, and saying
to myself, in rather a melancholy mood, 'This is the
way in which Nature gets her poets.   She has to mal-
treat rather savagely a great deal of very respectable
clay in the process, but I make no doubt that the clay,
sooner or later, finds its proper place in some other
condition: and, after all, THE POET IS THERE.'

Of course I must not be taken as meaning seriously

to say that this is the actual method according to which illustrious men are compounded and turned out of the laboratory of Nature. What I do mean is, I trust, sufficiently obvious, the rather that it has often enough been insisted on before—I mean that they belong to their time and are but specimens selected out of a multitude which clusters around them. A thousand influences cooperate with, a thousand accidents combine to impress each original mind, and nearly the same influences cooperate with, and nearly the same accidents combine to impress myriads of other minds and other temperaments, separated from the nobler ones by narrower or broader lines of demarcation. I hope I may say it without irreverence, 'they that run in the race run all, but one only receiveth the prize.' Mr. Ruskin would forbid the race. Is he sure that, having done so, he could always secure the prize for the most deserving? The very great are apt sometimes in youth to outgrow their strength, to exhibit more of struggle and contortion and awkwardness than some symmetrical rival, who is a better master of his genius, because his genius was never born to rise so high, and therefore never strives and ferments with such irregular and intermitting power. All this, however, has been brought home to the feelings and common-

sense of mankind by the world-famous story of the
Ugly Duck, so that I need not enlarge upon the
subject. I will content myself with reminding Mr.
Ruskin, that even if he could succeed in establishing
his prohibitory decrees, and in beating down free-trade
so far as poetry is concerned, he might still find himself
self-baffled in the end, by the defeat of his own object,
and the suppression of his own swan.

The second proposition to which Mr. Ruskin demands our assent is this: that as there is more first-
rate poetry than can be read or enjoyed in the length
of a single life, the attention of the world ought to
be concentrated upon that, and the lyres of all meaner
minstrels impounded at once, as you take away a gun
from a poacher. Whether this be quite the case,
unless he include in his *corpus poetarum* that huge
Calmuck Epic, of which every polite person among
the Calmucks is expected to know by heart forty-eight
books, at least, out of the three or four hundred which
lie open to his memory, I do not think it necessary
to inquire, because it is wholly irrelevant to the
matter in hand. He himself has told us, elsewhere,
with his usual eloquence, that the artist (and it really
matters not a jot whether such artist be poet, painter,
sculptor, or musician) becomes great, and earns his

glory, by being the man of men, the contemporary among contemporaries in his own day. He embodies their aspirations, he interprets their vague yearnings, he soothes their sorrows, he gives a voice to the dumb struggle of their passions, he lives, as they do, in the life of the present, instead of striving to create a future as yet unfelt by them, or to reawaken a past which they have forgotten. Now the complicated influences, which act upon our own time, may be less noble and less fruitful than those which acted upon the fellow-citizens of Dante or of Shakespeare, but still they have a nobility which belongs to themselves, and are entitled to bear their own natural fruit. This again brings us back to what I said before, that we must get our poets as we can, according to the methods which nature is determined to employ.

There is a dismal theory of the universe, that all the uncountable suns throughout space are smouldering down, gradually, but surely, into one perpetual night. More cheerful astronomers, however, are to be found, who encourage a hope that this is not altogether so; that what seems to us a void, is filled everywhere with dormant seeds of being—with, as it were, a diffused and impalpable vapour of heat and light and energy. So that everywhere, the great stars perish not, but are endowed with mysterious powers for drawing forth, and condensing, and assimilating to their own essence, the spirit of universal life which lies floating around them wherever they go; and for repairing, in this manner, the overflowings of incessant waste, from fountains of everlasting renovation. To this movement (if there be such a movement) of the heavens through space, we can perhaps liken the progress of Poetry through Time. At one season it may rejoice as a giant to run its course, in harmony with noble materials of inspiration, and with the heart of some great age; at another, it may have to toil across poorer and thinner regions of thought. But always, whether the element in which it moves be rich or poor, it is driven, by the law of its existence, to get as much life as it can for itself out of the surrounding atmosphere, or else to starve and die.

It is therefore idle to talk of the great writers of old, as being enough for the world, and that without any addition to their numbers. Men of mature age may return to them with delight, and interest themselves by observing how and where the poets who enchanted their boyhood approach to, and how and where they fall short of these, the acknowledged masters of their common art. But there is a yearning instinct in the youth of each generation, the mother, I believe, of all true poetry, which seeks ever to find in the songs which it loves and dwells upon, the reflection of its own passions and the echo of its own thoughts. In proportion as those passions are worth reflecting, and those thoughts are worth echoing, in that proportion, I apprehend, does the poetry of any particular time or country establish itself among the lasting possessions of mankind; but whether it be ephemeral or whether it be immortal, *have it you must.*

We now come to the remarkable dictum that unless the poetry of any poet be all good, it is none of it good. Surely this is a hard saying, and the lantern of Diogenes must be put into requisition, if we hope to find a writer of verses who is fit to live. Is all Shakespeare good? is all Homer good? is all Dante good? He must be an unflinching partizan who could answer these questions in the affirmative. Even, however, if we put aside such Di Majores, as soaring, in a region of their own, beyond the reach of criticism, I, for one, am not prepared to give up Lochiel and the Battle of the Baltic, the Last Man, and O'Connor's Child, and the Mariners of England, and some twenty other of Campbell's odes, because he wrote much hardly above mediocrity, and not a little which is hopelessly below par. I am not prepared to blot out the story of Margaret, and Lucy Gray, and Tintern Abbey, and the countless exquisite compositions which must occur to all who hear me, because Wordsworth was once ill-inspired enough to write, in honour of the Border damsel who saved her lover by the sacrifice of her own life, some flat, poor stanzas, which begin thus—

> 'Sweet Ellen Irwin, when she sat
>   Upon the braes of Kirtle,
> Was lovely as a Grecian maid
>   Adorned with wreaths of myrtle.'

And that on Scottish ground, too, and with the passionate music of the old lyrical cry ringing in his ears—

> 'I wish I were where Helen lies;
> Night and day on me she cries;
> Oh that I were where Helen lies,
>   On fair Kirkonnel lea.
>
> Curst be the heart that thought the thought,
> And curst the hand that fired the shot,
> When in my arms Burd Helen dropt,
>   And died to rescue me.
>
> Oh, think na ye my heart was sair,
> When my love dropt down and spak nae mair;
> I laid her down wi' mickle care
>   On fair Kirkonnel lea.

As I went down the water side,
None but my foe to be my guide,
None but my foe to be my guide,
  On fair Kirkonnel lea,
I lighted down my sword to draw,
I hacked him in pieces sma',
  On fair Kirkonnel lea.

I would my grave were growing green,
A winding-sheet drawn o'er my e'en,
And I in Helen's arms were lying
  On fair Kirkonnel lea.

I wish I were where Helen lies;
Night and day on me she cries;
And I am weary of the skies
  Since my love died for me.'

Now it may be said that I am dissecting words somewhat captiously: this might be so, if I thought Mr. Ruskin any nearer the truth in the spirit of these criticisms, than he is in the letter of them. As to their form, that, no doubt, is comparatively unimportant.

When he says that poetry not first-rate adds altogether to human weariness, in a most uncomfortable manner, I may imagine that I catch the tones of a famous voice, whose natural accent is a Scottish one—a voice which belongs not so much to Mr. Ruskin as to an elder if not a better dogmatizer. I may think that even if Mr. Ruskin be the appointed heir of our well-known Chelsea Elijah, it might have

been more discreet to wait, before wrapping himself
in the familiar mantle, until the prophet in possession had let it drop. But I am quite willing to
acknowledge that a man may state his case crudely
and violently, and yet be right in the main. Can we
say this, however, in the present instance? Honestly,
I think not. After all, people must be educated, or
must educate themselves, through the capacities they
have, and not through those which they have not.
Accordingly, one boy cannot write a letter to a school-
fellow without scribbling horses, and huntsmen, and
little wiry terriers, all over the paper; another steals
down in the grey of the morning, with his nightgown
still on, to pick out tunes upon the pianoforte before
it is wanted for those inevitable scales; a third, in
my day, used to know Marmion and the Bride of
Abydos, now he knows the Idylls of the King by
heart, and delights himself with flabby imitations of
Tennyson, or Byron, or Scott. Now, if you say to the
first of these lads, 'You will never become a Raphael
or a Titian, and therefore never let me hear of your
touching a pencil again;' to the second, 'Do you
suppose you can hereafter rival Beethoven or Mozart?
keep therefore away from the pianoforte, or consequences which I should deplore will be the result;'

and to the third, 'You are not a Shakespeare—no, nor even a Tennyson—therefore, if ever you stumble on a rhyme again, you must instantly be flogged;' you would, in my opinion, be going altogether the wrong way to work. Instead of clearing the mind, as you intend, for the ordinary purposes of life, you only sour the temper and darken the understanding with the dust and smoke of an extinguished faculty.

Leave, then, the young verse-makers alone; some of them, not always those whose apparent promise first meets the eye, are about to stand forth as the genuine poets of the on-coming time. In others, the impulse will gradually wear itself out, but not until it has imparted to the intellect a certain elasticity and glow of colour, which tends to heighten its attractiveness, and to increase its general power. But there is a third class, not usually of great importance, members of which, nevertheless, are lifted every now and then by the force of circumstances, and under the pressure of awakened passion, out of and above themselves; so that we get high poetry from men who are not really high poets, and owe more than one of those

'Jewels, five words long,
That on the stretched forefinger of old Time
Sparkle for ever——'

to writers, either wholly unknown, or at least comparatively obscure. For instance, what have we to do with Colonel Lovelace? He was a gallant soldier, without question, famous for personal beauty among his contemporaries, able, popular, and accomplished; but so were many others then, who are now totally forgotten. If the times had been smooth, he would have gone on glittering at the Court of Charles I, and polishing up his love ditties, till he got tired of that work, with very little interest for us. But the times were not smooth. Civil war swept down as a sword, cutting family ties and old affections asunder. Then came the partings, 'such as press the life out from young hearts'—the despairing appeals from sisters and sweethearts and mothers and wives, encountered with a resistance equally despairing on the part of brothers and lovers and husbands and sons. And I say that the spirit of England is stronger, and the literature of England richer even unto this day, because Colonel Lovelace was able to stand forth, for Puritan and Loyalist alike, out of the multitude of gentlemen and men of honour—to stand forth and fix in living words that answer to such appeals, which has to be given by all true men, and accepted by all true women, as implacable and final for evermore:—

'Tell me not, sweet, I am unkind,
   That from the nunnery
Of thy chaste breast and quiet mind
   To war and arms I fly.

True, a new mistress now I chase,
   The first foe in the field,
And with a stronger faith embrace
   A sword, a horse, a shield.

Yet this inconstancy is such
   As thou, too, shalt adore;
I could not love thee, dear, so much,
   Loved I not honour more.'

A manly sentiment indeed, certain to live on with the English language in its own manly words—words not unworthy to rank close up with that first great utterance of unselfish public duty, which yet speaks to the soul of man across the silence of three thousand years —

εἷς οἰωνὸς ἄριστος, ἀμύνεσθαι περὶ πάτρης.

But observe, if Colonel Lovelace's verse-making tendencies had been sternly repressed, this poem would never have seen the light. He is rather a voluminous author, and wrote a good deal, which nobody reads or is likely to read now; but he learnt thereby to use language as a tool, and to put his thoughts into shape. Had he not cultivated poetry as an art, before it seized upon him as an inspiration, the feeling would have been there for him, as it was there for many others

who gave it no permanent expression; but it must
have fallen back like a broken wave into the depths
of his own heart, and the literature of England would
have been all the poorer by the absence of one of its
poetical gems.

Up to this point I hope that we have gone on together. We all, I hope, agree in thinking, first, that
the course of poetry cannot be stopped by proscribing
future poets; secondly, that however desirable it might
be to have none but great writers, we cannot get these
except by a process of natural selection out of the
crowd of smaller men; and that, thirdly, each successive age will, without dethroning older potentates,
possess itself of its own sworn interpreters and guides.
Therefore it was that the tribes of Hellas, amid the
petty cares and struggles of a duller age, yearned to hear
of those heroic days, when their forefathers, led on by
children of the gods, established for ever the distinction
between the barbarian and the Hellene. Accordingly
the songs of Homer, which this yearning of theirs had
half created, were received at feast and game with
unfading enthusiasm, whereas recitations from the
philosophical poetry of Wordsworth would have fallen
idly and without music on their ears. Therefore the
patriarchs of Arabia, smitten by their overwhelming

sense of the personality of God, and the utter nothing-
ness of men, bowed down before the glorious inspiration of Job, with hearts which echoed every word of it
back. But the wide and tolerant gentleness of Shakespeare they would probably have resented as a personal
affront.

Different, however, as are the forms which at
different times poetry has put on, they seem for the
most part to be derived from a single source—that dissatisfaction, I mean, with what is present and close at
hand, which is one of Nature's silent promises to the
heart, one stimulus to the advancement of our race,
one evidence of the abiding greatness of man. Even
when the poet plunges headlong into lower elements,
and prostitutes his genius by investing frivolous pleasures or animal passions with his draperies of beauty
and grace, it is but an angry recoil from the pressure
of the Infinite—the ' desire of the moth for the star,'
driven back upon itself, and maddened by its bitter
disappointment. The imagination, indeed, not confined to poetry, but under the name of Hope, 'as broad
and general as the casing air,' has well been called by
some old writer—Simonides, I think—the nurse of life.
But who this nurse of life actually is, and what her
exact position with reference to the mental faculties

may be, is quite another question. A great deal has been thought and published upon the subject, by men eminent in different degrees, and at different times. They have, however, hitherto failed to land us in any definite conclusion.

Now, the first point to lay down, in order that we may escape from the mystification of mere words, seems to be that we must distinctly recognise as a fact that everybody possesses some imagination. We call one man imaginative as we call another muscular; not meaning thereby that weaker persons are without the same muscles, but only that they do not impress us with a special sense of their existence. I say this, however, with some doubt, and as it were tentatively, because there are critics of high authority who, when they speak of the imagination, connecting it with such names as Homer, Dante, or Shakespeare, speak of it in terms which might lead us to suppose that they look upon it as a separate faculty, by no means to be found, even as a germ, in average human creatures, but reserved for the peculiar favourites of Heaven. Just as the power of Samson, if I may follow up the analogy glanced at above, was infused into him, and him alone, by a Divine influence from on high, whilst that of Hercules, however gigantic, was the same in kind as the power of other men, 'diffused and manacled in joint and limb, and founded on the brittle strength of bones.' Now this view of theirs may be the right one. The larger cannot of course be comprehended by the smaller, and we know that there are shades of emotion rising up in many minds, quite naturally, which are wholly unintelligible to the rest of mankind. For instance, there is that strange state of feeling which seems to itself to recognise as familiar, places, persons, and expressions never seen or heard before. Upon some this weighs with such persistency and vividness of impression, that its absence from the souls of others surprises and bewilders them, whilst to those who have it not, the assertion of its existence is met by half-incredulous astonishment; so much so that we might almost fancy that the former, according to Plato's theory, were in the middle of their preordained transfigurations, whilst the latter were only entering upon their earliest phase of life. In like manner, the higher imagination may be some such peculiarity, only rarer in its manifestations, and belonging to the intellectual, rather than to the emotional side of human character. I can only say that, as at present advised, I can see no reason for supposing so. But if it be, it would seem hopeless, even for the possessors thereof, to analyse, and explain to the world of common sense, the nature of their incommunicable faculty. Voltaire's inhabitants of Saturn and Sirius, with their seventy-two and their thousand senses respectively, might as well attempt to make clear to the earth-born pigmy, whom they pitied as they talked, the secret of their complicated organisations. If, then, we are to examine this question at all, we must assume that it is within the ordinary jurisdiction of mankind, and take for granted, at present at least, that, vast as may be the difference between one imagination and another, it is still but a difference in degree, and not in kind.

There is, however, a new and original hypothesis, which it would be wrong to pass over in silence: that hypothesis, I mean, which has been advocated by Mr. Dallas, in his essay on 'The Gay Science,' with great ingenuity and zeal. He has done good service to all who busy themselves with investigation of mental phenomenon, by accumulating and discussing a number of recorded instances, in which the intellect is known to have worked, for the most part unconsciously, at times when the bodily frame was laid asleep. In this state it produces out of that work results sometimes natural to the producing mind, as when Coleridge, in an opium dream, created Kubla Khan; or as when a lawyer, with his eyes shut, in the middle of the night, builds up an elaborate opinion on some point of law; but in other cases, again, other results wholly foreign to it and unexpected, as when persons, ignorant of music whilst awake, pour out in sleep their unremembered strains, imitating with accuracy and skill certain melodies which have, somehow or other, forced themselves in upon a latent sensibility of the brain. This latent sensibility, when thus called into action, Mr. Dallas describes as 'the hidden soul,' and identifies it with the creative imagination. Since his book, which promises to be an interesting and a valuable one, is but half completed, it would be premature to condemn this theory, which may be reinforced by fresh arguments and additional explanations. But I must frankly confess that I do not understand it now. I do not see how the great works which are meditated and wrought out in full day-light, with a perfect consciousness both of the means employed and of the ends they are directed to accomplish, can be referred to the hidden soul. Nor, again, do I perceive in what manner the organised memory and methodical arrangement of facts, by the help of which a barrister grapples with his point of law, whether he grapples with it at his chambers or on his bed, can be ranked under the faculty

of the imagination. Nay, it appears to me, as far
as I can judge, that the hidden soul, which no doubt,
for most men (Mr. Dallas, I think, has established that
position), is more active than they could readily believe, executes its labours very much as the unhidden
soul executes hers, at other times. I do not think it
unlikely that some here, when boys at a public school,
may have done Latin verses in a dream. I have, I
know, more than once; though I never could remember
anything higher up than the last two. But they, and
I suppose their predecessors, were framed without any
mysterious agency at all—they were framed by the
same soul precisely, whatever that may be, which is
set apart for the manufacture of fifth-form longs and
shorts in an ordinary after twelve; nor could I ever
discover that they were appreciably better, or appreciably worse, than if I had hammered them out upon
the normal quarter of paper, whilst sitting at an
orthodox desk. I settled the matter for myself in
a careless sort of way, by supposing that different
portions of the brain were unequally asleep, and that
those portions nearest to wakefulness might exercise
their energies, more or less, without breaking that bond
which was yet enchaining the senses and the limbs.
Nor does it seem to me that the accidental circum-

stance of my remembering how I was engaged, instead of, as is perhaps more frequently the case, forgetting it altogether, can in any way affect the character of the mental operation itself.* At the same time, I readily admit that Mr. Dallas is an earnest student on all such subjects, and a conscientious thinker; I therefore wait with some impatience to hear if he has anything to add to his mental speculations. Meanwhile, I adhere to Shakespeare's much simpler creed that,—

---

* The last time when this happened to me (not very many years ago) may be worth record, as illustrating the instantaneous effects of a change in the mental attitude during sleep. I found myself one morning at Mrs. Holt's again, bent over the well-remembered wooden desk, and writing verses, for which my tutor was waiting, upon Spring. I got on smoothly enough till I came to this couplet,—

> 'Emicat omnis ager renovato flore rosarum,
> Et passim herbosâ nube virescit humus.'

Here my critical faculty came into play, I doubted about 'herbosa nubes,' but so completely was I the Eton boy once more that I put the doubt aside by saying, 'Oh, I think it will do, and if my tutor does not like it, he may alter it, and be hanged to him' (an improper speech of Philip asleep, for which Philip awake begs pardon of the excellent Provost of King's); but the little shift of thought, involved in this, woke me instantly with the two lines in question on my lips. The preceding ones had drifted irrecoverably (without, I fancy, leaving the world much poorer) into the abyss of space; if no such hitch had occurred, my belief is that I should have roused myself, at my usual hour, without any memory of the transaction at all.

> ' As imagination bodies forth
> The forms of things unknown, the poet's pen
> Turns them to shapes, and gives to airy nothing
> A local habitation and a name.'

From this point of view, the first constituent element
of the imagination seems to be a particular form of
memory, which presents its facts in groups, with all
their attendant circumstances and details retraced to
the life. It stretches out, as it were, into a spiritual
gallery, holding and exhibiting a long series of pictures
gathered from the past; one man recollects that such
a thing has happened, another exactly how it happened,
and this last kind of recollection is, no doubt, one of
the main foundations on which the imagination has
to rest. If we join to this a power of unlimited combination—out of all the contents of such a gallery,
a power, as Shakespeare calls it, of bodying forth from
the endless variety of things known, the forms of
things unknown, and of turning them, by the help of
language, into shapes—we have before us, I think, the
imaginative faculty in the rough. I do not, however,
say that he who possesses, or is possessed by such a
faculty, is therefore a poet. I understand that mathe-
maticians require a high degree of it to deal, for
instance, with the dimensions and configurations of
space, and probably with other parts of their science.

There is also the musical imagination, of which I am not qualified to speak; but, as far as my observation extends, music is more akin to mathematics than to poetry.

The radical difference, however, which separates the poetical imagination proper from other forms of the same faculty—from those, at least, which deal with articulate words, is that it is essentially and above all things suggestive. A mathematician may have to conceive the starry life and desert chasms of the universe by a mental gift, such as that which Dante put forth to drag before the inner eye his maps and ground-plans of hell; but when he comes to communicate the result of these far-stretching speculations, he has to unwind his story, link by link, and to pause at every step. The rhetorician may clothe what he has to say in purple and fine linen. He may dazzle all around him by the splendour of his diction; but still the object and duty of his art is to unfold and enlarge upon, and to hammer in, by repeated strokes, what he wishes to impress upon his audience. He leaves as little as possible to be supplied from within by any mental action of theirs; and the reason is clear, namely, that as the particular business of eloquence is to hurry the listener along with the speaker, any one

who stops to feel his own feelings, and to think his
own thoughts, becomes entangled in them, and is left
behind.   But the poet, on the other hand, is con-
tented to touch a chord, which then vibrates at will, as
its own sensitiveness may dictate; and according to
the number and intensity of the vibrations awakened,
legitimately awakened I mean, is the poetical power
shown.

The poet, of course, ought also to be an artist, and
must not overdo his work, or overstrain the attention
of his readers; so that passages of repose, and mixed
passages of rhetoric and poetry, or of thought and
poetry, are often well and wisely introduced into any
considerable work; but they do not, so far as it is
a poem, constitute its essence.   So, again, the rhetorician, when the ears of his crowd are caught, and their
hearts are hot within them, may often heighten the
effect of his appeals by a rapid flash of poetry; but any
speaker who, instead of expatiating upon topic after
topic as they arise in their order, should flit quickly from
one delicate suggestion to another, after the manner of
a poet, as an orator would be certain to fail.   To
illustrate what I mean, let us take two well-known
passages from Jeremy Taylor.   I choose a prose writer
to quote from, because the naked limbs, *disjecti poetæ,*

are easier to operate upon in the way of anatomy. Every one knows the famous paragraph in which he compares the swift passage from youth to age, and from life to death, with the opening, the blooming, and the fading of a flower:—'But so I have seen a rose newly springing from the clefts of its hood, and at first it was fair and full with the dew of heaven as a lamb's fleece; but when a ruder breath forced upon its virgin modesty, and dismantled its too youthful and unripe retirements, it began to put on darkness, and to decline to softness and the symptoms of a sickly age, till at night, having lost some of its leaves and all its beauty, it fell into the portion of weeds and worn-out faces.' Now the thought here is obvious enough, not to say commonplace. The comparison of the life of man to the flowers of the field can hardly have been an original simile much later than the age of Jubal. The whole beauty of the passage, a rhetorical beauty, consists in the exquisite accumulation of details, which must drive the meaning of this well-known metaphor home to the sense of the dullest peasant, and force him to acknowledge that the likeness is a real one. But, again, let us take this other sentence:—'I have read of a fair young German gentleman, who, living, often refused to be painted, but put off the importunity of his friends

by giving way that, after a few days' burial, they might
send a painter to his vault, and if they saw cause for it,
draw the image of his death to the life.' The Bishop
then proceeds to enumerate, rhetorically, the ghastly
circumstances of that condition, but he concludes, and,
as it were, locks his sentences together by a touch of
the purest poetry, and 'so he stands painted among his
arméd ancestors!' His arméd ancestors! That single
word, that short epithet, builds up for us in an instant
a feudal castle, frowning with all its towers above the
Danube or the Rhine, with its wide halls, its sounding
corridors, its stately picture-galleries filled with the
masterpieces of Albert Durer, of Holbein, and the like.
We know further how, in the midst of men and women
who seemed to move and breathe along its walls, that
fearful shadow in the midst was even then mocking
at their false pretences to life. We know how the
bereaved mother and forlorn sisters knelt continually
beneath, praying for the repose of the dead, and how
the shuddering vassals crossed themselves as they
passed. We know all this; but we read it by a light
which lives and spreads within, as soon as it has
been kindled for us from without. And therefore I go
on to say that we feel ourselves to be in the presence
of a great rhetorician, no doubt, but also in that of

a genuine poet. Nay, so completely does the inner-most poetry of a line lie in the soul, and not in the outward form of words, that the very same passage may be high poetry or simple prose according to the suggestions which it involves. When Ariel, in answer to Prospero's inquiries as to how it is possible that the affections of a man injured as he had been should be touched by the misery of his foes, replies at once, 'mine would, sir, were they human,' nothing can be more un-pretending than this brief speech considered as to its form of expression; but what interminable insights does it not open out into the world of spirits, and the infinite gradations of being!

Again, to use a more modern instance, Robert Browning's Duke of Ferrara, in that wonderful little tragedy of his, 'My Last Duchess,' dismisses the terror-stricken envoy from his future bride's father, in the following words :—

> 'Taming a sea-horse thought a rarity
> Which Claus of Innspruck cast in bronze for me.'

If we are to suppose this quiet observation to be ad-dressed to some fair-haired English Milordo who, with the mediæval equivalent for Murray in his hand, had blundered up against a courteous Italian prince, it would be absolute, not to say rather bald prose; but

coming, as it does, at the end of that dreadful series of
hints, through which the ambassador must convey to
the new wife, if he takes any interest in his own life,
without implicating the Duke of Ferrara, 'woe to him
if he does this,'—a warning not to be mistaken; it
is lighted up by a terrible significance from within.
We shudder to feel that if the innocent bride-elect
lifts a finger or raises an eyelash except in harmony
with the unspoken bidding of her lord, the grave which
holds the beautiful original of one veiled portrait has
room for her also, and that the picture-galleries of
Ferrara even yet are not without available space; and
acknowledge heartily, with how slight a motion of his
hand, the man of real genius can create an imperishable
dramatic effect.

And this brings us to another question much discussed and open to much discussion—the comparative
merits of the vigorous grasp, as opposed to the impalpable touchings of the poetical imagination. There
can be no doubt that where the vigorous grasp of
a subject is possible, such a grasp should always be laid
upon it; but there are regions of poetry, perhaps the
very highest, beyond the reach of the human eye, except
through fluctuating glimpses and visionary hints. And
a grander dream of suggestion may visit the heart of

an intelligent disciple, where the poet catches, or half catches, an evanescent ray from lights behind the sun, than if he had measured his distances and counted up his materials with the precision of an architectural draughtsman. When Alfred Tennyson in his 'In Memoriam' attempts to rest on the cheering belief that the soul of his friend, and of my friend, was removed for high purposes and events; and utters his passionate longing for faith, in these sublime words :—

> ' The wish, that of the living whole
> No life may fail beyond the grave;
> Derives it not from what we have
> The likest God within the soul?

> ' Are God and Nature then at strife,
> That Nature lends such evil dreams?
> So careful of the type she seems,
> So careless of the single life;

> ' That I, considering everywhere
> Her secret meaning in her deeds,
> And finding that of fifty seeds
> She often brings but one to bear;

> ' I falter where I firmly trod,
> And falling with my weight of cares
> Upon the great world's altar-stairs
> That slope thro' darkness up to God:'—

he would not, so far as I am concerned, have improved his picture by telling us that the stairs in question were of white marble, as if they had been

hewn out of the quarries of Carrara; and that each of
the steps was twice as large as those which led up to
St. Peter's Church at Rome.

We now come to a much contested point on which
it would ill become me to pronounce a confident
opinion, in the face of such thinkers as Coleridge, as
Wordsworth, as Ruskin, not to speak of others; the
distinction, I mean, deep and vital, which they profess
to have discovered between the fancy and the imagination. It would ill become me, I say, to pronounce
a confident opinion, but at the same time, as I am
bound here to be perfectly frank and open, I must at
once state, and, in venturing upon such a statement,
I am happy to find myself fortified by the high authority
of Mr. Dallas, that I cannot accept their conclusions.
To begin with the etymology of the words, though
I lay no more stress thereon than it deserves (it
indicates at least the original belief of mankind),
'imagination' is simply Latin for 'fancy;' 'fancy'
merely Greek for 'imagination.' In spite of this, however, I am by no means insensible to the convenience
of classing those inward pictures which spring up in
light minds, or at least in lighter moods of mind, apart
from those which embody the nobler and stronger forms
of passion and of thought.

To that extent, therefore, I willingly recognise the distinction which our English language, according to its later arrangement, establishes between them. To any further extent I do not recognise it. I believe that the picturesque procession of Queen Mab, which, in Romeo and Juliet, Shakespeare formed for the delight of his hearers, and which is usually presented to us as an admirable instance of poetic fancy, was seen by Shakespeare according to precisely the same laws of inward vision, as were called into action when Dante beheld those dilating flakes of fire which fell slowly upon the enemies of God, as the snow falls heavily among the Alps, without a sound. And yet I suppose none would deny that the Italian lines to which I refer compose a fine imaginative picture. Shakespeare from his memory, his reading, his powers of observation and combination, blended together one set of images into a bright and sparkling whole. Dante, from his memory, his reading, his powers of observation and combination, blended together another set of images into a gloomy and impressive whole. But I say the *modus operandi* was in both cases exactly the same. Two separate faculties were no more needed to call into life these two separate poetical creations, than we, under the laws of the physical world, need two retinas, one framed for glancing at a fire-fly, and the other for contemplating a fixed star.

To me, indeed, it seems that the upholders of the opposite theory would do well to examine themselves, so as to learn whether they have kept before their judgment with sufficient steadiness a truth which no one disputes in words, but which may often be, in the haste and tumult of thought, practically forgotten. Namely, that however expedient, however desirable we may consider it in discussions of this sort to talk of memory and imagination and humour and fancy, as if they were independent and self-existing substances, they are, after all, intimately and indissolubly united in one homogeneous mind. The composite life within is always one thing, and acts invariably in one mass. Like Wordsworth's cloud, ' it moveth altogether, if it move at all.' Hence the reason and humour of an imaginative man contain elements which the reason and humour of an unimaginative man do not contain; hence also the imagination of a humourist and logician is interpenetrated by logic and humour, and the mind acts as a whole under the combined influence of these three separate forces. Above all does one imagination differ from another, according to the proportions in

which a certain energy and glow of soul is mixed up
with it.

And here, unless I deceive myself, is the true practical difference between what the English people
choose *now* to call by the Greek name of fancy, and
what they prefer to speak of under the Latin name
of imagination. Imagination is fancy with ardour ·
of thought, and heat of passion burning through it.
Fancy is imagination, playing as the northern light,
and glittering without intensity and without warmth.
Nay, so absolutely, from my point of view, is this
the case, that the very same work of art may appear
to one critic fanciful, and to another imaginative,
according as they respectively perceive, or overlook,
in it the presence of passion. For instance, Mr.
Ruskin, in one of those eloquent passages which make
us proud of the English language, is giving due honour
to his favourite painter Tintoretto. In the course
of his panegyric, he presents to us, as the crowning
glory of that illustrious artist, his almost superhuman
imagination. A picture of Christ crucified is the one
upon which, above all others, he delights to dwell.
In this the fickleness of the Jews, and indeed the
evanescent character of all mere human love, is sym-
bolized by an ass's colt in the background, such a one,

we may presume, as the Saviour had ridden upon a few days before, feeding now upon withered palm-leaves, the same, no doubt, which had been strewed, in their freshness, across the triumphal path of the accepted Messiah. Now I feel sure that Mr. Ruskin is here perfectly right, but neither can I hesitate to believe, that the mighty Venetian of whom he speaks grew more and more inflamed by an overmastering impulse of sympathy as he brooded over his own work. The divine face of the suffering Mediator, visible only to him, must have pressed in upon his heart and filled it with a living glow of affection. Out of a re-action from this he must have flung upon his canvas, with all the magic power of genius, a fiery scorn and an inspiring hatred against those cowards who had deserted and those miscreants who had betrayed the Son of God. And thus arose, for all time, that which Mr. Ruskin has recorded as the sublimest achievement of imagination, yet accomplished by any painter-poet, among the sons of men. Otherwise, if we suppose the like point introduced by one of colder tempera-ment into a picture on the same subject, as a stroke of art, it might well be considered as too clever, too ingenious, too much under the same conditions of thought as Hogarth's happy incident of the spider's web woven across the poor-box, to be classed with the highest efforts of man's creative intelligence. In a word, I should say definitively that it was fanciful, and not imaginative.

I stated, at the opening of this Lecture, that one of the subjects which it might be expedient to discuss was, what are the effects which imagination indulged tends to produce upon the character at large? I have, however, trespassed upon your attention too long already, and must content myself by indicating my belief that the use of the imagination, as a moral element, is to fight against selfishness. This it ought to do, by giving life to an intelligent sympathy with the thoughts and emotions of others; whilst the danger to which it exposes men is, that if they give way to the habit of looking 'upon the world as a stage, and on all its men and women as merely players,' the heart may grow cold, even whilst the understanding is enlarged. It is obvious, however, that this is a matter which would require, if any justice is to be done to it, a lecture to itself. I shall therefore put it by for the present, and conclude by thanking you for the patience and attention with which you have listened to this somewhat ill-organized discourse.

PROVINCIAL POETRY.

LECTURE II.

PROVINCIAL POETRY.

When Monsieur De Talleyrand, if Monsieur De Talleyrand it were who is the author of the well-known saying, amused an ultra-civilized company of wits and diplomatists by telling them that speech was first given to man in order that he might conceal his thoughts, it is probable that he had in his mind Parisian French, Queen's English, very choice Italian, Attic Greek, Ciceronian Latin, and the like : that kind of diction, in a word, to which are liable, more or less, most of those books that no gentleman's library ought to be without. One main reason, in the opposite direction, which leads me to speak here of provincial poetry and provincial poets, is my belief that this celebrated sarcasm does not apply to those rustic dialects which have never diluted themselves, like the expanding circles of a pond, over the wide surface of literary com-

monplace. The words in use among uneducated men
are (I imagine) but few ; they accommodate themselves
to the every-day topics and elementary passions which
make up the daily life of the village or the farm. The
same subjects of conversation, if conversation it can be
called, recur at the same times, from week to week,
from month to month, from year to year. And the
talk of the alehouse, or the blacksmith's shop, seldom
passes out far beyond them. Hence when a labourer,
still more when a labourer's wife, happens to possess
an energetic understanding, a lively imagination, or
a vehement temper, she has to struggle up to eloquence
by making all the language within reach bend under
her till it cracks. Every phrase is, as it were, double-
shotted with meaning. Vivid metaphors are pressed
into their place, not to decorate a sentence, not to
round a period, but, with the true object of all such
illustrations, to quicken and fortify the sense. She
pounces upon them, and drags them towards her from
every quarter, so that she may bridge over the shortest
road home to the hearts and intellects of her audience.
Such a woman I met not so very long ago in one of our
northern districts. She was boiling up with eager
wrath against an oppressive squire, who, according to
her, had treated a deserving tenant with shameless

injustice. It was clear that pour out her emotions
upon somebody she must; and perhaps it occurred to
her that I, as a stranger and a bird of passage, was
a safer confidant than any of her particular friends. I
know nothing of the facts of the case, and therefore
neither acquit nor condemn the supposed delinquent.
Her story, at any rate, ran thus:—The tenant in
question was one who, like Tennyson's *Northern Farmer*,
had a passionate sense of his duty to the land. If she
represented him truly, he worked early and late, paying
his rent to a moment, and improving his fields with
a zeal that never slackened, not so much in the hope of
conciliating his landlord, or of increasing his worldly
substance, as to feel his life keen within him, and to
satisfy the natural instincts of his soul. But though
admirable in these respects, he was not altogether the
discreetest of men, or, as she put it, 'He wor an
oonhandy kind of chap, who let his toongue wagg in
pooblic-hoose.' Now this ill-advised wagging of the
tongue, in that dangerous part of the hamlet, unhappily set in motion certain scandals, of which it is
unnecessary to say more, than that the lord of the
manor objected to their public discussion among his
humbler neighbours. Some pickthank contrived to let
the little great man know what had taken place, and

he, so she informed me, was ungenerous enough to
wreak a mean revenge. All this she flung forth in
her fiery Yorkshire, which crackled and rung as she
gave it out, (Yorkshire, compared with which my
pottering dictionary-English is as the outer to the inner
rainbow,) and ended her impassioned declamation (of
the truth or justice of which, I repeat, I know nothing)
in the following words:—' He broake him in no time at
a'. He blaacked him reet awa'.' Now you or I should
probably have said, he never rested till he had accomplished his ruin, or some such platitude. This woman,
however, had but little of such Norman-English at command. From her very poverty she was compelled to
make herself rich. From her very incapacity to find
ordinary words, strong enough to hold her meaning,
she was forced into a noble image ; at least by the
power of that phrase, ' He blaacked him reet awa','
she has left, sculptured on my imagination ever since,
the form of her sorrowing friend, walled round, without
a gleam of sunshine, by the darkness of despair, buried
alive, so to speak, under the gloom of his unmerited
misfortunes.

On another occasion, a stalwart ploughman, believing in himself, and honourably conscious that he
never gave less than a day's work for a day's wages,

refused to acknowledge any obligation to a master, for whom, neither in point of ability nor in point of character, did he feel any respect, and compressed his burst of resolute independence into the following weighty sentence:—'I'se neither debt-bound, nor awe-bound till him.' Again, a quaint old gardener, whom I knew well, took the measure of his master, a clever but indolent man, in these words:—'Sir Thomas is nae fule, but he's t'ignorantest mànn as is; he knows nought about ought.' The same worthy, complaining to a married woman, one of the daughters of the house, that his walls got no rest from busy little fingers (he never, even in a dream, considered the fruit as belonging to anybody but himself), she endeavoured to console him, by pointing out that in both generations, her's and the next, the family had overflowed with girls. 'We might,' she said, 'have been all boys, and where would you have been then?' But he, deeply meditating on these things, shook his head, and replied,—'Na, lass; na, then, I should have got shut on you whiles.' In plain English, I should have got rid of you, except when you were at home for the holidays. He felt, much as a Sicilian or North African of old might have preferred a flying inroad of pirates or Moors to the steady exactions of his Roman Proconsul, that, with the public school for an ally, he could endure a transitory storm of boys, if only he were spared the constant tribute levied upon him by permanent young ladies. Now, such massive bits of vernacular speech, wherever we light upon them, teach us that a non-literary tongue may, within certain limits (narrow enough no doubt when compared with the larger aims of language), possess advantages peculiar to itself. The principal of these seems to be that a vigorous mind has to impress a portion of its own strength and life upon the few forms of utterance which constitute its whole vocabulary ; otherwise there would not really be enough of them to get on with at all. On the other hand, men brought up mainly upon words, men who have all the conventional expressions and accredited phrases from the elegant extracts ready at call, are apt to be overwhelmed by their allies; they are apt, sometimes even when there is real power, to be embarrassed and weighed down by great lumps of commonplace diction, much of which, like the copper money that hampered poor Correggio to death, has but little, except bulk and abundance, to recommend it to mankind. Dr. Johnson, for instance, if he had been born in Yorkshire or Dorsetshire, and had published his imitations of Juvenal in either of these dialects, would never, I am sure, have started off in the tenth satire with so vague and futile a personification as—

> 'Let observation, with extensive view,
> Survey mankind from China to Peru.'

The high road of the national language we will consider, if you please, as built to sustain the pressure of the whole English mind—to find room for the passage up and down of all great thoughts, all wide-reaching imaginations, all stormy passions, which enter into our national life. But still there may be certain shy graces of idiom and feeling which, like wild roses, or thorn-blossoms, or lilies of the valley, are more likely to be found among the nooks and windings of a Devonshire or Dorsetshire lane. When, therefore, poems full of beauty and power, like Mr. Tennyson's 'Northern Farmer,' or the lyrics of Mr. Barnes, are given to the world, it would be a mistake to consider them as originating in mere whim and caprice on the part of their authors. We have heard that when my friend Lord Houghton read the 'Northern Farmer' to his tenants, and ex-constituents, round about Ferrybridge and Ponte-fract, they rose at him as one man, shouting together, 'That caps a',' and begged to be informed—a recognition of merit which speaks volumes for the right-hearted population north of Trent—where the book, which contained so fine a poem, might be summarily bought? I do not wish to step out of my province, but I cannot help remarking, that our statesmen, having first opened wide the doors which were formerly locked, and removed the shutter-bars originally intended to protect the house, are now making haste to tell us that they know little of the crowds sure to swarm in; but that it is everybody's instant business to educate them, so that they may not push. If this be so, the story which I have just told indicates that there are veins of feeling still unworked, modes of **access** to the deeper thoughts and emotions of our fellow-countrymen yet almost unexplored; and these, as a step in the right direction, it may be as well to occupy at once. If, therefore, in order to commence the poetical part of the people's parliamentary education, we need no more than that a channel should be cleared out for those well-springs of speech, any one of which might have been the main feeder of our English tongue—if men, whose daily thoughts and words are too remote from those of our established poets to be in any degree impressed by them, are yet to be reached and taught, so far as poetry can be made a teacher, by the help of their native dialects,—the **fact,** I apprehend, is an important one. Under such circumstances we cannot, I am sure, be ready enough to hail Mr. Barnes, Mr. Waugh, and other labourers in the same field, with due reward, ample honour, and immediate recognition. Nay, even if we put aside such practical aims, as foreign to the scope of a professorship like this; from a philological point of view such labours are full of interest and value. By turning up the subsoil about the roots of our language, we may strengthen the trunk, and possibly enrich some of the branches with unexpected fruit. If, to descend to minutiæ—if, by the help of provincial poets, we could recover for ordinary use such adjectives as 'silvern,' etc.—recover them, I mean, without worrying our readers by any sense of pedantry or strangeness (nothing is worth that), we should get rid of a defect in idiom to which we have been hurried, through our metropolitan impatience of delay. When substantives, such as 'silver' and the like, are thus put upon double duty, I think it is a mark of poverty, or stinginess, in the establishment to which they belong; reminding us somewhat of Molière's 'Avare,' in which, as we know, Harpagon's cook was his coachman also; but I do not think we should, on that account, have been tempted to accompany the miser in a drive, and I am sure that we should have refused, one and all, his

invitations to dinner.   It is an odd instance, by the
way, of the unequal manner in which time and custom
act upon language, that whereas 'silvern' has drifted
entirely, or all but entirely, out of reach,—so that
Mr. Tennyson rightly personifies the evening star as
'Sitting under *silver* hair with a silver eye,'—the corre-
sponding epithet 'golden' still keeps its head above
water, though somewhat hardly pressed.   We talk of
a gold watch, gold plate, and so on, but we write about
golden hair, golden hours, golden children, and the like ;
though what 'golden children' may mean is not so easy
to say—'possibly the German equivalent for what we
call yellow-boys,' as I once heard suggested to a student
of Schiller's lyrics, who stuck at the phrase.   Instances
of this kind are numerous enough : one word perishes,
another, apparently with no particular reason for out-
lasting it, lives on.   Now a good deal of light may be
thrown upon the language if we search, among the provincial varieties of speech, for these vanished or vanish-
ing forms and idioms.   Though any one of them would,
I am sure, repay investigation, the Dorsetshire variety
in which most of Mr. Barnes's poems are written, is
the one which it is most natural for me to examine at
present.   Its participles want the hard final *g* of ours :
for instance—

> ' The light of waves a *runnén* there
> Did play on leaves up over head,
> And fishes scaly sides did gleam,
> A *dartén* on their shallow bed.'

Now, upon the whole, I do not prefer this grammatical form to our own; the English last syllable lends itself better to a keen and ringing melody, and carries within itself a greater appearance of strength. But sometimes, where graceful sentiment is aimed at, where pathos, in its lighter aspects, is what we require—as in some rustic idyll or tender song—if we could only give the Dorsetshire participle a brevet and local rank, to act as Queen's English for the nonce, we should, I think, be richer in point of diction than we are. Still more do I envy Mr. Barnes his old plurals in *-en*, such as housen, cheesen, furzen. Everybody knows what an intrusive, ubiquitous creature is the unmanageable English *s*. Every one who writes verses has been bothered about *s* pure and *s* impure. And though we Britons have to put a bold face upon the matter, and to maintain that the cacophony in question does not signify at all; it is only because we cannot help ourselves, and have given up all hope of a remedy. Now if once more — in accordance with Horace's dictum that 'multa renascentur, quae jam cecidere'— we could call back from oblivion and disuse that

valuable termination in *-en*, it is impossible to say
what metrical triumphs might not be achieved. We
might even hope to allay, if we could not wholly
quench, the disembodied hiss which floats round a
church, whenever the school children pause in their
hymn. I fear greatly, however, that this cannot now
be done; I fear that a language, so long as it lives,
must roll on like a river, which becomes broader, and
deeper, and of greater importance, at each stride of its
onward course; separating hostile kingdoms perhaps,
or bearing huge three-deckers down to the sea; but
which yet, alas! also leaves behind, at every bend,
more and more, the flower-crowned banks and sparkling purity of its parent brook. Nay, to the annoyance
of literary men, I believe that whenever Horace's
anticipations are realised, whenever his proposed renaissance does take place, it takes place as a necessity,
and not as a luxury of language. I doubt whether Mr.
Tennyson, with all his genius, and all his popularity,
could re-awaken one strong preterite which has really
lapsed; whilst railway navvies, with a sublime un-
consciousness, like that of the brewer's horse, who
undertook (through a godfather, I admit) to draw a
thousand inferences at once, have disinterred, and
brought into daily use, the sound old English verb

'*to shunt*'—a verb which had slept, somewhere or other, like the annual toad of our coal-mines, since it was last alive and awake for poets who flourished before Chaucer.

If, however, determination can do anything—if the laws of human speech are in any degree to be influenced by the human will—here is a proper occasion for its exercise. Men more sanguine than I am might think that the power of varying our hissing plurals, by a recurrence to the old plurals in *-en* which yet linger in the provinces, is not absolutely lost and gone. If so, let us hope sooner or later to see sportsmen shooting their fifty brace of grousen on the 12th of August, Mr. Gladstone and Mr. Disraeli fighting out their differences in full housen, and young ladies engaged for twenty successive dancen, even from the time of this present Commemoration. But no, alas! *volat irrevocabile verbum,*—all I can say is, if it were possible to accomplish successfully this literary feat, he who accomplished it would deserve £4000,—ay, from the most economical of governments — much better than the gentleman who patented that method of punching holes between postage-stamps, which to me, I speak humbly as a blind and awkward man, appears a success—only for the inventor.

I have dwelt at some length on the possible philological value of such poetical studies, because I find that
among young people who are at first disposed to admire
the exquisite lyrics of Mr. Barnes, this admiration is
followed at once by a hot fit of wrath, and a sense
of being cheated, as soon as they discover that he
is a scholar and a gentleman. A popular writer—De
Quincey, I think—tells a story of his ill success in
lending 'The Vicar of Wakefield' to his landlady's
daughter, somewhere among the Westmoreland lakes.
At first, the girl took intense interest in the tale,
accepted the *dramatis personae* as real men and women,
and loved and hated them with all the proper emphasis
of youth; but, alas! suddenly it was revealed to her
that the book was a work of fiction. Now that was
a portent, the idea of which had never crossed her
innocent mind. Accordingly she became furious at
the supposed deception, looked upon De Quincey as
bankers look upon a man who has tried knowingly to
utter a forged bill of exchange; and, as for Goldsmith,
if she could have resuscitated him, and had her will,
she would have consigned him to Appleby jail as a
rogue and a vagabond, for obtaining sympathy under
false pretences   Just so fared the unfortunate Mr.
Barnes, at the hands of those to whom I refer. Oh!

said they, he is a gentleman after all, is he? Oh! we thought he was a ploughman. Oh! we don't care a bit about his poetry now. I endeavoured to convince them they were entirely in the wrong; but of that strategical operation I have always observed that, however skilfully and zealously it may be undertaken, it is apt, with regard to young and old alike, to fail of success in the most unaccountable manner. With you, however, who are not committed to any opinions on the subject, I hope to do better. Now, when a man of great natural genius, like Burns (God forbid that I should call Burns a provincial poet; but I may perhaps be allowed to use him for purposes of illustration), thinks and feels, and writes what he thinks and feels, in one dialect, after having been imperfectly educated in another, he is apt to attach a fictitious value to the long words and polyglot phrases which he may have gathered from his dialect of education. Let us take an instance: when Burns, in one of his most charac-teristic outbursts, carries us off our critical feet by this lyrical impulse—

> 'Auld Nature swears, the lovely dears
> Her noblest work she classes, oh!
> Her 'prentice hand she tried on man,
> And *then* she made the lasses, oh!'

the spirit, grace, and sparkling originality of the two

last lines charm us away from examining the two first;
but, if we refuse to listen to the voice of the charmer,
it cannot be denied that the conception of nature,
classing her lovely dears, is an intrusion, what geolo-
gists call a 'fault,' of school English, cutting awkwardly
across the vein of his inborn Scottish idiom. But
when a scholar like Mr. Barnes, who, besides being
thoroughly acquainted with the way of thinking, and
the way of talking, which prevails in his native district, adds research to that familar knowledge, traces
the expressions which he finds about him home to
their proper origin, and looks at them by the light of
comparative philology, this criticism does not apply.
Such a man, when he writes, can trust himself safely
to the impulses of his own mind, and will probably
give us better Dorsetshire, better Yorkshire, better
Scotch, as the case may be, than the clever peasant
or artisan who has learnt but little outside his native
tongue, and therefore overvalues that little. Such a
peasant is in danger of fancying that he rises above
himself, whenever he inserts, among his own idioms,
a word of four syllables derived from the Latin—whenever, to recall an old Joe Miller, he edifies his village
hearers by using that 'blessed word Mesopotamia.'

Having thus endeavoured to persuade you that you

are not bound to despise Mr. Barnes, because, instead
of being an ignorant man of genius, he is a learned
man of genius, I shall now proceed to call your attention to the poems which he has written. I do not
mean to confine myself to him altogether; but he
merits our particular attention. Mr. Barnes, with
an accurate estimate, I think, not so much of his
own powers, as of the powers and resources of his
Dorsetshire Doric, has confined himself to the lyrical
interpretation of such simple emotions as arise out
of the simple drama of an average country life. I
refer this absence of ambitious aim, in his little
odes, to the nature of his dialect, rather than to any
deficiency in himself; because I do not choose to
believe, though some such assumption is constantly
made, that the art of doing one thing very well implies that you are to do everything else particularly
ill. We all remember Horace's encomium, which
strikes us now as such an inadequate one—

> ' Molle atque facetum
> *Virgilio* annuerunt gaudentes rure Camoenae.'

It is clear that he looked to Varius as the heroic
bard of the time, and never suspected for a moment
that in his ingenious asthmatic friend, who wrote

such graceful verses about ploughs, and olives, and
bees, and Corycian old men, lay hid the author of
the national epic. But whatever Mr. Barnes' reasons
may be—want of power, want of will, or a scientific
measurement of the capabilities and non-capabilities
of his own provincial tongue — as a fact he has
attempted nothing inconsistent with the character
which he has assumed—that, namely, of a small Dorsetshire farmer. He dwells lovingly upon the lights
and shadows which play among the wooded coverts
of his native hills, upon the bells of his village
church, upon the dear old mill :—

> 'Oh, joy betide the dear old mill,
> My neighbour play-mate's happy home,
> With rolling wheel and leaping foam
> Below the overhanging hill.
>> Where wide and slow
>> The stream did flow,
> And flags did grow, and lightly flee,
> Below the grey-leaved withy tree;
> Whilst clack, clack, clack, from hour to hour
> Did go the mill by cloty Stour.'

I must here pause to explain the word 'cloty'—the rather
that it illustrates something which I said, at the outset
of this lecture, as to the compensations which belong
to a non - literary language; I mean, that when a
peasant speaks of anything within the circle of his

daily occupations, he gives it, as a distinguished friend
of mine acutely observed to me, a special name to
itself. A sheep, for instance, of a certain age—I am
sure I do not know of what age—which we should
describe at length, he pithily calls a tegg. A yellow
water-lily, to put which clumsily before our readers
we require three words, he marks off at once as a
'clote,' whilst the river upon whose breast it lies floating, becomes, for him, the '*cloty* Stour.' And thus he
condenses into two syllabes a rural picture which it
would take, I believe, two lines to paint in English
proper. To return, however, as the French proverb
has it, to our teggs, Mr. Barnes does his work among
the ordinary scenery, the ordinary joys and sorrows of
a commonplace English county. And here his position, as we must admit, contrasts unfavourably with
that of Burns. Burns had a proud national history to
appeal to; there were, in every direction, national
sensibilities, founded on a haughty sense of blood and
of race, ready to answer such an appeal; whereas anything emphatically English is somewhat out of Mr.
Barnes' reach, because what he has undertaken to
deliver is, not the universal English, but the local
Dorsetshire mind. However, even in a commonplace English county, love and death are as busy as

over the regions beyond, and the true poet, having
them to deal with, requires but little else. Moreover, paradoxical as it may seem to say so of one
who uses such a dialect, Mr. Barnes has done much
to atone for a certain inevitable monotony in the
choice of his subjects—a limitation of ideas and
images, forced upon him through the narrowness of
the path which he has chosen to tread—by cultivating,
in the execution of his short poems, a most exquisite
finish of style. He has felt, I think very justly, that
anything like slovenliness of diction, metrical harshness,
nimiety (if I may use a word which I am sure I have
seen somewhere) would be more intolerable in him,
than in writers who make use of average English
like the rest of us. Accordingly, as a rule, his little
pieces exhibit a delicate grace and a completeness not
unworthy of Horace. It is time, however, to allow
our poet to speak for himself. Some of the poems
are short comic dialogues, intended to set forth, in
that form, the characteristic features, as they appear
to him, of his Dorsetshire neighbourhood. But whatever merit they may possess from that point of view,
they do not strike me as being among his happier
efforts, and in no degree approach to the grim pathos
and dramatic humour of the 'Northern Farmer.' It is

through his own pathos however, but pathos generally
of the lighter and more sentimental kind, that he takes
his proper rank—a high rank, I think, among contemporary writers of verse; and indeed, though I say this
as generally true, it would be unfair to deny that he
sometimes rises into a higher mood, and gives way to
deeper impulses of feeling and of thought. I propose
now to read to you one or more of his shorter poems,
premising only that I shall read them so as to be understood. The Dorsetshire dialect, I am happy to say,
admits of this without difficulty; in a more northern
one, it could perhaps hardly have been managed.
Indeed, except where the local word is used as a
rhyme, nothing is lost by transferring Mr. Barnes' lines
into our common tongue—they pass, without an effort,
into good and simple English. In the following little
ode, for instance, which he calls 'The Echo,' if you will
only bear in mind that 'slooe' is the Dorsetshire form
of our 'sloe,' and 'sheen' of the verb 'to shine,' you
have ready for your ears some beautiful English verses.

THE ECHO.

'About the tow'r an' churchyard wall,
    Out nearly overright our door,
A tongue ov wind did always call
    Whatever we did call avore.

F 2

The vaïce did mock our neämes, our cheers,
    Our merry laughs, our hands' loud claps,
An' mother's call "Come, come, my dears"
                            —*my dears;*
    Or " Do as I do bid, bad chaps"
                            —*bad chaps.*

' An' when o' Zundays on the green,
    In frocks an' cwoats as gay as new,
We walk'd wi' shoes a-meäde to sheen
    So black an' bright's a vull-ripe slooe,
We then did hear the tongue ov air
    A-mockèn mother's vaïce so thin,
" Come, now the bell do goo vor pray'r"
                            —*vor pray'r;*
        " 'Tis time to goo to church; come in"
                            —*come in.*

' The night when little Anne that died
    Begun to zickèn, back in May,
An' she, at dusk ov evenèn-tide,
    Wer out wi' others at their play,
Within the churchyard that do keep
    Her little bed, the vaïce o' thin
Dark air, mock'd mother's call " To sleep"
                            —*to sleep;*
        " 'Tis bed time now, my love, come in"
                            —*come in.*

' An' when our Jeäne come out so smart
    A-married, an' we help'd her in
To Henry's newly-varnish'd cart,
    The while the wheels begun to spin,

> An' her gay nods, vor all she smil'd,
>   Did sheäke a tear-drop vrom each eye,
> The vaïce mock'd mother's call, "Dear child"
>   —*dear cbild;*
>   "God bless ye evermwore; good bye"
>   —*good bye.'*

The four last lines of the third stanza are, in my judgment, exquisite above the rest :—

> ' Within the churchyard that do keep
>   Her little bed, the vaïce o' thin
> Dark air, mock'd mother's call " To sleep,"
>   —*to sleep;*
>   " 'Tis bed time now, my love, come in."
>   —*come in.'*

The manner in which this ominous echo, 'come in,' breathing forth, upon the doomed child, its phantom-like summons from her future home within the grave, yet softens itself into the likeness of a mother's voice calling her child to sleep, can hardly be too much admired. It imparts a spiritual grace to the whole poem, and teaches us, better than many sermons, how that place within the churchyard is, after all, but a place of quiet, ' where the wicked cease from troubling, and the weary are at rest.'   In spite, however, of the charm and impressiveness of this affecting stanza, Mr. Barnes feels that to finish thus would react, with too much solemnity, on the primal conception of this little piece, and

so jar upon his fine artistic perceptions; he therefore skilfully rounds off these suggestions of his
memory by introducing, after the burial, a bridal,
wherewith to end; but still, in order to chime in
with the key-note from which he started, it is not
the glow of triumphant love, nor the joyous revel of
the wedding-bells, to which he invites our attention,
but the gentle regrets and natural tears of the maiden,
as she departs, into a new home, from her mother's
clinging embrace. He leaves us, therefore, cheered
with a gleam of brightness and a touch of pleasure,
but the brightness, in order that it may not be out of
harmony with his original theme, is a subdued one,
and the pleasure not without melancholy.

The next poem which I shall read to you is 'The
Rose in the Dark,' p. 32; in this case, it is unnecessary to make any preface at all.

THE RWOSE IN THE DARK.

'In zummer, leäte at evenèn tide,
  I zot to spend a moonless hour
'Ithin the window, wi' the zide
  A-bound wi' rwoses out in flow'r,
Bezide the bow'r, vorsook o' birds,
An' listen'd to my true-love's words.

' A-risèn to her comely height,
  She push'd the swingèn ceäsement round;
And I could hear, beyond my zight,
  The win'-blown beech-tree softly sound,
On higher ground, a-swayèn slow,
On drough my happy hour below.

' An' tho' the darkness then did hide
  The dewy rwose's blushèn bloom,
He still did cast sweet aïr inside
  To Jeäne, a-chattèn in the room;
An' though the gloom did hide her feäce,
Her words did bind me to the pleäce.

' An' there, while she, wi' runnèn tongue,
  Did talk unzeen 'ithin the hall,
I thought her like the rwose that flung
  His sweetness vrom his darken'd ball,
'Ithout the wall, an' sweet's the zight
Ov her bright feäce, by mornèn light.'

Every one, I think, will agree with me in looking
upon this as a country love-idyll exquisite of its kind.
It is also a good instance of Mr. Barnes' fine taste
in knowing when and where to stop, in discerning
how much poetical embroidery a little incident of this
kind will bear, so that he may not overwork his subject, or overload it with ornament. 'The Snowy
Night' is a companion picture to the 'Rose in the
Dark,' only somewhat keener and livelier in point of
colouring: it carries with it a Christmas sparkle of

December stars, instead of the fragrant gloom of a breathless evening in June. No preliminary instruction is needed, except that you ought to be told the meaning of the Dorsetshire word 'lew'—it means 'screened,' 'sheltered.'

A SNOWY NIGHT.

'Twer at night, an' a keen win' did blow
     Vrom the east under peäle-twinklèn stars,
All a-zweepèn along the white snow;
     On the groun', on the trees, on the bars,
Vrom the hedge where the win' russled droo,
     There a light-russlèn snow-doust did vall;
An' noo pleäce were a-vound that wer lew,
     But the shed, or the ivy-hung wall.

'Then I knock'd at the wold passage door
     Wi' the win'-driven snow on my locks;
Till, a-comèn along the cwold vloor,   .
     There my Jenny soon answer'd my knocks.
Then the wind, by the door a-swung wide,
     Flung some snow in her clear-bloomèn feäce,
An' she blink'd, wi' her head all a-zide,
     An' a-chucklèn, went back to her pleäce.

'An' in there, as we zot roun' the brands,
     Though the talkers wer maïnly the men,
Bloomèn Jeäne, wi' her work in her hands,
     Did put in a good word now an' then.
An' when I took my leave, though so bleäk
     Wer the weather, she went to the door,
Wi' a smile, an' a blush on the cheäk
     That the snow had a-smitten avore.'

The last poem with which I shall trouble you is
'The Turnstile.' In this you have only to be tolerant
of 'goo' for 'go' and 'overjayed' for 'overjoyed.'

THE TURNSTILE.

'Ah! sad wer we as we did peäce
The wold church road, wi' downcast feäce,
The while the bells, that mwoan'd so deep
Above our child a-left asleep,
Wer now a-zingèn all alive
W' t'other bells to meäke the vive.
But up at woone pleäce we come by,
'Twere hard to keep woone's two eyes dry;
On Steän-cliff road, 'ithin the drong,
Up where, as vo'k do pass along,
The turnèn-stile, a-païnted white,
Doo sheen by day an' show by night.
Vor always there, as we did goo
To church, thik stile did let us drough,
Wi' spreadèn eärms that wheel'd to guide
Us each in turn to t'other zide.
An' vu'st ov all the traïn he took
My wife, wi' winsome gaït an' look;
An' then zent on my little maïd,
As skippèn onward, overjay'd
To reach ageän the pleäce o' pride,
Her comely mother's left han' zide.
An' then, a-wheelèn roun', he took
On me, 'ithin his third white nook.
An' in the fourth, a-sheäkèn wild,
He zent us on our giddy child.
But yesterday he guided slow
My downcast Jenny, vull o' woe,

An' then my little maïd in black,
A-walkèn softly on her track ;
An' a'ter he'd a-turn'd ageän,
To let me goo along the leäne,
He had noo little bwoy to vill
His last white eärms, an' they stood still.'

Now this little poem, as a representation of quiet
sadness—sadness not yielding to despair, but nevertheless clouding the common daylight, and tinging
each familiar object with the shadow of its own black-
ness, is, so far as I can judge, unsurpassed in its way.
At the same time, I own that I have some difficulty in assigning to such a poem its proper place
on the scale of poetic excellence. A pathetic wail,
like the one I have just read, like Mrs. Hemans'
'Graves of a Household,' like many others which you
will easily recall, is sure of producing its full effect
—sure, I may say, of becoming an universal favourite.
A critic, no doubt, may find it hard to determine how
much of its influence is derived from instincts which
are alive in all hearts at all times, from sympathies
which tremble at a touch ; and how much from the
real genius shown by its author ; but, whatever he
may decide, we may feel sure that he will not be
listened to, especially by the young, who have rather
a turn for playing with sorrow, as children play with

fire until they have been burnt by it. Accepting, accordingly, their verdict for the present, I think we may fairly claim for 'The Turnstile' a high place in the very first rank of such charming compositions. I might multiply my quotations from Mr. Barnes indefinitely. Out of his three volumes, in the Dorsetshire dialect, many selections might be made of equal merit with the above; still, I think those which I have cited are characteristic specimens of the poet; so that a just notion may be drawn from them, both of what he usually aims at, and how he has succeeded in his attempts. At the time, moreover, when I began to turn this lecture over in my mind, several laudatory articles referring to him, which have recently appeared, were still unwritten. I do not, however, regret the labour which I have given to the subject; he deserves, unless I deceive myself, all and more than all, the notice which he has obtained; and I am happy to find the conclusions, at which I had arrived in this matter, fortified by the unanimous concurrence of so many able critics. It is surely no light praise for an author, by one and the same work, to render valuable services to philology, and to secure, without requiring a particle of indulgence on any ground of dialect, the renown of a distinguished poet.

There are other provincial poets, besides Mr. Barnes, of whom it might be proper to say something, notably Mr. Waugh, whose beautiful lyric 'Come Home to the Children and Me,' has made its way into the hearts of his keen-minded Lancashire fellow-country-men. It is not, however, so easy to read off into English as the Dorsetshire idylls of Mr. Barnes, and therefore I shall not attempt it; the rather that I wish to call your attention to a much older ballad, which connects itself with some interesting specula-tions as to the manner in which epic poetry is born, and grows. I mean the well-known legend of Chevy Chase. Not only is this a provincial poem, but it is written, says Bishop Percy, in the broadest and coarsest northern dialect; at a time, too, when that northern half of England, if compared with the southern and western counties, was insignificant in point of wealth and population. And yet men found these rugged verses so full of fire and authentic force—so gallantly do they appeal to the strong English pulses that beat in Northumberland and in Cornwall alike, so rich are they in all those qualities which make war noble—that in a hundred years or so after its first publication, this rough Border lay was stirring the heart of Sir Philip Sidney like a trumpet, and taking its place, no longer provincial, among the recognised trophies of our English literature. I say of our English literature, because, though I am aware that there exists a Scottish version of the tale, for me a single stanza decides the proprietorship at once:—

> ' Our Scottish archers bent their bows,
> Their hearts were good and true,
> At the first flight of arrows sent
> They four-score English slew.'

Now this is a manifest, I may add a most unskilful adaptation and distortion of the lines. The spear or the axe, not the bow, was notoriously the Scottish weapon. We all must remember the gasp of patriotic despair through which Sir Walter Scott describes the pitiable equipment of his Hebridean archers, before the fight of Flodden:—

> ' but oh!
> Short was the shaft and weak the bow
> To that which England bore.'

Again, when Marmion, the grave and cautious ambassador from England, is taunted by James IV, and endeavours, in his answer, to check those unbridled passions of the king which are hurrying him to instant war, how does he proceed? Why, his warning begins, his warning ends, with an ominous allusion to the invincible arrows of England:—

> ' Much honoured were my humble home,
> If thither brave King James should come;
> *But Nottingham has archers good,*
> And Yorkshire men are stern of mood,
> Northumbrian prickers wild and rude;
> And many a banner shall be torn,
> And many a knight to earth be borne,
> *And many a sheaf of arrows spent,*
> Ere Scotland's king shall cross the Trent.'

Whether, however, this stern old song be in its original form Scotch or English, matters little. Both nations have a right to be proud of it. Earl Douglas frankly offers to peril his life, so that the blood of meaner men may not be spilt in his private quarrel. Earl Percy leans upon his hand—

> ' And sees the Douglas de ;
> Then takes the dead man by the hand,
> And says, woe is me for thee.
> To have saved thy life, I'd have parted with
> My landés for years three ;
> For a better man, nor of heart, nor of hand,
> Was not in all the north-countree.'

And so these two champions stand always together on the same level in our affections. They represent equally the highest form of middle-age chivalry, the highest type, I hope I may add, of our English character. Nor has that type, I trust, died out as yet upon our English soil.

I have heard, on the authority of an eye-witness, how in one of the fiercest and most dubious of our Peninsular struggles, a young French officer, superb of stature and brilliant in horsemanship, after rallying and remodelling his scattered brigade, came down, with the aspect of Henry of Navarre, waving a white handkerchief two lengths in front of that plunging cloud of cavalry which threatened to sweep the motionless battalions before it—into headlong ruin. But no, the English squares were too firmly rooted, the English volleys too true. Among the first who dropped, under their withering impact, was the gallant Frenchman. His baffled followers at once melted away into defeat. Still, even then, our advancing soldiers, with the light of victory on their brows, and the white heat of battle burning in their veins, bent for a moment in sadness over the stately form of their fallen foe, and muttered gloomily to each other, 'Poor gentleman, what a pity!' I could not but feel, when this anecdote was first told to me, that these men also, though the technical period of chivalry may be gone for ever—that these men also were born English knights, spiritual heirs, as we well may call them, to the generous Percy, and his high-hearted Northumbrian bard. It was not, however, so much to remind you of the merits of this

familiar poem, merits which the criticism of Addison
in the 'Spectator' has ratified for all generations of
Englishmen, as to make some remarks upon its epic
character, that I have referred to it here. In the first
place, we shall find that it sprung as it were from the
soil, among the ancestral woodlands of those knights
whose heroism it proclaims, whilst it deplores their
untimely fate. In the next place, we may remark that
the author, though he deals with real men and real
manners, is careless altogether about the actual truth
of his facts; he kills people who were not killed, con-
fuses one skirmish with another, and treats accurate
chronology with placid contempt. And yet how wrong
we should be, (having historical access to other sources
of information, we are sure of that,) if we denied that
there was a substantial basis of well-grounded belief
below this old Border song. The persons introduced
into it, the events described, the known national results
with which it manages to connect itself, all inform us
that there lurks a vanished history beneath, as certainly
as the rose-tinted clouds, that hang over the sunken
sun, testify to the previous existence of daylight.

And here, if I may be permitted to digress for a
moment, I would add that the same conclusion is to
be arrived at, through mistier labyrinths of doubt, and

with a fainter confidence of having really landed ourselves at the goal, if we compare the Arthurian Tales
with the monkish chronicle of Nennius. In that
writer's bitter invective against Mael-Gwyn, who has
on reasonable suggestions been identified with the le-
gendary knight Lancelot, we discern a faint outline
of the glorious personal qualities, as well as of the
characteristic faults, which blend themselves into the
impressive portrait, as drawn for us by his poets, of
that mediæval Achilles. It seems as if eminent men
left an ineffaceable mark upon their times, as if, however completely the truth of history may be over-
shadowed and blotted out by bewildering myths and
traditions—however absolutely the truth of circumstances may perish, the truth of character nevertheless
will survive.

To go back, however, to Chevy Chase. In the reigns
of Elizabeth and James I, the patriotism of England
became intensified in all directions, particularly in the
Scotch direction; the men of Devon and of Somerset
would be as keen against the 'daughter of debate,' or
the poisoner Kerr, as any native of Bamboroughshire or
Otterburn; so that the glowing stanzas of Chevy Chase
would make a welcome for themselves, in any part of
England, as soon as they were understood. In order,

however to get this opening for them, the language had
to be somewhat changed, and immediately the required
adapter arose. We have, as it happens, the two diminutive Iliads ready at hand, and whenever we please
can compare them together. We see how the younger
poet has dealt with the older, and accordingly may
conjecture, if we choose, how such a process is apt to
take place at other times. It must be confessed that,
in this instance at any rate, the poem is not improved
by it. I once travelled by rail in the same carriage
with an enthusiastic and impassioned French cook;
for three mortal hours did he hurl at my head a
divine and conspicuous Philippic against the besotted
Philistinism of the British kitchen-maid. Would that
there had been, in my seat, to listen sympathetically,
instead of me—my eminent predecessor. Among other
profound truths, this artist explained with overwhelming eloquence, and at great length, how the outer leaves
of lettuces, celery, and the like imbibe from the sun
and the life-giving air a higher flavour and a finer
energy than those which are shrouded within; but
though, Cassandra-like, he everlastingly warned and
adjured, the infatuated young woman in question
would, under some foolish pretext of cleanliness or
tidiness or immemorial custom, keep on trimming

and maiming their vegetables in spite of him. Somewhat after their fashion, the re-caster of Chevy Chase into English, whilst removing the rough border outside and husk, has pared away a little of its native freshness and pith—a little of that spirit and wild fragrance which it had drunk in from the self-sown forests and heather-clad fells of the North. But after all there is not much to complain of, all the best verses, all the happiest images, all the most striking thoughts, are substantially reproduced. There is but one observation, I think, sufficiently important in itself to call for a critical observation—the modern re-adjuster gives way to a momentary impulse of national spite, from which the old warrior-minstrel was wholly free. The spurious lines, I admit, have great force :—

> ' And the Lord Maxwell in likewise,
>   Did with the Douglas die,
> Of twenty hundred Scottish spears
>   Scarce fifty-five did fly;
> Of fifteen hundred Englishmen
>   *Went home* but fifty-three,
> The rest were slain in Chevy Chase,
>   Under the greenwood tree.'

These lines, I have said, are forcible and full of spirit; but still I am glad that the genuine Northumbrian harper knew better than to fail in respect towards such gallant adversaries, of whom he had already said,—

> ' Hardier men, nor of heart nor of hand,
>   Were not in Christianté.'

His closing picture is, I think, at once simpler and more noble in its simplicity than that of his south-country interpreter. According to him, both parties alike, after struggling on with unflinching courage throughout the long summer day, cease fighting, and that only from utter exhaustion, when the moon rises and the vesper-bell begins to sound:—

> ' They took off on either hand
>   By the light of the moon,
> Many had no strength to stand
>   On Cheviot the hills aboone:
> Of fifteen hundred archers of Inglonde
>   Went away but fifty and three,
> Of twenty hundred spearmen of Skotlonde
>   But five and fifti.'

And now, before I conclude, seeing that I hold a brief for provincial poets in general on this occasion, I should like to ask you a question: Is there no other well-known lay, besides 'The Hunting of the Cheviot,' which started into life among outsiders and refugees?

no other which, though careless of historical facts, yet
from the impressive truth of its characters, above all
from the noble proportions and intense life of the
central one, gives sufficient evidence of a basis of
history beneath? no other which, though it dealt with
alien traditions, and celebrated the triumphs of a clan
beaten and dispossessed by Sparta, stirred, nevertheless, the heart of a Spartan Sir Philip Sidney like a
trumpet? Under his auspices it insinuated itself
gradually into every corner of the land — into the
metropolitan cities and the remotest colonies alike.
Its provincialism sloughed itself away as the serpent
sloughs its skin: it became national, it became a bond
of union, it became a kind of Bible to all who spoke
any one of the numberless dialects of Hellas. And
now this old Æolic ballad, which began its career as
the Hellenic Chevy Chase of some obscure Smyrniote
rhapsodist or rhapsodists, stands forth to endless generations as the poem of the world. I can easily imagine
the disgust of the fashionable Court minstrels, from
Argos and Mycenæ and Corinth and Lacedæmon, who
thought it a stretch of condescension when they attended
the festivals of meaner states, at their unexpected reception. They came to see and to conquer; but the
beautiful maidens of Delos and the other Ægean isles

turned away from their brand-new Dorian hexameters
to listen, delightedly, to 'that blind old fiddler from
Chios, who sings about those effeminate Æolian princes
and their trumpery Asiatic expedition.' Some one of
them, perhaps, may have anticipated, more or less, the
candour of Monsieur Falconet, who, after comparing the
beauties of his own faultless model for Peter the Great's
equestrian statue, with the countless defects of that inferior animal upon which Marcus Aurelius sits, an em-
peror for ever, above the steps of the Capitol at Rome,
stopped, took a pinch of snuff, and ended his lecture
thus: 'Et cependant, Messieurs, il faut avouier que cette
vilaine bête est vivante, tandis que la mienne est morte.'
In some such spirit, possibly, the laureate of Temenus,
or the favourite rhapsode of Cresphontes, may have
checked the sneers of those hangers-on and parasites
by whom he was sure to be surrounded. He may have
said to them,—'Nay, nay; you are too hard on the
old man: there is often something fine in what he
declaims; and could he correct himself of that horrible
habit of dropping his h's, and of the other vulgar Ion-
isms which disfigure his style, I am certain that I could
make something of him.' Oh, sacred but forgotten
poet, I have no doubt that you could. He, however,
has managed to do without you, and has made some-

thing of himself—so much, indeed, that we who are not provincial poets look upon him as the light of the past, the creator of Hellas, the bard of bards, the inexhaustible well-head—

> ' A quo, seu fonte perenni
> Vatum Pieriis ora rigantur aquis.'

But were I Mr. Barnes, Mr. Waugh, or any member of their special literary guild, I should insist upon contemplating him from a different point of view—I should claim him as my particular ἄναξ ἀνδρῶν—as the captain and patron-saint, if I may so speak, of my own poetical brotherhood; and, if ever a hostile critic were ill-advised enough to decry my pretensions by saying, ' After all, you do not write English; you are only a provincial poet,' I should reply, without hesitation, ' True, so I am; so also in his day—was Homer.'

DR. NEWMAN'S

'DREAM OF GERONTIUS.'

LECTURE III.

DR. NEWMAN'S
'DREAM OF GERONTIUS.'

A POET is not always interesting to his readers exactly in proportion to his artistic eminence. The distinction drawn by Wordsworth at the opening of the 'Excursion,' between what he calls 'the vision and the faculty divine' and what he calls the accomplishment of verse, does not apply itself only, as he applies it there, to those who write and to those who refrain altogether from writing. It enters also into our comparative estimate of certain different classes among literary men. With regard to some, we should say, that what they give to the world is, more emphatically, an exhibition of talent, of intellectual brilliancy, of pure literary power; whilst, as to others again, we cannot but feel that their efforts come upon us as suggesting something more, as

outpourings from unsounded depths within the character, as irrepressible utterances of the hidden soul.

Now, in the earlier stages of society, the true and
born poet was not looked upon, I apprehend, as a
literary man at all; he belonged to a race apart (ἄνευ
μανίας οὐδεὶς ποιήτης), and was ranked accordingly among
prophets rather than among authors; he was a favoured
servant upon whom a precious burden was laid; a chosen
interpreter, to whom noble messages were entrusted—
messages which he was driven, under the pressure of
a self-consuming enthusiasm, to communicate in music
to man. But as civilisation rolled down from those
august heights and clouded solitudes, where, according
to the common belief of nations, her original fountain-
head derived itself from God; as she flowed into
a thousand circulating channels, and fertilised new
ground, the arts of life gradually assumed a more
practical and definite form. When this took place,
the poet was, in a great degree, unmantled and dis-
crowned—perhaps at present I ought rather to say, was
disestablished and disendowed;—he had, whatever the
proper phrase may be, to retire into the background.
Sophists, rhetoricians, orators, and statesmen all thought
that they could teach the people how to live and what
to wish for, much better than solemn old gentlemen

who kept crooning their mystic hexameters, in harmony with the motions of a staff. Philosophers, in
their turn, maintained that the right to bore mankind
with discussions about τὸ ἕν and the pure reason, was
indisputably theirs; whilst historians made it clear
that the necessary twist could be given to facts more
succinctly and more plausibly in prose than in verse.
Poetry, therefore, though it still continued to live and
to please, ceased to be that exhausting burthen, that
painful wrestling with the powers of the universe, by
which its earlier votaries were at once ennobled and
overwhelmed. Still, however, some rays from the re-
tiring sun-god were refracted around the image of the
bard; and, even to this day, there lingers a belief, true
or false, that when a poet, real, original, and unmistakeable, rises upon us, his genius, his inspiration, as we
call it, is something special, something differing not in
degree but in kind from any inspiration which urges
on the orator, the statesman, or the mathematician.
When, therefore, we turn to our present imaginative
writers, who come forward as artists and creators to
enchant us with the graces and varieties of a beautiful literature, a half thought crosses the mind now and
then whether the harp which they have inherited
retains all her original strings; whether the chord of

mystery which at first gave a tone of strange power and
earnestness to the whole instrument, has not somehow
or other relaxed itself, and silently mouldered away.
If, then, at such moments we find in our path some
lonely and single-minded searcher after wisdom,—

> ' Whose soul is like a star, and dwells apart,'—

if we find one for whom life is no arena upon which
brilliant accomplishments may be displayed, or glittering crowns of victory arrived at—no place for easy
pleasure, or even the most innocent self-indulgence,
we are surprised and startled into reverence. We,
perhaps, may be wasting our time in frivolous pleasures
or unsubstantial pursuits; but, to him, his life has
ever proved a problem which all the years of it are
too short to solve—an arid desert massed up with
mirages and phantoms, through which he has to
struggle, in order that he may bring himself face to face
with his own ideal of the truth. Such a man—and
I call Dr. Newman such a man—if he writes verses,
writes them because he cannot help himself; the
travail of his heart must come out somehow, or else it
will tear him to pieces; and in his restlessness he discovers that verse, for him, is the natural outlet of
feeling. From his thoughts any idea of mere literary

success is a thousand leagues away. The subjects
which he chooses are not those most susceptible of
poetical embellishments. No; they are his own doubts
and struggles, the glimpses of light and the oppressions
of darkness which alternately cheer and sadden his un-
participated existence. To put it better than I can, he
grapples, not as an imaginative exercise, but in deadly
earnest with

> ' Those obstinate questionings
> Of sense, and outward things,
> Fallings from us, vanishings,
> Blank misgivings of a creature
> Moving about in worlds not realised:
> High instincts, before which our mortal nature
> Doth tremble, like a guilty thing surprised.'

From such a man we may be as far removed in
spirit and in feeling as if he were an inhabitant of the
Dog-star; but still we find ourselves, whenever we meet
him, in the presence of something unquestionably
noble. Moreover, if we regard him as a poet, though
others may delight us more, though his intellectual
gifts for that particular purpose may be comparatively
unimportant, still the fibre of intensity is always alive
within him; and over him the sense of intercommunion with something higher and deeper than man

> ' Broods like the day, a master o'er a slave—
> A presence that is not to be put by.'

It is not wonderful, therefore, if we think sometimes
that he may be united to the rapt singers and prophets
of old by links of feeling, and touches of privilege,
which obtain no entrance into more brilliant souls;
it is not wonderful, therefore, if we pause sometimes
to consider whether it be not to such as him, rather
than to such as them, that we ought to look for any
fragments of the lost and forgotten tune, for any last
faint echoes upon earth from that primeval melody
which arose in heaven when 'the morning stars sang
together, and all the sons of God shouted for joy.'

Now, if the distinction I have here taken be a sound
one—if Dr. Newman, by some delicate thread of connection, be affiliated to the older instincts, and the
more prophetic half of the poetical character—if for
him the imagination be not an intellectual plaything,
not a mere musical instrument, but the appointed
spiritual energy by the help of which he raises himself,
at intervals, to glance over the imprisoning walls of
sense and matter into the spiritual world beyond—
then surely he deserves from us, as a man of high
and unusual nature, the most attentive consideration.

I am not here, of course, to claim for him a literary
station as high as if he were a Tennyson or a Browning;
or, indeed, to deny that Tennyson, throughout his 'In

Memoriam' and elsewhere probably, is visited by that remoter and more authentic inspiration of which I have been speaking; but still, for Tennyson, as for others,—

> ' The rainbow comes and goes,
>   And lovely is the rose;
> The moon doth with delight
>   Look round her, when the heavens are bare;
> Waters on a starry night
>   Are beautiful and fair;
> The sunshine is a glorious birth,
>   Albeit he know, where'er he go,
> That there has passed away a glory from the earth.'

For Dr. Newman, on the other hand, the inaccessible muse Urania is almost his only patroness; from her eight earthlier sisters he gets hardly any assistance. Nay, unless I misconceive his philosophy, he scarce believes in any real rose, in any actual rainbow; the stars themselves are little more than phantom lights, visionary flashings of that great dream, woven between the soul and God, which men agree here to call for the moment our visible and material universe. Now to us, originally of coarser texture, and who have knocked about the world ever since, who have gone sessions, squabbled with attorneys as revising barristers, and done work for the Poor Law Board, much of this is almost inconceivable. The children and

champions of compromise, we undergo a sense of in-
significance and degradation which creeps into the
marrow of our bones when, as in the 'Apologia,' we
stumble upon a man who, really and earnestly sincere,
has lived always in, for, and by the spirit alone. His
love of truth is so keen, so subtly keen, that the will
answers to every breath of logical impulse, just as our
telegraph-wires acknowledge the lightest pulsations of
an electric current. We may gasp with astonishment,
when we find that a casual phrase of St. Augustine's
has upset, as if it were a house of cards, some cherished
theory which the labour of years had gradually wrought
into shape; we may smile when we perceive how
simple, how child-like in many ways was that powerful
mind, beneath whose sway the hearts of so many 'were
moved to and fro, as the trees of the wood are moved
by the wind;' but still the more we know, the more
we honour the man, the more do we accept him as
a strange, an abnormal, a solitary, but still as a
beautiful soul. Among other matters, more important
no doubt, but less within my province, if we read his
poetry, we read it with affectionate respect, not so
much because it is exquisite in point of art, as because it is essentially spontaneous, spiritual, and deep.
A good deal of it, doubtless, awakens no echo in our

sympathies, it does not speak to us, possibly because our sense of hearing is not of the requisite compass; but we all of us, in our degree, have been vexed and harassed by inward struggles; we all of us have known the weight of darkness upon our life, and therefore we can all feel that in this prayer—this cry—for light, there is an intense reality and truth which lend to it no ordinary charm :—

THE PILLAR OF THE CLOUD.

'Lead, Kindly Light, amid the encircling gloom,
    Lead Thou me on!
The night is dark, and I am far from home—
    Lead Thou me on!
Keep Thou my feet; I do not ask to see
The distant scene,—one step enough for me.

I was not ever thus, nor pray'd that Thou
    Shouldst lead me on.
I loved to choose and see my path, but now
    Lead Thou me on!
I loved the garish day, and, spite of fears,
Pride ruled my will: remember not past years.

So long Thy power hath blest me, sure it still
    Will lead me on,
O'er moor and fen, o'er crag and torrent, till
    The night is gone;
And with the morn those angel faces smile
Which I have loved long since, and lost awhile.'

I have entered upon these preliminary details, and

dwelt upon the inborn peculiarities which Dr. Newman
himself has disclosed to us, because all his poems,
'Gerontius' among the rest, grow out of his whole
character. They are the expressions of a nature, not
the developments and elaborations of an art. It is
remarkable how, more than once, in his 'Apologia,'
this strange man recurs, with something like fear, to
a haunting sense that all the outward aspects of matter
are phantasmal and unreal: a sense which seems to
have been about his path and about his bed from early
childhood. I have known the same feeling, or one
like it, in others. I have known men, yes, and young
children also, with such an impression, seldom given
out, but always on cross-examination found to be
lurking at the heart. We poco-curanti who think
life too short to be wasted on metaphysics, and who
refute Berkeley in the style of Dr. Johnson, by kicking
at a stone or a foot-ball, are apt, whenever we run up
against such weird mystics, to feel dissatisfied with
ourselves and every one else. We may go on further-
more to reflect (though that Buddhist creed implies the
unimportance rather than the unreality of matter) how,
at this very day, the absolute majority of mankind
believe, under ancestral traditions beyond a date, in the
transmigration of souls, and grow thereupon still hotter

and more flurried and more uncomfortable. We have
even been known, for a quarter of an hour, to question
whether all wisdom and all knowledge of human nature
has condensed itself, as to time, within the latter half
of this nineteenth century; and as to space, within
some twenty streets round about Piccadilly and Pall
Mall. Luckily for our peace of mind this unnatural
modesty does not last long But even when we have
recovered our legitimate self-esteem, it may not be
without profit to study the effect of such anomalous
temperaments upon religion, upon politics, upon life.
Our present business is with literature—with poetry,
indeed—more especially the poetry of Dr. Newman.
Now, original as he is, he cannot, any more than
smaller men, escape from the conditions of his age.
When he first became known, the influence of Wordsworth was perhaps at its highest; there was a surfeit
of Byron; there had been a reaction from Scott;
Tennyson, as yet, was below the horizon. I should
therefore expect to find, as one result of Dr. Newman's
scepticism with regard to matter, that he would remain
comparatively unaffected by much in Wordsworth that
produced a deep impression upon others. I should
have previously imagined, for instance, that Dr. Newman would be somewhat hard and cold to the beauty

and influence of the outer world. I think, upon examining this point, that these anticipations of mine
are realised more or less. We all know, at any rate,
what the opposite tendency—the tendency, I mean, to
see life in everything, and to spiritualise for himself all
the manifestations of matter—have produced for us in
Wordsworth. It has indeed so informed his poetry,
that in spite of a religion keen, unintermitting and
profound, he has been grumbled at by sound divines as
a Pantheist. Speaking, however, not as a theological
but only as a poetical critic, this is a heresy, if Wordsworth were a heretic, which I cannot bring myself to
regret; under that stimulus he pursues Nature as if
she were his mistress, and colours every description of
her with a living glow of love. Dr. Newman, on the
other hand, so far as I can judge from the book which
I hold here, is not much interested in what for him
has but little reality, and dwells but seldom on the
earthly outside of things with any warmth of personal
affection. Now this, in my judgment, is a grave
defect. I think a want of sensuousness in a poet (and
I say so openly, because the poetry of abstract thought
is not likely to be undervalued at present,) fatal to
very high eminence in that department of literature.
Wordsworth, it may be said, has clothed deep and

original views with enduring poetry. True; but he
was enabled to do so just because he united a character
peculiar in its passion, no doubt, but still intensely
passionate, with a great faculty of thought :—

> 'The sounding cataract
> Haunted him like a passion ; the tall rock,
> The mountain, and the deep and gloomy wood,
> Their colours and their forms, had been to him
> An appetite, a feeling, and a love.'

And therefore it is that the dry bones scattered about
the 'Excursion' and the 'Prelude' have had strength
given them to stand up on their feet and live. Nay,
without referring again to what Wordsworth says of
himself, how is it that Coleridge describes the inspiration of his friend?

> An orphic song indeed,
> A song divine of high and passionate thoughts,
> To their own music chanted.'

It is this double refraction of passion and of thought,
fused into one flash of blended light, which gives their
life and character to his poetical diamonds; but still
it is in the passion rather than in the thought, if we
could but disentangle them, that we should find, I
believe, the quickening spirit of the gem. Hence I
think Dr. Newman in his earlier poems has suffered
somewhat by assigning too much weight to Words-

worth's power of thought, without sufficiently taking into account the more poetical and less imitable qualities by which it is relieved. The same criticism may be directed with even more propriety against other esteemed writers who have enlisted, during the last thirty years, in the 'Wordsworth's own Cumberland meditators;' they may knit their brows like their illustrious colonel, but they cannot mimic ' the beatings of his heart.'

I once knew of two young ladies, both fond of poetry—both Wordsworthians to the tips of their fingers. The first had drunk in so deeply her poet's views of intercommunion with the life of the universe —views which suffered nothing to lie for him inert and dead—that in her universal sympathy she even out-Wordsworthed Wordsworth ; she could not rest till she had clothed her very gowns with a personal identity and an individual character. She baptized them accordingly, as fast as they came home from her milliner, with sonorous names of heroes and of kings. Hence a girlish friend sitting with her was startled by the sudden irruption of a stern though affectionate maid: 'Now, Miss, you have gone and torn Castor, and Pollux is as dirty as the ground; you have nothing left for Sunday but old Lysander, and yet, you know, I told you over and over again how wrong you were to leave Superbus behind.' Her rival inclined to the austerer side of the Great Man's intellect, and was found to have jotted down in her commonplace book the following awful entry: ' Resolved, for the future, to think clearly, comprehensively, and profoundly on all subjects.' This at the first aspect may appear the more noble proceeding, but I am convinced that if they intend to follow as poetesses in the steps of their master, the gownswoman of the two was in the right.

Nay, even as far as that master himself is concerned, I will make a clean breast of it, and confess that in spite of the width of thought and glow of feeling which distinguish him from his numberless imitators, I hardly look upon him as taking rank among the normal summits in the orthodox range of Parnassus, but rather as standing, with respect to such mountain brothers of song, like a peak of Teneriffe, apart, and unsympathising and alone.

To return, however, to our immediate subject. Any comparative insensibility to the beauty of nature, or to those outward aspects which stimulate the imagination of the passionate and sensuous poet, is in the ' Dream of Gerontius ' of less importance. The region through which it moves is filled with the dry colourless light of

infinity, and not by those fluctuating rays which tinge
our human atmosphere. I should say, therefore, that
Dr. Newman, in grappling with such an awful subject
as immortality and the state of the soul after death,
had chosen well for himself; if such a statement did
not somewhat imply that this fine poem had originated
in an artistical pursuit of literary excellence, instead
of springing up spontaneously out of the innermost
fountains of a deeply religious mind.

However this may be, the massiveness of thought,
the purity of feeling, and the austere grandeur of
imagination which distinguish Dr. Newman, find
here an appropriate place. In a more secular poem,
I should expect that, either from the natural bias of
his understanding, or perhaps from the collapse of all
slighter emotions under the pressure of intense thought,
a certain dryness and stiffness of style would have
made themselves felt, and felt disadvantageously. Dr.
Newman, however, is here dealing with high matters,
fitted to call forth that deep-seated zeal and fire which
always lay in the heart of his character—a zeal and fire
which, in their instinctive rebellion against his pre-
conceived plans for being calm and tranquil and
reserved, often lend a subtle and peculiar charm to
his writings. Besides, what I have called above an

austere imagination, that is, a faculty of which the
business is to conceive and body forth great architectural wholes of thought, without frittering itself away
on the details of ornamentation, is the only form
of the imaginative intellect suitable to a drama so
solemn as 'Gerontius;' and, in that respect, Dr. Newman is eminently strong.

And now I must ask your pardon, if I detain you
at this point for a moment, by a short analysis of
the poem which we are examining. I can hardly
doubt that every one of you is at least as well acquainted with it as I am myself. But still, the old
maxim that half the failures in love, in war, in
trade, in every department of life, have as their cause
the taking things for granted, claims a hearing,
and must be attended to. 'Gerontius,' then, is a religious drama which describes a dying Catholic, not
apparently a man of any special or exceptional holi-
ness, but one who has struggled worthily through a
long series of years, and is now before the gates
of Death. He still is, as he ever has been, a
dutiful and pious son of his mother Church; but
his senses are shaken by pain, and by his human
terror of the grave; his senses, moreover, half spiri-
tualized as the strength of the flesh ebbs away from

them, detect on the air around and in the soul within,
hostile and malignant emanations bent to poison his
latest breathings, and to beat down that sacred hope
which falters more and more as it approaches its
fulfilment. Still he is supported against these unseen
enemies by faith; and when his earthly destiny has
accomplished itself, departs in peace. Immediately he
finds that he is borne along by some protecting power,
through sneering demons and sympathizing angels, up
to the Throne of Judgment itself. The dramatic element is made up of a colloquy between him and this
glorious creature to whom he has been entrusted. In
order, however, to make head against the monotony
which would ensue if this were all, the dialogue, as it
proceeds, is from time to time relieved by the choral
hymns of the seraphs whom they pass, interrupted by
the malevolent utterances howled at by them by demons,
who would fain impede their progress; and solemnly
closes with a lyrical valediction sung by that immortal
guide over the awe-stricken soul; which then is left,
after having been at once cheered and blasted by a
single glimpse of the Most High, to cleanse itself from
those disfiguring stains which forbid its immediate
entrance into heaven. Of the doctrines involved in
this striking production it is unnecessary to say more

than that there is nothing, except the bare idea of purgatory (a theological and not a poetical blemish), which need prevent any Christian, or, indeed, any one who believes in the providence of God, from valuing it according to its deserts. It is built mainly upon those noble foundations which were laid eighteen hundred years ago, and which are still the common inheritance of Christendom, the common centre of our European civilization.

It is probable, indeed, that the first idea of composing such a dramatic work may have been suggested to Dr. Newman by the Autos Sacramentales of Spain, and especially by those of the illustrious Calderon; but, so far as I can learn, he has derived hardly anything from them beyond the vaguest hints, except, indeed, the all-important knowledge that a profound religious feeling can represent itself, and that effectively, in the outward form of a play. I may remark that these Spanish Autos of Calderon constitute beyond all question a very wonderful and a very original school of poetry, and I am not without hope that, when I know my business a little better, we may examine them impartially together. Nay, even as it is, Calderon stands so indisputably at the head of all Catholic religious dramatists, among whom Dr. Newman has recently

enrolled himself, that perhaps it may not be out of
place to inquire for a moment into his poetical methods
and aims, in order that we may then discover, if we
can, how and why the disciple differs from his master.
Now there is a great conflict of opinion as to the
precise degree of merit which these particular Spanish
dramas possess. Speaking as an ignorant man, I should
say that, whilst those who disparage them seem rather
hasty in their judgments, and not so well informed as
could be wished, still the kind of praise which they
receive from their most enthusiastic admirers puzzles
and does not instruct us.

Taking, for example, the great German authority on
this point, Dr. Lorinzer, as our guide, we see his poet
looming dimly through a cloud of incense, which may
embalm his memory, but certainly does not improve our
eyesight. Indeed, according to him, any appreciation
of Calderon is not to be dreamt of by a Protestant.
'Even learned critics,' says he, 'highly cultivated in
all the niceties of æsthetics, are deficient in the knowledge of Catholic faith and Catholic theology without
which it is impossible properly to understand Calderon.'
And yet, without being Greeks we feel the Iliad, without
being Parsees the Shahnama comes home to us, without
being Mahometans the songs of Arabia quicken our

pulses with their lyrical impulse and fire; Berserker poets, Hindoo poets, even Chinese poets speak a language not unintelligible to our ears:—

' One touch of nature makes the whole world kin.'

However true, therefore, these Teutonic dicta may be, we cannot be expected patiently to acquiesce in them. Dr. Lorinzer then goes on to say, ' that old traditions which twine round the dogma like a beautiful garland of legends, deeply profound thoughts expressed here and there by some of the Fathers of the Church, are made use of with *such incredible skill* and introduced *so appositely at the right place,* that (I presume) even ordinary imaginations are awakened to the charm of the poetry, even ordinary understandings roused up to enter into the depth of the thoughts.' Oh, no ! I beg your pardon, I have misread the learned German. He does not finish his sentence in that way at all. What he does really say is this, ' are made use of with such incredible skill, and inserted so appositely at the right place, that —frequently it is not easy to guess the source from whence they have been derived.' The learned German's notion of incredible dramatic skill, and exquisite appositeness of introduction, seems to be that the exercise of these high faculties should leave spectator or reader, as the case may be, in hopeless perplexity and confusion. According to this method of reasoning, the logical objection against Calderon ought to be taken thus, that though often most meritoriously difficult, he falls short of absolute perfection in this, that it is sometimes possible to understand his meaning. Nevertheless, these scenes so unfathomably profound, these sublime enigmas, which exact, like the handwriting on the wall, a specially inspired interpreter to decypher them, were composed in the first instance to gratify, and did gratify, the uneducated populace of Madrid. I should like to have Calderon himself up, even for half an hour, if it were only that he might criticise his critics.

At the same time, Dr. Lorinzer's knowledge of his subject is so profound, and his appreciation of his favourite author so keen, that for me, who am almost entirely unacquainted with this branch of literature, formally to oppose his views, would be an act of presumption of which I am, as I trust, incapable. I may, however, perhaps be permitted to observe, that with regard to the few pieces of this kind which in an English dress I have read, whilst I think them not only most ingenious but also surprisingly beautiful, they do not strike me as incomprehensible at all. We must accept them, of course, as coming from the

mind of a devout Catholic and Spanish gentleman who
belongs to the seventeenth century; but when once
that is agreed upon, there are no difficulties greater than
those which we might expect to find in any system of
poetry so remote from our English habits of thought.
There is, for instance, the 'Divine Philothea,' in other
words, our human spirit considered as the destined
bride of Christ. This sacred drama, we may well
call it the swan-song of Calderon's extreme old age,
is steeped throughout in a serene power and a mellow
beauty of style, making it not unworthy to be ranked
with that Œdipus Colonæus which glorified the sun-
set of his illustrious predecessor; but yet, Protestant
as I am, I cannot discover that it is in the least obscure. Faith, Hope, Charity, the five senses, Heresy,
Judaism, Paganism, Atheism, and the like, which
in inferior hands must have been mere lay figures,
are there instinct with a dramatic life and energy
such as beforehand I could hardly have supposed
possible. Moreover, in spite of Dr. Lorinzer's odd
encomiums, each allegory as it rises up is more neatly
rounded off, and shows a finer grain than any of the
personifications of Spenser; so that the religious effect
and the theological effect intended by the writer are
both amply produced—yes, produced upon us, his

heretical admirers. Hence, even if there be mysterious treasures of beauty below the surface, to which
we aliens must remain blind for ever, this expression,
which broke from the lips of one to whom I was
eagerly reading the play, 'Why, in the original, this
must be as grand as Dante,' tends to show that such
merits as do come within our ken are not likely to
be thrown away upon any fair-minded Protestant. Dr.
Newman, as a Catholic, will have entered, I presume,
more deeply still into the spirit of these extraordinary
creations: his life, however, belongs to a different era,
and to a colder people. And thus, however much he
may have been directed to the choice of a subject
by the old mysteries and moralities (of which these
Spanish autos must be taken as the final development
and bright consummate flower), he has treated that subject, when once undertaken by him, entirely from his
own point of view. 'Gerontius' is meant to be studied
and dwelt upon by the meditative reader. The autos of
Calderon were got ready by perhaps the most accomplished playwright that ever lived, to amuse and stimulate a thronging southern population. 'Gerontius' is,
we may perhaps say for Dr. Newman in the words
of Shelley,—

> 'The voice of his own soul
> Heard in the calm of thought.'

whilst the conceptions of the Spanish dramatist burst
into life with tumultuous music, gorgeous scenery,
hurrying processions, and all the pomps and splen-
dours of the Catholic Church. No wonder, therefore,
that our English auto, though composed with the same
general purpose of using verse, and dramatic verse, to
promote a religious and even a theological end, should
differ from them in essence as well as in form. There
is room, however, for both kinds in the wide empire
of Poetry, and though Dr. Newman himself would be
the first to cry shame upon me if I were to name
him with Calderon even for a moment, still his
mystery of this most unmysterious age will, I believe,
keep its honourable place in our English literature
as an impressive, an attractive, and an original production.

If we proceed to examine it in detail, I think,
though I speak diffidently, that the finest thing it
contains is the early soliloquy of Gerontius when
he finds himself, as he believes at first, alone with
infinity. The whole of this speech is so real and
so plausible, that we accept it at once as the natural
continuation of his earthly career, and seem to feel
with him that his actual position, however new and
previously unimagined, has nothing in it to awaken

either surprise or confusion.   I will now, with **your
permission,** read it to you at length :—

> '**I went** to sleep; **and now I am** refresh'd,
> **A** strange refreshment: for I feel in me
> **An** inexpressive lightness, and a sense
> **Of** freedom, as I were at **length** myself,
> **And ne'er** had been before. How still it is!
> **I hear no more the** busy beat of time,
> **No,** nor **my fluttering breath, nor** struggling pulse;
> **Nor** does **one moment differ from the next.**
> **I had a dream; yes;—some one softly said**
> " He's gone;" and then a sigh went round the room.
> And then I surely heard **a** priestly voice
> Cry "Subvenite;" and they knelt in prayer.
> I seem to hear him still; but thin and low,
> And fainter and more faint the accents come,
> As at an ever-widening interval.
> Ah! whence is this? What is this severance?
> **This** silence pours a solitariness
> **Into** the very essence of my **soul;**
> And the deep rest, so soothing and so sweet,
> Hath something too of sternness and of pain,
> For **it drives** back **my** thoughts upon their spring
> By a strange introversion, and perforce
> I now begin to feed upon myself,
> Because **I** have nought else to feed upon.
>
> Am I alive or dead? I am not dead,
> But **in** the body still; for I possess
> A sort of confidence, which clings to me,
> That each particular organ holds its place
> As heretofore, combining with the rest
> Into **one** symmetry, that wraps me round,
> And makes me man; and surely **I** could move,

Did I but will it, every part of me.
And yet I cannot to my sense bring home
By very trial, that I have the power.
'Tis strange; I cannot stir a hand or foot,
I cannot make my fingers or my lips
By mutual pressure witness each to each,
Nor by the eyelid's instantaneous stroke
Assure myself I have a body still.
Nor do I know my very attitude,
Nor if I stand, or lie, or sit, or kneel.'

The rest of the work is much in the same key as the above: it is grave and subdued as to tone, somewhat bare of ornament, but everywhere weighty with thought. It is written also with Dr. Newman's usual mastery over the English language, and moves along from the beginning to the end with a solemn harmony of its own. I am here referring to the blank verse; the speeches rather. The lyrical portions (with the exception of two, on which I shall touch by-and-by) are, in my judgment, less successful. The strains as they flow forth from the various ranks of angels are not, if I may use a somewhat pedantic word, differentiated by any intelligible gradations of feeling and of style, and, indeed, do not move me much more than those average hymns which people, who certainly are not angels yet, sing weekly in church. The interlocutory blasphemies of the demons are still worse.

I cannot help pronouncing them to be mean and repulsive.

I am aware that here there is room for a wide difference of opinion; I know that German critics of renown will tell you that the fiends of Dante or of Tasso are more to be admired than those of 'Paradise Lost.' But, though I do not wish to enter into any abstract discussions on the nature of good and evil, or on the metaphysical effects consequent on utter alienation from God, I yet feel that, poetically speaking, what they say is not true. I stand here in an English University, as an Englishman—an English Philistine, if you will—and profess myself, on that head at least, incurably Miltonic. I do not forget that another class of thinkers, very different from German critics, have arrived, by a separate road, at something like the same conclusion, and that our Miltonic Hades has been condemned by intelligent English divines. The silent valley where the lost spirits sing—

'With notes angelical to many a harp;'

the intellectual pleasures reserved for them when they reason high—

'Of fate, free-will, fore-knowledge absolute;'

the noble palace, for which

> ' The blazing cressets, fed
> With naphtha and asphaltus, yielded light
> As from a sky,'

are thought of, as opening avenues to something more like comparative happiness, than is consistent with the appointed prison-house of misery and sin. Excellent men, therefore, speak of such fine imaginations as dangerous and deceitful; just as if these sublime visions of our great Puritan poet had lent some colour of plausibility to the hypothetical plans of that Yankee pedlar who, on being asked, when he returned from a business tour in Texas, what kind of a place it was, is said to have replied, ' Wall, stranger, if Hell and Texas both belonged to me, *I* should sell Texas.' Now, whatever may be the moral or theological force of these objections, upon me as a poetical critic, and nothing more, they do not tell with any weight. When I look at the question from my own point of view, I think that if you degrade one who 'was

> ' Of the first
> If not the first Archangel,'

into an imp, you destroy, to our apprehensions, his personal identity at once; he is no longer the same being; no longer an antagonist powerful enough to dispute with Michael; no longer the centre of the hostile system—a spiritual anti-sun, as it were, raying out that darkness which maintains to the end its fierce though unequal battle against the immeasurable light.

Nay, even if Milton had never existed, I should still consider the fiendish shapes of the 'Inferno,' who are like nothing so much as the harsh ushers and malignant young bullies of an ill-conducted private school, to be wanting altogether in dignity and effect.

I sympathise with both clauses of Wordsworth's noble line—

> ' Calm pleasures there abide, majestic pains ; '

and therefore I turn away, not without a sense of relief, from Dr. Newman's gibbering devils, to the melancholy grandeur with which Byron, in his 'Heaven and Earth,' reproduces our Miltonic idea of a fallen spirit :—

> ' Son of the saved,
> When thou and thine have braved
> The wide and warring element,
> Shall thou and thine be happy? No!
> Thy new world and new race shall be of woe.
>
>   *   *   *   *
>
> And art thou not ashamed
>   Thus to survive,
>   And eat, and drink, and wive,
> With a base heart so far subdued and tamed
> As even to hear this wide destruction named?

Who would outlive their kind
Except the base and blind ?

' There is not one who hath not left a throne
 Vacant in heaven, to dwell in darkness here,
Rather than see his mates endure alone.
   Go, wretch, and give
 A life like thine to other wretches—live !
And when the annihilating waters roar
 Above what they have done,
Envy the giant patriarchs then no more,
And scorn thy sire, as the surviving one,
 Thyself for being his son.'

In justice to Dr. Newman, however, I must admit
that the passage wherein the guardian angel explains
to Gerontius why the hellish outcries by which they
are assailed are now ineffective and contemptible, is
finely conceived and vigorously expressed :—

    ' In thy trial-state
Thou hadst a traitor nestling close at home,
Connatural, who with the powers of hell
Was leagued, and of thy senses kept the keys,
And to that deadliest foe unlock'd thy heart.
And therefore is it, in respect of man,
Those fallen ones show so majestical.
But, when some child of grace, Angel or Saint,
Pure and upright in his integrity
Of nature, meets the demons on their raid,
They scud away as cowards from the fight.
Nay, oft hath holy hermit in his cell,
Not yet disburden'd of mortality,
Mock'd at their threats and warlike overtures :

Or, dying, when they swarm'd, like flies, around,
Defied them, and departed to his Judge.'

The two rhymed pieces which stand out from all the others as deserving of high commendation are, first, the final utterance of Gerontius after his momentary interview with the hidden power of God: it is full of a sad and yearning melody, well calculated to infuse into our hearts the lesson which Dr. Newman designed it to convey. The other lines to which I referred are those which contain the farewell of the guardian angel, who, in a strain of solemn and tender pensiveness, fitly closes the drama. It may suffice, perhaps, if I read the former of these two, which, upon the whole, I prefer :—

'Take me away, and in the lowest deep
　　　There let me be,
And there in hope the lone night-watches keep,
　　　Told out for me.
There, motionless and happy in my pain,
　　　Lone, not forlorn,—
There will I sing my sad perpetual strain,
　　　Until the morn.
There will I sing, and soothe my stricken breast,
　　　Which ne'er can cease
To throb, and pine, and languish, till possest
　　　Of its Sole Peace.
There will I sing my absent Lord and Love :—
　　　Take me away,
That sooner I may rise, and go above,
And see Him in the truth of everlasting day.'

I think I have now said all that I had to say about
the 'Dream of Gerontius;' but perhaps I may venture
to add, in conclusion, that little as I sympathise with
the actual opinions, or even with the methods of
reasoning which characterise Dr.. Newman, it has
nevertheless been a real pleasure to me to recall the
days of my youth, and to feel that he deserved then,
and has ever since continued to deserve, the admiring
reverence with which he filled the men of my generation. He has bared his heart before the crowd, and
all who will may see how true, and pure, and tender
a heart it is.

There may be others whom we looked up to likewise, who have surrendered their souls to a bitterer
antagonism and a more hostile zeal; who pain us,
now and then, by assuming a somewhat unsympathetic
demeanour—by seeming to undervalue the memories
that lie behind them, and the ties which they compelled themselves to break. If such there are, it is not
for us to blame them; we know too well how keen the
edge of these disputes, how envenomed the spirit of
these religious differences, is and ever must be; but
though we blame nobody, it is still lawful for us to
rejoice, that one the most eminent of his class, should
not, in spite of an unwavering devotion to his new

creed, even wish to forget the years when he worked
and flourished at Oxford; that by *him,* at any rate, the
old influences are yet spoken of with genuine respect,
the old friends with undiminished affection; that of
him, at any rate, we may yet fairly say, in words which
are hacknied no doubt, but hacknied only because
they cannot be improved upon—

'Cum talis sis, utinam noster esses.'